D0721379

THE
YARDBIRDS

Celebrating the end of the first
US tour, Rolling Stone Discotheque,
New York City, September 1965.

THE
YARDBIRDS

ALAN CLAYSON

*THE BAND
THAT LAUNCHED*

Eric Clapton

Jeff Beck

Jimmy Page

Backbeat
Books

THE YARDBIRDS

ALAN CLAYSON

A BACKBEAT BOOK

First edition 2002

Published by Backbeat Books

600 Harrison Street,

San Francisco, CA94107

www.backbeatbooks.com

An imprint of The Music Player Network United
Entertainment Media Inc.

Published for Backbeat Books by Outline Press Ltd,

115J Cleveland Street, London W1T 6PU, England.

www.backbeatuk.com

ISBN 0-87930-724-2

Art Director: Nigel Osborne

Design: Paul Cooper

Editorial Director: Tony Bacon

Editor: Paul Quinn

Production: Phil Richardson

Dedicated to the memory of Lord David Sutch.

Origination and Print by Colorprint (Hong Kong)

02 03 04 04 06 5 4 3 2 1

CONTENTS

YOU CAN'T JUDGE A BOOK BY ITS COVER

Because a Boy Scout patrol leader I admired had said they were his favourite group, The Dave Clark Five became mine too. Taking the mildest disparagement of them as a mortal insult, I supported the Five as others would a football team – until the age of 16, when I could barely bring myself to admit I'd developed a preference for another outfit on the same record label.

At first I'd found The Yardbirds an unprepossessing bunch, visually, but they crept up on me in the twilight of their three-year run in the Top 40 – around the time the Five's 'Tabitha Twitchit' was unleashed on an unsuspecting public in 1967. Man, that song was awful. Its twee narrative and corny horn arrangement caused even snowblinded disciples like me to start listening in advance to successive DC Five discs before purchase. It wasn't even 'so bad it was good' – though I was filled with a sort of appalled amazement that they'd had the gall to insert a desperate recycling of the thump-thump 'Glad All Over' hook.

Contrasting with this artistic nadir was The Yardbirds' 'Happenings Ten Years Time Ago' – reckoned in retrospect to be "possibly the greatest 45 ever released" (according to Tom Hibbert's *Rare Records: Wax Trash And Vinyl Treasures*). It was the latest from a Yardbirds in uncertain transition before their decline. When their next A-side, 'Little Games', was issued, I wondered how they'd lumbered themselves with such a pig's ear of a song – even if it was nowhere near as horrible as 'Tabitha Twitchit'. They hadn't even penned it themselves, having felt obliged to look to outside composers again after 'Happenings Ten Years Time Ago' had struggled in the previous autumn's charts on both sides of the Atlantic. Perhaps, I thought, 'Little Games' was just a holding operation, something to mark time while they either regained a muse in keeping with contemporary market suitability, or else waited, like Mr Micawber, for something to turn up. Thus the seasons of pop would revolve in time-honoured growth, death and rebirth, and the group, if they kept their nerve, would bloom again in a fertile spring.

Still, I acquired a copy of 'Little Games' to go with other Yardbirds items that had also been collected via, let's say, 'illicit means' at a time when I was still haemorrhaging income on Dave Clark produce. After 'Tabitha Twitchit', though, I transferred my allegiance to The Yardbirds to such an extent that I set about getting hold of everything – past, present and future – on which The Yardbirds, collectively and individually (and anyone associated with them) had ever breathed.

During this vain endeavour, an acquaintance called Nicholas shoplifted 'Mr Zero' – a solo single by Keith Relf – on my behalf during a visit to London. I did the same with an import copy of 'Shapes Of Things', which had a picture sleeve and, crucially, a flipside otherwise unavailable in Britain. Such an action might have landed me in juvenile court, but I had to have that disc, just as I had to have the copy of the *Yardbirds* LP (alias *Roger The Engineer*) which turned up in the deletion rack of my local record shop in a country town in Hampshire.

Twelve-inch vinyl albums were not impossible to steal, but I chose instead impassioned haggling with the young woman behind the counter, who let me take it away for 15 shillings – most of a week's newspaper-round earnings. Having invested that amount of cash, I intended to spin it until it was dust: sometimes concentrating, say, only on the lead guitar or bass, then just the words. Next, I might play it at the wrong speeds – or backwards if the Dansette could be rigged up to do so. I was determined to get my money's worth.

At that point, as well as listening to the music itself, I began to become preoccupied with its creators, seeking insights into artistic conduct and clarification of obscurer lyrical by-ways, and generally searching for information about what made The Yardbirds tick. Scrutinising the diminishing number of articles, interviews and snippets of news about them in the music press, I made myriad private observations that lifted me from the armchair and back to the records – not merely the grooves, but the labels and packagings where I found much to notice, study and compare.

I wasn't as evangelical about The Yardbirds as I'd been about the Five. It was a deeper, more inward-looking intrigue, which had less to do with a misfit's imprinting of his sub-cultural perversities on other teenagers than what I considered to be my 'aesthetic direction'. Insidiously, through received advice from The Yardbirds and like icons, I evolved into an even more 'awkward' adolescent: I had an increasingly intense ten-year running battle about haircuts, church and other issues with my mother, who swore she'd die of shame if ever I appeared on stage with a pop group. She survived that – and the Dansette noise from my bedroom – partly, I imagine, through the discovery that our household might not be the only one containing someone like me.

As it happens, east to the Isle of Thanet, an older lad named Richard MacKay had been even more deeply moved by The Yardbirds. Decades later, Richard remained unswerving in his loyalty. As founder and editor of *Yardbirds World*, the magazine for those with an insatiable appetite for all things Yardbird, he would sum up his opinion of the group in this way: "From the moment I heard their first record, 'I Wish You Would', in 1964, I was hooked. They were obviously not following the latest trends, they were setting them. And Eric Clapton, Jeff Beck and Jimmy Page were the best guitarists around. Yet to my mind The Yardbirds made names for their successive guitarists, not the other way round, because the main ideas stemmed from the other members, namely Jim McCarty, Paul Samwell-Smith, Chris Dreja and the late Keith Relf."

What began as a hobby for Richard mutated into a craving, an obsession, almost a religion. Take it from one who's been there: you file, catalogue and gloat over your treasures. You talk with great authority about your interest, and are baffled at why others don't find it as absorbing. Your attic floor groans beneath the weight of vinyl, tapes and memorabilia.

In the early 1980s my own enthusiasm for the group wasn't exactly dead and buried either. Even 31-year-olds with pregnant wives continue to worship idols and overdraw on a misspent youth – and The Yardbirds were about to assert their ancient power once more.

I first crossed paths with the remarkable James Stanley McCarty in 1981 when he was drummer with Ruthless Blues at Angie's, a club in Wokingham, not far from my home near Henley-on-Thames. With Steve Maggs – future supremo of Audio Art, a 'new-age' record label – I buttonholed him after the soundcheck to pick his brains about Keith Relf for a fanzine Steve wanted to produce.

Over the next 15 years I graduated from Jim's interviewer to his sometime songwriting collaborator – and, most surreal of all, rehearsing with what amounted to an ersatz Yardbirds, and sitting in with The McCarty Blues Band during their residency in a London pub. In reciprocation, Jim has served as careers advisor, father confessor and a major catalyst in the recovery of my own artistic confidence.

Through him I also made contact with Paul Samwell-Smith, and Keith Relf's widow, April, and his sister Jane – who had been recruited into Renaissance, and later Illusion. By the late 1980s she'd resurfaced as featured vocalist with Stairway, Jim's new-age ensemble. Jane even sang a lyric I penned for the 1996 Stairway track 'Raindreaming'.

When I got wind of a Yardbirds reunion in 1994, I began running for office in earnest. Was it so unreasonable, I asked myself, to embrace the unbearably exciting hope that, in view of recent events and connections, I might become a Yardbird? I'd already 'sat in' with Jim's band, after all – albeit panicking on devil-may-care keyboards, and creating havoc with stomach-churning modulations and flurries of bum notes. (Chris Dreja had been there too and, surprisingly, he'd had less of a clue about some of the numbers – all the hits plus a lot of R&B – than I had.) I rang Jim to ask point-blank if I could be Keith. I didn't get the job. One thing that could have gone against me is my way with a mouth-organ, which is as naive as my two-fingered typing...

I was invited to Jim's 50th birthday party, in July 1993, at the 100 Club in central London. For days beforehand I'd been wringing my hands about what I ought to wear and how to behave – the etiquette at these galas can be crippling. But the celebration of Jim's half-century was no ordeal of luvvie conviviality, and I soon began to enjoy myself like I would at any other party with dim lights, finger food, chit-chat and records.

In the queue for the buffet were various Kinks and Pretty Things, as well as former Yardbirds, Renaissance figures, Stairway-farers et al loosening up with coded hilarity and mutual nostalgia about bohemian haunts around Teddington Lock when the world was young. They seemed so far away now: Kingston Art College, L'Auberge Cafe, Eel Pie Island, the Craw Daddy and, of course, the G Club where Alexis Korner's Blues Incorporated had presided over the beatniks, weekend dropouts and those in the throng awaiting destinies as Rolling Stones, Downliners Sect-ers, Manfred Mann men – and Yardbirds.

The historian in me drank it all in. Details were eased from my memory bank and were laced with secondary research and further first-hand reminiscences when I wrote this book – which also redresses a common imbalance by focussing heavily on members of the group other than the triumvirate of guitar heroes, and includes the period between the sundering of The Yardbirds in 1968 and an apparently permanent reformation in the 1990s, so bringing the story up to date.

Essentially this is a rather personal telling of the Yardbirds story, at times more of an extended meditation than a strict chronological biography (though you will find a full diary of their activities near the end of the book). It endeavours to place in a historical context the professional strategies of a group who, even more than breaking barriers in pop, at times so detached themselves from its mainstream that only restrictions such as the common chord and rock instrumentation put much of their music in the realm of 'pop' at all.

Alan Clayson, April 2002

CHAPTER 1

HAPPENINGS TEN YEARS TIME AGO

*"There were four rock bands in the world
that really counted, and The Yardbirds
was one of them."*

SIMON NAPIER-BELL

For the Tibetan monk out there who's never heard of The Yardbirds, I ought to recount the old, old story for the trillionth time... The dominant musical emphasis of the British Beat Boom was on songs, but most consumers of today's cultured 'contemporary' pop for the over-forties have taught their children to regard The Yardbirds less as combined figureheads and background forces of 1960s pop (though we'll see later just how influential they were) than as a springboard for the nurtured prowess and neo-deification of three of their lead guitarists. Just as, let's say,

THE YARDBIRDS

Them and The Equals are recalled respectively as Van Morrison's and Eddy Grant's old groups, so The Yardbirds are the combo in which Eric Clapton, Jeff Beck and Jimmy Page cut their teeth before moving onwards and upwards.

While the over-attention paid to the virtuoso guitarists contributed to the group's self-destruction, the varying degrees of whimsical fretboard elasticity, masterful technique and outright craziness were among the ingredients that transformed The Yardbirds from a Home-Counties blues appreciation society to the point where even Simon Napier-Bell, a disgruntled former manager, found it in him to admit in an otherwise waspish 1982 autobiography (*You Don't Have To Say You Love Me*), "There were four rock bands in the world that really counted, and the Yardbirds was one of them."

"Interest in the group's six-string heroes has tended to displace the often less-tangible innovations of the other members"

Indeed, although Eric Clapton, Jeff Beck and Jimmy Page have racked up heftier commercial achievements since, I firmly believe none of them has left as insidious a legacy to pop as they did when each was a humble Yardbird – and this despite the relatively primitive technology of the time.

Sensational though they were, interest in those six-string heroes has tended to displace the often less-tangible innovations of the other members – even vocalist Keith Relf at the central microphone, but particularly the group's 'quiet blokes' at the back, who didn't have that much going for them until they found their feet as composers.

In particular, Paul Samwell-Smith on bass, and Jim McCarty, toiling over his drum kit, posed no limelight-threatening challenge to anyone. Yet they composed nearly all The Yardbirds' most enduring songs and, with general factotum Chris Dreja, were principal advocates in the realisation of extraordinary musical visions. These were seen most blatantly in the pioneering of extended improvisation (the famous Yardbird 'rave-ups'), deliberate electronic feedback and the imposition of symphonic tempo changes, Gregorian chant and other eruditions onto the group's musical grid. With The Kinks, The Yardbirds were also the first pop explorers of Indian sounds (with Beck's mock-oriental twang more like the real thing than the real thing).

Initially the ceiling of The Yardbirds' ambition had been modest. After preludes by individual members in skiffle, mainstream pop and gutbucket ethnic blues, The Yardbirds smouldered into form, circa 1963, with singing mouth-organist Relf, drummer McCarty, lead guitarist Anthony 'Top' Topham, Dreja on rhythm guitar, percussion and occasional piano, and Samwell-Smith on a customised home-made bass guitar.

The five clung onto their day jobs and college courses while delivering souped-up rhythm & blues – R&B – in bohemian haunts around the western edge of London. I gather from my teenage sons that 'R&B' doesn't mean the same now as it did when I was a lad. My concept of the stuff was derived from

The Yardbirds, the Downliners Sect, Them, The Pretty Things, the Stones and lesser beat groups of the 1960s who attempted to emulate – with varying levels of success – the John Lee Hookers, Slim Harpos and Howlin' Wolves from the speakeasies and juke joints of black America.

After 16-year-old Topham had been ousted by the older Eric 'Slowhand' Clapton – no more eloquent an instrumentalist but possessing a stronger stage presence – The Yardbirds took over from The Rolling Stones as house band at Richmond's Craw Daddy in 1963, and were soon earning enough to go fully professional.

Just as the Stones had pushed R&B-derived pop into the hit parade, The Yardbirds – if lacking 'image' beyond a generalised arty aura – were well placed to do likewise. Signed to an EMI subsidiary, their second single, a 'surf' revival of Sonny Boy Williamson's 'Good Morning Little Schoolgirl', gained a toehold on the Top 50 in October 1964; and 1964's atmospheric *Five Live Yardbirds* album shifted sufficient copies to serve as a holding operation during the months preceding a final recording session with blues purist Clapton.

Uneasy about his colleagues' more upmarket outlook, Eric flew the nest to join John Mayall's Bluesbreakers just before the release of 1965's catchy 'For Your Love' – with Samwell-Smith in control at the studio console – which turned out to be a domestic chart-topper and global million-seller.

Respected session musician Jimmy Page (the group's first choice as Eric's replacement) recommended Jeff Beck of The Tridents. As shown by his inspired use of exotic phrases, unprecedented legato effects and abrasive passagework, the charismatic new recruit was no Clapton duplicate. Beck was to display further eclecticism and unpredictability in compatible amounts during The Yardbirds' two-year golden age as they ventured into areas far removed from their R&B core.

'For Your Love' precipitated more adventurous smashes – 'Heart Full Of Soul', 'Evil-Hearted You', 'Still I'm Sad' (their first self-penned A-side), 'Shapes Of Things' and 'Over Under Sideways Down' – all hybrids of instant familiarity and musical experiment.

Even a solo 45 by Relf made the UK Top 50 – just. But fast comes the hour when fades the fairest flower. It may be dated from the resignation of the gifted Samwell-Smith, a month before the release of 1966's outstanding *Yardbirds* LP. While Paul became a full-time record producer for such diverse future clients as Jethro Tull and Carly Simon, the others soldiered on for another year, after persuading Jimmy Page to step in – initially on bass, but soon reverting to a more apt role as co-lead guitarist, as soon as Dreja was able to switch to the four-string.

> *"Beck was to display further eclecticism and unpredictability during The Yardbirds' two-year golden age"*

Apart from a cameo in Antonioni's *Blowup* flick and soundtrack, the only recordings credited to this Beck-plus-Page edition were the overtly psychedelic 'Happenings Ten Years Time Ago' and its UK flipside, 'Psycho Daisies'.

During a harrowing North American tour, the erratic Beck was sacked, and with a consequently increased stake in The Yardbirds' ebbing fortunes, Page suggested making use of Mickie Most, renowned manufacturer of chart ballast, for the discs that punctuated the group's continued downfall. Forbidding much elaboration – and favouring session hirelings over established personnel – Most's A-sides were to include 'Little Games' and a US-only heist of Manfred Mann's 'Ha Ha Said The Clown'. Other sub-standard efforts that reflected a creative impasse led to the break-up of The Yardbirds after an engagement at Luton Technical College in 1968.

That same year, Cream – with Eric Clapton, drummer Ginger Baker and bass guitarist Jack Bruce – enacted a more premeditated disbandment. Clapton was then railroaded into the Blind Faith 'supergroup' before throwing in his lot with the less illustrious Delaney & Bonnie & Friends.

Meanwhile, guided by Mickie Most, Jeff Beck had entered the UK Top 40 thrice – with 'Hi Ho Silver Lining', 'Tallyman' and 'Love Is Blue'. Lead vocal on 'Tallyman' was shared with Rod Stewart, whom Beck, a hesitant singer, had enlisted into The Jeff Beck Group for an outstanding US concert debut.

Tracks from the Beck ensemble's *Truth* LP – and from The Yardbirds' valedictory *Little Games* – were repertory blueprints for Page's new Yardbirds, renamed Led Zeppelin for an eponymous debut album that had them stereotyped as the ultimate 'high energy' rock band – though by 1970's *Led Zeppelin III* a quasi-pastoral approach had infiltrated the modus operandi.

> *"Sub-standard efforts that reflected a creative impasse led to the break-up of The Yardbirds in 1968"*

This acoustic emphasis had in fact been pre-empted by 'Henry's Coming Home' – the *ultima Thule*, the rarest of prizes for collectors of Yardbirds artefacts – a poor-selling 1968 single by McCarty and Relf, reunited under the name Together. This anticipated the following year's more lucrative Renaissance (not to be confused with an act called The Renaissance, then clients of NEMS, the agency set up by the late Brian Epstein) with Relf's singing sister Jane and former members of The Nashville Teens and The Herd. Though McCarty co-wrote much of 1972's *Prologue* album, he (like the Relfs) had by then left Renaissance to fend for themselves.

On vocals and keyboards, Jim was to form Shoot for a solitary LP, *On The Frontier*, while Keith emerged as the producer behind Medicine Head, also returning to the stage as this duo's bass guitarist. He stepped further into the limelight with Armageddon, a short-lived hard rock unit of mystical bent.

Relf had had less to prove than Clapton, who on his first solo collection – titled simply *Eric Clapton* – either couldn't or wouldn't be as flashy as before. Neither was he quite ready to function outside the context of a group, hence his subsequent nominal leadership of Derek & The Dominoes, who split as Eric's drug addiction worsened.

Jeff Beck had been off the air too, having parted from Rod Stewart et al before suffering serious injuries in a road accident. On recovering, he assembled another Jeff Beck Group for two albums before linking up with The Vanilla Fudge's Tim Bogert and Carmine Appice. But this trio petered out, mostly through lack of new material and Jeff's growing dislike of heavy metal.

Now that Beck had thrown the race, Led Zeppelin ruled stadium rock, even when, amid rumours of Page's dabbling in the occult, they retired from the road for over a year prior to a world tour to promote their sixth album, 1975's *Physical Graffiti*.

Beck's offering that year was *Blow By Blow*. He was now so captivated by jazz-rock that, declining a post with The Rolling Stones, he then recorded *Wired* with former Mahavishnu Orchestra keyboard player Jan Hammer – with whom he toured and surfaced as one of few rock guitarists who could handle fusion music convincingly. As Jeff would tell you himself: "Whether there's one thing I've done that sums up Jeff Beck and my approach to the guitar, I couldn't say – because as soon as I reach my destination I'm off somewhere else."

After *There And Back* with Hammer, Beck's *Flash* was more in keeping with passing trends. Then came a liaison with Malcolm McLaren on *Waltz Darling*, and the more characteristic Jeff Beck's *Guitar Workshop*.

Though increasingly less adventurous, Eric Clapton's career rolled on despite his personal troubles, and his solo albums continued to sell well to devoted followers and register in the charts, particularly in the United States.

Page's Led Zeppelin saw out the 1970s with big-selling records too, but after drummer John Bonham's passing in 1980 they disbanded, save for rare one-off reunions. Page has since taken on film soundtracks and membership of The Firm (with Bad Company's Paul Rodgers). Before teaming up once more with Robert Plant, he issued 1988's solo album *Outrider*, and a disappointing album with former Deep Purple frontman and chanteur David Coverdale.

> *"In 1983 an act called The Yardbirds played the Marquee during the club's anniversary celebrations"*

In 1983, Jimmy and Jeff Beck had been intrigued when an act called The Yardbirds played the Marquee during the club's anniversary celebrations. Chris Dreja, Jim McCarty and Paul Samwell-Smith presided over the frontline antics of John Knightsbridge (guitarist with McCarty's pub-rock band Ruthless Blues), mouth-organist Mark Feltham and Medicine Head's John Fiddler. The latter's presence was a poignant touch – he was standing in for his old mentor and colleague Keith Relf who'd died in 1976 after being electrocuted, just when the first Renaissance line-up was planning to reform as Illusion.

This briefly reformed Yardbirds entered the studio under the guise of Box Of Frogs. Aided by guest spots from Beck and Rory Gallagher, and by the big-name respects paid to the mid-1960s edition of The Yardbirds (via, for instance, David Bowie's overhaul of 'Shapes Of Things' in the mid-1970s), the first Box Of Frogs album hopped to Number 45 in the US charts. There was, nonetheless, a tacit understanding that this arguable confirmation of The Yardbirds' posthumous popularity was blighted by a more glorious past.

Since Box Of Frogs, McCarty has been linchpin of various blues bands – including one with Top Topham – and has participated in the artistic *faux pas* that was the British Invasion All-Stars, a merger with shellbacks from The Nashville Teens, The Downliners Sect and The Creation.

Drawing on The Yardbirds' inspired spirit of old, Jim kept the faith as mainstay of Stairway, Britain's best-loved new-age outfit (founded with Louis Cennamo of Renaissance), and with a *cause célèbre* of a solo album, *Out Of The Dark*. The reference points of both projects are similar to those attempted by his previous incarnations – 'Turn Into Earth' from the *Yardbirds* album was featured in Stairway's concert repertoire. Though mainly instrumental, vocal pieces such as 'Lavender Down', 'Bird Of Paradise' and 'Aquamarine' were as strong in their way as any in the Yardbirds or Renaissance canon.

The man-in-the-street, however, was only aware of Stairway to the same small degree as he was of a simultaneously-functioning Jim McCarty Band which, in the early 1990s, contained the fine lead guitarist Ray Majors (ex-Mott The Hoople) and 28-year-old bass player 'Detroit' John Idan. One evening at the 100 Club they were augmented by Chris Dreja for what was billed as another one-off Yardbirds reunion.

> *"In spring 2002 The Yardbirds were still touring on the Sixties circuit with the likes of The Troggs"*

The wheels of the universe came together again on a sturdier footing in 1994. Second-billed to The Blues Band at an auditorium in Brentwood, Essex, a permanently reconstituted Yardbirds consisted of Jim's pub trio plus Dreja and Laurie Garman from The Diplomatics on harmonica. John Idan – Scott Walker-handsome and a gen-u-ine American – added some teen appeal to the otherwise middle-aged line-up, and took the lion's share of lead singing, in a ghost-of-Keith voice that got attractively rougher during an intense 40-minute recital that included 'For Your Love', 'Shapes Of Things', 'Over Under Sideways Down' et al, as well as R&B set-works such as 'I Ain't Got You', which less than about two per cent of the onlookers might have recognised as a 1964 B-side. All that most fans, old and new, wanted were the ambles down a trailblazing Memory Lane.

In spring 2002 The Yardbirds were still touring on the 'Sixties' circuit with the likes of The Troggs and The Spencer Davis Group. No-one could pretend the reformed group can recreate what it must have been like when *Five Live Yardbirds* was taped in 1964, or when Beck and Page broke sweat with on-stage duelling during the 'Happenings Ten Years Time Ago' period. Even so, today's Yardbirds might stagger the type of people who attended Eric Clapton's Albert Hall seasons out of little more than habit – and their support could perhaps facilitate such a promising outfit's ascent from the netherworld of nostalgia.

Yardbirds

THE PICTURES

An ad for a couple of early 'Yard-Birds' gigs at Studio 51 (4th/6th October 1963) – just days before Anthony Topham left (1). Publicity shot (April 1964), with Dreja, Clapton, Samwell-Smith, McCarty and Relf posing in a blustery Hyde Park, central London (2). Surreal times in the back garden of Lord Ted Willis in leafy Kent (13/5/1964); the former TV script writer had berated the current "candyfloss" pop culture, so PR-minded Giorgio Gomelsky brought the band round to his house to prove him wrong...

FIVE LIVE

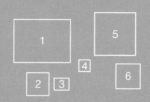

	1		5
		4	
2	3		6

Nervy early TV performance on *Ready Steady Go*, performing debut single 'I Wish You Would' (22/5/64). Is Eric scared, or just wearing a neck brace? (1). Away from the glamour of TV, there were still many more mundane boards to be trod around the country: this rare shot from August '64 shows stand-in Mick O'Neil of The Authentics fronting The Yardbirds instead of a temporarily ailing Keith Relf (2). Evidence (from October '63) of the band's residency at the famed Craw Daddy R&B club (3). Debut UK album, *Five Live Yardbirds* (31/12/64) featured live recordings from earlier in the year at London's Marquee club (4). Keith in better health, but poor knitwear, in January '65 (5). Now fully fledged recording artists, the boys signed on to the pop treadmill (6).

JEFF'S
BOOGIE

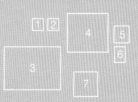

Sleeve of US album *For Your Love* (5/7/65) – a compilation featuring the big hit padded out with early rarities, with Jeff pictured at the keyboards on the cover (1). *Having A Rave-Up With The Yardbirds* (US Nov '65) had a sleeve that implied more of a tea dance than a rave-up, and included 'Heart Full Of Soul', 'You're A Better Man...' plus recycled extracts from the *Five Live Yardbirds* set (2). A '65 PR shot of the five looking hip, if slightly glazed (3). Performing on *Ready Steady Goes Live* (April '65), a month after Beck joined the group, with Dreja here on maracas (4). One of Beck's first PR shots – the suit, tie and haircut didn't last (5). The infamous Kinks tour, May '65 (6). By now everyone looks more casual about being on *Ready Steady Go*, Oct '65 (7).

21

On *Ready Steady Go*, 18/2/66, performing 'Shapes Of Things' (1). One of the group's less flattering publicity shots, early '66, with Beck looking the least gawky in fringed, suede jacket (2). Striking cool poses while recording US TV show *Shivaree* (3/1/66) at the height of their fame; they played 'Heart Full Of Soul' and 'I'm A Man' (3). The *Sonny Boy Williamson & The Yardbirds* LP was released in Jan '66, with a photo of the Beck line-up on the sleeve, but was recorded during Clapton period back in Dec '63 at the Craw Daddy club (4). A stripey look while in sunny Italy for the rather inappropriate San Remo Festival, Jan '66 (5).

SHAPES & STATES

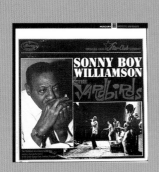

READY STEADY GO

ROGER
THE ENGINEER

The classic *Yardbirds* album (July '66), also known as *Roger The Engineer*, thanks to Chris Dreja's cover artwork (a warped caricature of the LP's engineer Roger Cameron), was issued in mono (1) and stereo versions – of which (2) is a 1980s re-issue in yellow sleeve. Considered their best overall studio work, it was released in the US (with two tracks missing) as *Over Under Sideways Down* (see p27). By now old hands on the *Ready Steady Go* TV series (4/3/66), they're seen here plugging new single 'Shapes Of Things' (3). One of the better shots of Jim on drums, at the same *RSG* show (4). In May '66 they were back at the Rediffusion studios for the launch of the 'Over Under Sideways Down' single (5). Jeff lets rip on his Les Paul (6).

25

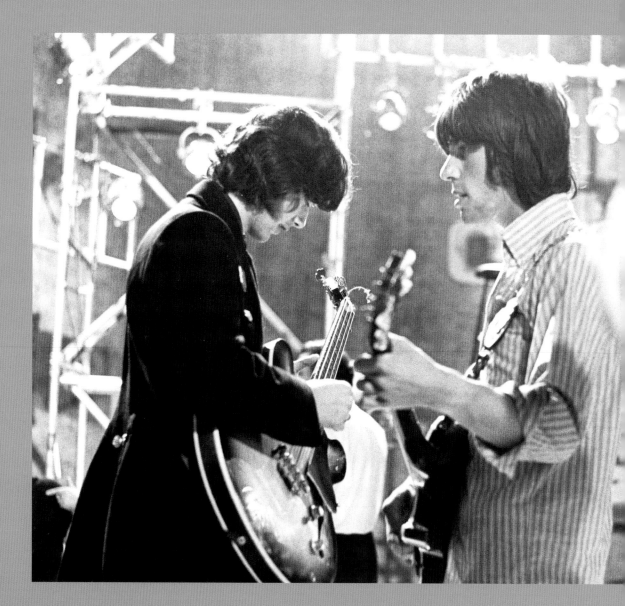

PAGE FOUR

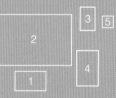

The short-lived line-up with both Beck and Page lasted only a few months, from June '66, with Page initially replacing Samwell-Smith on bass. On 22nd July they taped two tracks ('Farewell' & 'Lost Woman') for *Ready Steady Go* (1). Page and Beck tuning up (2). Keith adds handclaps (3). Autograph hunters form a queue between takes (4). The sleeve of US-released *Over Under Sideways Down* (5), a rehash of *Yardbirds/Roger The Engineer*, with pre-Monty Python cut-outs replacing Chris's cartoon doodlings on the sleeve, and without the tracks 'Rack My Mind' and 'The Nazz Are Blue' (the latter used as a US B-side).

PAGE SIX

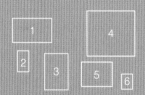

A "great show" by all accounts at the Fillmore
Auditorium in San Francisco (23/10/66) – also a
relatively rare photo of both Page (left) and Beck
(right) playing guitar together on-stage (1). First
date of Yardbirds fourth US tour, 21/10/66, at
the Comic Strip, Worcester, Massachusetts (2).
Page and McCarty on-stage at Ventura High
School, California, 27/8/66 – Beck was ill, so
Jimmy borrowed his Les Paul Standard guitar,
which may have inspired him to get one of his
own (3). More publicity shots of the Beck + Page
line-up (4, 5 & 6), probably taken during the US
tour in November 1966, Beck's last appearances
with The Yardbirds.

Melody Maker

JULY 20, 1968   1s weekly

YARDBIRDS SPLIT

YARDBIRDS, who have been together for five years, have split into two groups.

Lead guitarist Jimmy Page and bassist Chris Dreja will add two new members and continue as the Yardbirds; vocalist Keith Relf and drummer Jim McCarty will add a bassist and guitarist and be known as Together.

Reason for the split: differences over musical policy. "There were no personal differences among the boys," said a spokesman. "It is just that Keith and Jim are following an entirely different musical line from Jimmy and Chris."

OLD FOR NEW

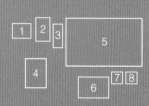

After Beck's departure, the four-piece embrace a more psychedelic 1967 look (1 & 6). Poster for dates at the Fillmore Auditorium (23–25/5/68) on final US tour (2). News of the band's split broken in *Melody Maker* (25/10/68) – Dreja and Page to continue as Yardbirds (though Dreja opted out) while Relf and McCarty to form Together (3). Last known reference to Yardbirds in the 1960s – a Surrey University gig (25/10/68) by the line-up that soon changed its name to Led Zeppelin (4). The new Yardbirds line-up played their first UK gig at The Marquee on 18/10/68 – l to r: Jones, Plant, Page, Bonham (5). *Little Games* (24/7/67) was The Yardbirds' last studio album (7). Sleeve of rare *Live Yardbirds* LP, recorded 30/3/68 in New York but not released till 1971, as a Zeppelin cash-in.

ONE MORE TIME

	1	2
	3	
		4

The 21st century Yardbirds in action on their 2002 UK tour: Gypie Mayo on lead guitar (1); John Idan on bass and vocals, watched by Chris Dreja on rhythm guitar (2); Alan Glen on harmonica and percussion (3); and stalwart Jim McCarty on drums (4).

"The Yardbirds aren't a nostalgia band. The excitement, the energy still winds me up, and I'll always be a fan of The Yardbirds as much as I am a player. It's a band I'd be proud to take anywhere."

CHRIS DREJA

CHAPTER 2

EVER SINCE THE WORLD BEGAN

"The school headmaster put a stop to our music straight away – because it was dirty. He thought that anyone in rock'n'roll must be involved in sex and drugs."

PAUL SAMWELL-SMITH

Now we must set off on the historical scenic route, beginning where London bleeds into the county of Surrey – because The Yardbirds' background was, like that of so many icons of the Swinging Sixties, privet-hedged suburban.

Thus we find ourselves in the glum post-war neighbourhoods bordered by the respective drones of London Airport (later Heathrow) and the Great West Road, the mudbanks of the Thames and the clattering railway commutations to Waterloo – no different to many other arcadia of meadows and woodland

now buried beneath an urban sprawl. We're roaming a residential hinterland of raw red brick built by-the-book amid small-time light industry, concrete rows of lock-up garages and tangles of shopping precincts; crumbling Victorian town houses holding each other up like drunkards; tree-lined up-market avenues and windswept acres of playing fields; arteries of traffic distracted by advertising hoardings; and industrial zones of engineering, electronics and chemical works with giant chimneys levelled at the skies like anti-aircraft guns.

> *"Music theory was taught almost as a kind of mathematics, through cross-legged banging of assorted percussion"*

Parking lots formed from bombsites are evidence that the encroaching renewal programme has been assisted in places by the Luftwaffe. As an insensible babe-in-arms, the oldest Yardbird – Keith Relf, born in Richmond, Surrey in 1943 – may have watched formations of the RAF zooming towards the German bombardment of the docks where the horizon glowed with ton upon booming ton of death and destruction. Prised into the world a few weeks after Keith, Jim McCarty had opened his eyes in Liverpool, the grimy pivot of Victorian commerce that had been blackened further by the same hostile shadows from mainland Europe.

An only child, Jim did not dwell on Merseyside long enough to catch and hold the glottal Scouse drawl that would sound ambiguously alien and 'common' in Teddington where, short-trousered and gabardine-raincoated, he began his formal education at Stanley Road Primary School.

As it was for most baby-boomers under an unimaginative and frequently terrifying regime, music theory was taught almost as a kind of mathematics, through cross-legged banging of assorted percussion, and the diagrammatic representation of a dotted crotchet using three of the third-pint bottles of lukewarm milk provided by the Welfare State at mid-morning school playtime.

For families such as the Relfs and McCartys, the more lugubrious post-war realities could be shut off, however fleetingly, when you turned your back on London's outer conurbations for what was described as 'the countryside': for instance the village of Ripley – where Eric Clapton was born – or olde-world Cobham with its ivy-clung walls, tea-shoppe gentility, and a guarantee that nothing would happen there, year in, year out. Deeper into the heart of rural Surrey, apple-cheeked hikers emerged from birch woods to view a storybook landscape melting into a touch of mist towards the Sussex coast.

Only the cascading pylons need remind you of the existence of Hampton, Morden, Gunnersbury and all the rest of the overlapping vicinities between Staines and Croydon where all those in the most illustrious edition of The Yardbirds were growing up. Here a newly-wed couple might start married life in one of their in-laws' homes, front doors slammed on the pervading smell of soiled nappies and over-cooked cabbage, and streets were roamed by gangs of a menacing if narcissistic teenage cult, identified by seedy-flash finery and quiffed glaciers of brilliantine. The first Teddy Boy murder was committed on a London heath in 1954 – but by the following March a highlight of Scottish singing comedian Jimmy Logan's act at the London Palladium was a gentle send-up actually entitled 'Teddy Boy', with complacently tuxedo'd accompaniment from The Geraldo Orchestra, and not a trace of rock'n'roll.

Everybody laughed at first. There was nothing new about bored adolescents, with hormones raging, wondering what to do until bedtime. Yet as the 1950s got out of neutral, grandmothers everywhere pleaded for calm amid blazing rows between parents and once-tractable children over music of increasingly loud, racy and North American persuasion issuing from wireless and wind-up gramophone.

Its titles were infiltrating the recently-established New Musical Express record and sheet-music sales charts – and soon the hunt was on for more money-making morons who modelled themselves on Mr E A Presley, a hillbilly shouter from Tennessee.

Copying Elvis, or one of the other rock'n'roll 'maniacs' from the States, was how any teenager in the mid-1950s world gave himself the best chance of being elevated to at least regional renown. Off-the-cuff examples were France's Johnny Halliday, Mickie Most from South Africa and Australian Johnny O'Keefe.

There were plenty more in Britain. Originally from Isleworth, just over the river from Richmond, Vince Taylor (Brian Holden to his mates) was to put himself forward as a second Gene Vincent; Danny Storm from the Middlesex side of the Great West Road devised a stage act that coincided in every detail with that of Cliff Richard, the kingdom's foremost Elvis duplicate; and Wee Willie Harris was bruited as Greater London's very own Jerry Lee Lewis.

Like Lewis, Harris pounded the piano, but the majority of would-be rock'n'rollers were trying to master an instrument once mainly associated with Latinate heel-clattering. Most would grapple with shaping rudimentary chords before giving it up as a bad job, but the fingertips of a substantial minority hardened with daily practice.

A certain Geoffrey Arnold Beck had been taking the trouble to learn properly even prior to the coming of Presley. Born in 1944 in Wallington near Croydon, Surrey, Jeff had endured membership of a church choir and two years of piano lessons, but confesses, "I didn't listen." Then came the day in 1951 when he heard, bursting from the radio, a disc featuring the novel multi-tracking of Les Paul and his self-designed electric guitar. "I remember asking my parents what that strange noise was. They told me it was all fake, just studio tricks – but I'm sure it was the first music that really caught my attention."

"Jeff Beck endured membership of a church choir and two years of piano lessons, but says he 'didn't listen' "

If not as highly regarded as Les Paul, the most omnipotent of Britain's amplified pickers was a 30-something Londoner named Bert Weedon. Fretboard executants like Beck, Dave Edmunds and George Harrison began by positioning as-yet uncalloused digits on taut strings while poring over exercises prescribed in Bert's best-selling *Play In A Day* manual, before moving on to its *Play Every Day* companion, with pieces by virtuosi such as 'gypsy jazz' exponent Django Reinhardt, and Chet

Atkins, who had first refusal of virtually all recording sessions in Nashville, the Hollywood of country and western.

As disparate in style and artistic appetite as Reinhardt and Atkins, a generous litter of hit parade contenders would be spawned by Surrey during the next decade, when the sky became the limit.

While Petula Clark, Manfred Mann's Michael d'Abo and Pink Floyd bass player Roger Waters were connected to the county by mere accident of birth, The Yardbirds are among those who will be eternally Surrey, as The Beatles are Liverpool. Yet they all had to fight the same battle for attention because, then as now, the industry of glamour, fame and pop clotted in London – seat of these islands' handful of major record companies. So the mountains had to come to Mohammed.

Even as close as the city's outskirts, the possibilities of making a living as a musical entertainer belonged only to idle speculation, something dreamed of while sharing a communal cigarette behind school bicycle sheds. If you didn't tramp a well-beaten path uptown – as the likes of Cliff Richard and Wee Willie Harris had – you might as well give up, and try harder for academic qualifications instead of just waiting for Friday to roll around. But who wanted to be full-steam-ahead for dull and respectable old age when there was even the possibility of a more enchanting alternative, no matter how remote?

> " 'Musician' no longer meant sitting in the fourth row of violins and cranking out Beethoven all your life"

'Musician', you see, no longer meant sitting in the fourth row of violins and cranking out Beethoven all your life, or indeed conforming to any school dictates about what was and wasn't 'decent' music. For Paul Samwell-Smith, a first-former at Hampton Grammar in 1954, and Christopher Dreja, still at junior school in Surbiton, 'The Ballad Of Davy Crockett' and Frankie Laine's quasi-religious 'I Believe' were more meaningful than Brahms' 'German Requiem'.

In those days you'd have had quite a search for anything wilder on the BBC Light Programme than the likes of *Ken Sekora's Jazz Club*, Friday evening's *Radio Rhythm Club* and infrequent spins of Fats Waller, Hoagy Carmichael and the odd blues opus between the Mantovanis, unchained melodies, Mambo Italianos and doggies in the window. On TV, *Round About Ten*, with its inclusion of Humphrey Lyttelton's Jazz Band, was as hot as it got.

Anthony James 'Lonnie' Donegan, a Glasgow-born Londoner who at the time led his own Tony Donegan Jazz Band, later recalled: "I first heard blues on *Radio Rhythm Club*. There'd be one 'folk' song per programme. Sometimes it was a blues."

Perhaps the most crucial local band at the time was The Crane River Jazz Band, formed in Cranford, Middlesex with trumpeter Ken Colyer. "They were the first band to get that authentic New Orleans feel," noted Lonnie Donegan. "Ken had joined the merchant navy just so he could jump ship in New Orleans. Had he not done that, British pop wouldn't be what it is today." Traditional jazz ("trad"), as spearheaded by Ken, turned out to be a stepping stone to skiffle and all that followed. "Chris Barber had a band too," Donegan continued. "All of us used to get together at the Prince Alfred at Mile End and play all night. From this emerged the first professional English jazz band, named after Chris. With Ken, Chris and I being into Leadbelly and all the other Afro-American music, we featured this with the band, and it all got mixed up."

Stravinsky had been sincerely loud in his advocacy of jazz as early as 1913, but to sniffier grownups the world over it was part of the depraved cacophony subverting all that was good and true. All the same, some unadulterated rhythm & blues (R&B) from black North America had crept onto white radio playlists, notably in Fats Domino's ambulatory lope and the sly lyricism of Chuck Berry – the most conspicuous giant of classic rock'n'roll to fly in the face of the traditional demarcation line that existed between composer and artist. Meanwhile, Bill Haley & The Comets, a paunchy dance combo from Detroit, had got lucky in 1955 with a clangorous Xerox of Sonny Dae & The Knights' R&B original, 'Rock Around The Clock'.

"Rock'n'roll, when she was originally spoke, was rhythm & blues," said Lonnie Donegan, "and God knows what that was either. Country blues brought to the city and played through an amplifier?"

A passion for such 'music' – if that's what you called it – would bring puffy smiles to the lips of do-gooders in cardigans who presided over hearty pastimes intended to distract young minds from nature's baser urges. When not inside youth club, scout hut or YMCA for ping-pong, scout gang-show rehearsals or 'Brains Trusts' quizzings on current affairs, you were meant to be out brass-rubbing, Bob-A-Jobbing or booting around a soaking-wet leather football.

Many schools and youth clubs at the time had jazz societies, who might dare to devote perhaps one meeting per term to, say, 'Blues and Jazz-Influenced Pop'. Seats of learning were still generally divided along educational lines: for the type of parents that cared less about their offspring's happiness than the approval of their own peers, a child passing the 11-Plus examination, and thus gaining a place at a (usually single-sex) grammar school, was as desirable a social coup as it was an academic one. The Secondary Modern school was where 'failures' like Eric Clapton, Jeff Beck, Anthony Topham and Chris Dreja went – after going to pieces on that day-of-days that decided your future back in the 1950s.

Jeff Beck did manage to construct a crude solid-body guitar during woodwork at Sutton East Secondary ("but I had a row with my dad, and he tossed it out into the garden and busted it"). Over at Hollyfield Road School for Boys & Girls, Chris

"Chris Dreja was to become renowned for his self-taught knack with Jelly Roll Morton-esque honky-tonk piano"

Dreja was to become as renowned for his self-taught knack with Jelly Roll Morton-esque honky-tonk piano as soccer captains, raffia prizewinners and class bullies were in their chosen spheres.

Not-so-liberal establishments included the all-boys Leatherhead Grammar – where Keith Relf was little more to the headmaster than a name on a register – and Hampton Grammar, where short-back-and-sides and 1950s 'quiet' style of dress were applauded tacitly by teachers as marks of masculinity and sobriety. Intellectually stultifying pop music was regarded with malevolent neutrality at best. Paul Samwell-Smith was to recall: "There was a lot of opposition. Our music master was quite good, but the head put a stop to it straight away – because it was dirty. He thought that anyone in rock'n'roll must be involved in sex and drugs."

As a contrast to this, Bill Haley and his tubby old troupers finally landed on these shores in 1957 during a world tour. Chuck Berry was first experienced less directly by the world beyond the States when he appeared in *Jazz On A Summer's Day*, a US film documentary about a turn-of-the-decade outdoor festival. Duck-walking with his crotch-level red guitar, Chuck offended jazz purists but captured the imaginations of European adolescents who were to turn to long-players like 1958's *One Dozen Berries* or an imported *Chuck Berry Is On Top* as regularly as monks to the Bible, savouring – as I would later with Yardbirds – the tactile sensation of handling the cover, and finding no liner-note syllable too insignificant to be interesting.

> *"The fascination increased in proportion to the grimness of adult scowls at the noise and loutish excess of rock'n'roll"*

The fascination increased in proportion to the grimness of adult scowls at the noise, gibberish and loutish excess of the rock'n'roll epidemic from across the Atlantic. When, in 1959, Chuck served the first of two jail terms that would put temporary halts to his career, his incarceration, coupled with a dearth of alternatives, only boosted his cult celebrity. Berry's 'Carol', 'Reelin' And Rockin'', 'Too Much Monkey Business', 'Memphis Tennessee', 'Let It Rock', 'Little Queenie' and all the rest were to be prominent in the repertoires of all British beat groups that mattered – and were often the redeeming features of many that didn't. Pretty Thing-in-waiting Phil May remembers he used to go and watch Bern Elliott & The Fenmen, the Medway Towns' answer to Cliff Richard & The Shadows, "but I would be waiting for them to play their two Chuck Berry numbers."

Of all the events that coalesced to spur on the British beat boom, perhaps the most paramount was when Buddy Holly & The Crickets undertook a British tour in March 1958. Making up for a manifest deficit of physical attractiveness, Holly possessed other talents – not least of which was an ability to write, with various Crickets, songs tailored to his elastic adenoids, demonstrating how rock'n'roll could be simultaneously forceful and romantic. Moreover it didn't have to be complicated. Most Crickets originals were inspired reworkings of R&B-style clichés, as exemplified by 'Not Fade Away', built around Bo Diddley's trademark shave-and-a-haircut-six-pence drum rhythm.

Among those schoolboys who found Buddy and his Crickets' stage act and compact sound instructive were Mick Jagger, Jeff Beck, Keith Relf and Eric Clapton, who – independently of each other – all caught the show in and around London. Obvious evidence of this is The Rolling Stones' maiden Top Ten strike with 'Not Fade Away', and Blind Faith's later investment of 'Well... All Right' (a Holly B-side) with a snake-charmer riff, altered lyrics and a typically elongated instrumental work-out over the fade.

After Holly played the Liverpool Empire, John Lennon and Paul McCartney's early efforts as composers became less of a sideline – though their Quarry Men was a group as much in artistic debt to the ubiquitous Lonnie Donegan, who'd been crowned 'King of Skiffle' circa 1957 (on the strength, he confesses, of "doing impressions of Broonzy, Leadbelly, Josh White and Lonnie Johnson, as well as Woody Guthrie, Hank Snow, Hank Williams...").

Though Lonnie's skiffle was derived from the rent parties, speakeasies and Dust Bowl jug bands of the US Depression, its closest relation in primeval rowdiness, rockabilly, gripped the American teen infinitely tighter. Among rockabilly's brand leaders were Johnny Burnette & The Rock'n'Roll Trio, whose 'Train Kept A-Rollin'' was later recorded twice by The Yardbirds – in 1965 and for 1966's *Blow Up* film soundtrack, albeit thinly-disguised as 'Stroll On'. (It was to resurface as a stage fixture of both Jim McCarty's blues bands and the latter-day Yardbirds.)

Rockabilly and skiffle shared the same three bedrock guitar chords. For those readers unfamiliar with song structures, it's at least worth being aware that certain chord cycles recur ad nauseam throughout pop. An astonishing number of pop songs (and practically all blues and most folk songs) use what's called a three-chord-trick – which means they're simply built around three related chords: first position (I), fourth position (IV) and fifth position (V); say E, A & B. 'Hang On Sloopy' is one example of how the three chords might be combined, but you'll hear them linked together in many ways.

> *"Having figured out simple chord arrangements, 1950s British teenagers would form skiffle combos"*

A 12-bar blues will often use those same three chords, but the defining element is that they're spread over a set number of bars – in one of several possible sequences, but always resolving back to the root chord at the end of the 12th bar – and this format is then repeated over and over. 'Too Much Monkey Business' is an example, but you can point to countless blues or rock'n'roll tracks from Robert Johnson to Status Quo.

The other classic rock/pop variation is the I-VIminor-IV-V ballad cliché (including many Fifties and Sixties classics like Ben E King's 'Stand By Me', Sam Cooke's 'Wonderful World', and the Righteous Brothers' 'Unchained Melody'). More often than not these are augmented by a 'middle-eight' or 'bridge' passage (often something like IV-I-IV-V). Variations on these structures often require comparatively little instruction.

Having figured out these simple chord arrangements, a 1950s British teenager could (and generally did) form a skiffle combo with friends. Aspirant skifflers would be everywhere, stretching out limited repertoires at wedding receptions, youth clubs, church fetes and birthday parties, only too pleased to entertain for as little as a round of fizzy drinks.

As well as an embarrassment of slashed acoustic guitars, at the core of skiffle's contagious backbeat were tea-chest-and-broomstick bass, a washboard tapped with thimbles, dustbin-lid cymbals, biscuit-tin snare drum and further vehicles of musical effect fashioned from everyday implements. Like punk a generation later, anyone could try skiffle – and the more ingenuous the sound, the better.

For most participants, skiffle was just a bit of fun, and attempts at composition, even within professional outfits, usually provoked howls of affectionate derision: "Listen, you can't beat the Yanks at that game any more than you can at anything else. We don't need more than the American stuff we're doing already – and if we did, could a twit like you come up with anything of the necessary calibre?"

In the teeth of ridicule, some would-be Gershwins might continue to grapple with their muse, and a capacity to try-try-again would occasionally result in a song superior to some of the non-originals. An example was the climactic 'Shakin' All Over', written and recorded by Johnny Kidd & The Pirates – formerly The Five Nutters, house band at a Willesden skiffle club in north-west London, but by then an established act guaranteed engagements six nights a week. The track was initially earmarked to be buried on a B-side, but famously knocked teen idol Cliff Richard's 'Please Don't Tease' from the UK Number One spot in August 1960.

"Attempts at composition, even within professional outfits, usually provoked howls of affectionate derision"

With bass, drums and just one guitar behind him, Johnny had patented a prototype: later entities such as The Big Three, The Who, Cream, The Jimi Hendrix Experience and (in an eventual incarnation) The Yardbirds would all be based around an instrumental 'power trio'. The Pirates were also among the first big groups (in Britain at least) to feature one of those new-fangled electric basses, which radiated inestimably greater depth of sound than any bull fiddle, and certainly anything knocked together from tea-chest, broomstick and string.

This new hire-purchase debt matched those for the amplified guitars and orthodox dance-band drum kit that had superseded the finger-lacerating acoustic six-strings and pots-and-pans percussion which were fast becoming old hat.

Skiffle groups now filled interval slots for jazz bands at Ken Colyer's Studio 51, London's oldest jazz club, not to mention headlining sessions down in the Heaven & Hell, Le Macabre, the Safari and other all-skiffle basements within the square mile bordered by the bustling consumer paradises of Park Lane, Piccadilly, Shaftesbury Avenue, Charing Cross Road and Oxford Street.

All were fizzling out as the decade closed, but bitten belatedly by the skiffle bug, Chris Dreja thrummed a tea-chest bass during lunchtime work-outs at Hollyfield until he scratched together five shillings for an acoustic guitar from a local pawnshop. Full barre chords proved painful, Chris reflected, as, "the strings were about an inch off the fretboard – but it gave me incredible strength and steadiness in my left hand."

More idiosyncratic still was Jeff Beck's way with a guitar – he defied parental disdain and, with commendable application, plus a shop-lifted pickup, and strings sometimes made of household wire, he manufactured a second electric instrument: "I just put the frets on wherever I thought they should go – we had to guess from photographs – so I was hitting a lot of strange notes." For almost two years Jeff practised in his bedroom and "fiddled with the dial of the shortwave band on our radio for hours. That was my first amplifier too. It was barely audible, but that was enough for me to feel, 'Hey, I'm on the radio'."

The acceleration of puberty found him looking for an entree into pop, which came when he teamed up with a school friend: "His mum and dad helped us out financially, and I think our first gig was at a fairground, playing Eddie Cochran stuff that nobody was particularly interested in hearing."

By implication, such displays were generally for the benefit of performers rather than audience. Though Beck and Dreja had as-yet-unspoken fancies about making their way as professional musicians, few other teenagers paid serious attention to what they'd been persuaded to understand was a vocational blind alley. Rock'n'roll, skiffle, whatever, could not be permitted to assume unrealistic proportions. It was a folly, to be cast aside when you resigned yourself to being a 'credit' to your parents through achievement by effort – meaning that if you beavered away and kept your nose clean, you might be on the board of directors in ten years and chairman by the time you were 40...

CHAPTER 3

DRINKING MUDDY WATER

"I went ballistic when I heard the electric sounds of Jimmy Reed. It wasn't regimented. It was pure emotion, feel. That was probably what shaped me forever – and partly what shaped The Yardbirds too."

CHRIS DREJA

Far from seeing it as a long-term career option, one of the strongest motives for even the most ill-favoured oik to be in a pop outfit was that he had licence to lock eyes with short-skirted 'birds', with urchin faces and pale lipstick, who'd lost enough of their *sang froid* to ring the stage front, ogling with unmaidenly eagerness the enigma of these untouchable boys-next-door – untouchable at least until a tryst could be sealed with a beatific smile, a flood of libido and an 'Alright then, I'll see you later'.

At that time there was still nearly always a distinction drawn between the

Bass player Paul Samwell-Smith

vocalist and the 'accompanists' – if there was a group, its role was simply to back the singer. Often the instrumentalists would be relatively anonymous musical foils for a glamorous if bland frontperson.

In the effectively enforced calm that followed the rock'n'roll storm in the mid 1950s, the hit parades of North America – and subsequently everywhere else – became constipated with the harmless and ephemeral likes of Bobby Rydell, Bobby Vinton, Bobby Vee… Bobby This and Bobby That were interchangeably doe-eyed, hair-sprayed, conventionally good-looking, and manipulated by handlers who had taken heed of the increasing market unreliability of Jerry Lee, Gene, Chuck and the remainder of the decaying decade's wild men – apart from King Elvis, courtesy of his post-army release schedule of Italianesque warblings and lightweight tunes with saccharine lyrics and jaunty rhythms.

Yet, following a 1960 chart-topper with 'Apache', it was Cliff Richard's backing Shadows who most moulded musical direction for the post-skiffle pop group around Britain. In the back-street palais of Cork or Aberdeen it was by no means unusual to witness a quartet happily presenting a set consisting exclusively of deadpan Shadows reproductions, complete with synchronised footwork from a two-guitars-bass-drums line-up that was soon to be the 1960s beat group stereotype.

"Hank Marvin was the inspirational source for the fretboard fireworks of Jeff Beck and others"

And while it had also sparkled beneath the fingers of Buddy Holly, the Fender Stratocaster will be forever associated – in Britain anyway – with Hank B Marvin, more the public face of The Shadows in his black horn-rims than, say, nondescript drummer Tony Meehan. Through metallic picking, copious use of tremolo arm and insinuated belief that tone lay in the hands of the guitarist rather than effects pedals, Marvin was the inspirational source for the fretboard fireworks of Jeff Beck, Ritchie Blackmore and others, who started looking out for opportunities in groups that aspired to be proficient Shadows copyists.

Hank Marvin copyists like Jeff and Ritchie were two-a-penny around 1961. A Tony Meehan was much rarer. Around London's south-western suburbs (as everywhere else), mere ownership of a drum kit was sufficient to attract overtures for your services from all over a district which, while not yet exploding with pop, appeared to have more and more groups enjoying parochial fame by the month.

While sticksmen were vexingly few and far between, you didn't need radar to locate their whereabouts. Taking on an onerous summer job to pay for it, 15-year-old Jim McCarty attacked a second-hand kit of indeterminate make for hours daily – and while his trial-and-error crashing irritated the entire terrace, it brought forth hand-and-foot co-ordination, accurate time-keeping and the naive genesis of a personal style.

He had pledged himself to The Country Gentlemen, an outfit containing Brian Samwell-Smith, his younger brother Paul, and a moveable feast of other Hampton Grammar sixth-formers. The group had named themselves after the Gretsch Country Gentleman, a guitar played by no less than Chet Atkins, but also desirable for its sleek action and bright, clean sound, particularly in the recording studio.

For the Gentlemen, getting a record out was not the far-fetched afterthought it might have been for less ambitious groups. Their playing experience to date involved a trivial round of mainly high school hops and pubs – where the law forbade minors to consume any drink more alcoholic than cherryade. But being enormous within the immediate vicinity of Hampton Grammar was not enormous enough for the Gentlemen – even if their stock-in-trade was the same Top 20 preferences and Shadows instrumentals that could be heard in the country's most out-of-the-way village institute. The group were especially pleased with their renditions of 'Shakin' All Over' and 'Apache', but it was 'With Love', a 'Bobby-ballad' confected by the Samwell-Smiths, that was to be the earliest musical archive of the fledgling Yardbirds.

Since the Gentlemen didn't have the power to enchant a record label manager enough to send even an underling a few miles west to hear them, the only way forward seemed to be to immortalise themselves on tape. A lot of fiddling with microphone positioning while the reel-to-reel's valves warmed up in a bass guitarist's parents' lounge resulted in an arrangement of 'With Love' to be packaged and mailed by registered post (and without much hope) to each of the four big record companies – Decca, EMI, Pye and Philips – in turn.

Then a miracle occurred. Within weeks, in autumn 1961, 'With Love' landed on the desk of EMI recording manager John Schroeder – one of a deluge of 'demos' that thumped onto EMI's doormat with every mail delivery. Incredibly, instead of yawning and clicking it off halfway through the first chorus, Schroeder rubbed his chin and re-ran the tape. 'With Love' wasn't exactly a masterpiece of song, but these Country Gentlemen weren't obvious no-hopers. It would do no harm, he supposed, to summon them to the firm's studio complex in St John's Wood so he could get an idea of how well they might come across on vinyl.

> *"In Autumn 1961, 'With Love' landed on the desk of EMI recording manager John Schroeder"*

Nervous merriment subsided to virtual silence as the van containing the Gentlemen nosed up Abbey Road and bounced into the asphalt car park of the Edwardian facade that fronted the studios. Reined by fear, Brian and Paul lilted the vocal harmonies with cautious accuracy after the condescending control room intercom called them to order. In the drum booth, Jim's headphoned ears tingled between takes with the leakage of murmured intrigue from Schroeder's glass-fronted empire of editing blocks, blinking dials and jack-to-jack leads.

Afterwards, the Great Man grinned cheerfully and waved farewell as the boys commenced a crestfallen drive home. "It didn't work," sighed self-denigrating McCarty, "because of me. Schroeder reckoned that Tony Meehan would have made a better go of it."

Accustomed to on-stage inconsistencies of tempo caused by the mood of the hour, drummers were most prone to behind-the-scenes substitution in the studio. "The reasons were purely financial," explained ex-Johnny Kidd drummer Clem Cattini, the first dyed-in-the-wool rock'n'roller to emerge as a familiar figure on London's recording scene. "You were expected to finish four tracks – two singles – in three hours. A group might take a week to do two titles – not because they were incapable, but because sessions are a different mode of thinking to being on the road. You can't get away with so much. You need more discipline."

Having someone like Meehan or Cattini 'ghost' his drumming would, therefore, have been no slight on Jim McCarty, and he was not to be the victim of any heartless sacking, as Pete Best would be under similar circumstances when The Beatles arrived at Abbey Road for the first time a few months later. Such a situation didn't arise for the simple reason that The Country Gentlemen were soon to throw in the towel anyway.

Sodden with bitter fulminations in the murkiest corner of Richmond's L'Auberge cafe, none of them would ever concede that groups who frequented the Top 20 were any better than they. Yet what else could the Gentlemen do? Post the tape to the producer of the Light Programme's weekly pop magazine, *Saturday Club*, then when he gave a thumbs-down, send it to the booking agents at Mecca, Top Rank or some lesser leisure corporation controlling a ballroom circuit?

> *"None of them would concede that groups who frequented the Top 20 were any better than they"*

So inward-looking was the UK music industry that there seemed to be few realistic halfway points between obscurity and the Big Time – and a policy of territorial defence was epitomised by a closed shop of venues, which became obvious as soon as you tried to get above yourself by contacting a promoter you didn't know. Visitors of hit-parade eminence notwithstanding, work tended to be doled out only to acts from the same district – for instance The Emeralds were to Camberley (on the opposite border of Surrey) what the Gentlemen were to Richmond. Why bring outsiders over when our own lads can do the job just as well for a fraction of the cost?

Besides, various parents were whining about looming GCE A-level exams at school, and prevailing upon their offspring – with some success – to be sensible. Shackled to homework on a fine spring evening, a Country Gentleman would glower through working-class-posh lace curtains at a dismal, futile and inflexible eternity. Was this all there was: exams and then a stagnant river of a rest-of-your-life, flowing towards the Eldorado of a bonus in your wage packet and a retirement gold-watch to tick away the seconds before you went underground?

A 'proper' job was an unappetising prospect for Jeff Beck too, as his final hour at Sutton East crept closer. In every sense of the phrase, he played for time. He had surfaced in a succession of fly-by-night parochial Shadows as an exceptional Hank Marvin imitator, famous too for note-for-note duplications of solos by Chet Atkins and Merle Travis – whose fresh approach to C&W picking had evolved through playing on guitar bluegrass breakdowns written for banjo.

Beck was more taken, though, with the more abandoned rockabilly of Cliff Gallup, guitarist with Gene Vincent's Blue Caps (a player Jeff once described as "like Chet Atkins on acid"), and Eddie Cochran, whose songs had dominated Jeff's first public engagement. A multi-talented Oklahoman Elvis, Eddie's 'Twenty Flight Rock', 'Summertime Blues' and other singles outlining the trials of adolescence had garnered a plenitude of British covers.

Although Cliff Gallup had left the Blue Caps at the end of 1956, it was as if all Jeff Beck's birthdays had come at once in

"It's intriguing to tally just how many groups from every phase of mid-1960s pop had roots in art schools"

spring 1960 when Cochran co-starred with Vincent on a 'scream circuit' trek around Britain: 'A Fast-Moving Anglo-American Beat Show'. His dark locks bleached then to a fair tousle, just like Eddie's, Beck wasn't the only local guitarist to follow the tour, as far as finances would allow. He would learn what he could – albeit from a distance – about a terse resonant technique, and pick up important details like Cochran's use of an unwound ultra-light third string – the secret of his agile bending of middle-register 'blue' notes.

Apart from Vince Taylor and Johnny Kidd, other Britons in cultural debt to Gene Vincent included Shane Fenton (who in the glam-rock era changed his name to Alvin Stardust), and Cal Danger and Kerry Rapid, who were under the aegis of Bob Potter, an entrepreneur based in Camberley. A Potter showcase over the county line in Aldershot so impressed Jeff Beck that afterwards he was emboldened to ask Potter point-blank if he could join The Emeralds, now the all-purpose accompanists to Danger, Rapid and the other singers in the troupe. After the formality of an audition, Jeff left home to play lead guitar in something as near as dammit to Gene & The Blue Caps.

Next, Beck threw in his lot with The Crescents, Shadows imitators from Farnborough. After a few weeks, he'd moved on to Him & The Others. Then came The Bandits, and a return to Kerry Rapid as one of his backing Blue Stars, as Jeff drifted from pillar to post, from group to unsatisfactory group, all arriving at the same commercial and artistic stalemate.

During this period Jeff Beck was ostensibly on a two-year course at Wimbledon School Of Art, though his career there wasn't especially glorious. It's intriguing to tally just how many groups from every phase of mid-1960s pop had roots in art schools. John Lennon, for instance, was the most famous and notorious Old Boy of Liverpool's Regional College of Art. Down south, both The Rolling Stones and The Pretty Things were hatched in Sidcup Art School in Kent, just as The Rockin' Berries, The Animals, The Kinks, The Creation, The Bonzo Dog Doo-Dah Band, The Move and The Pink Floyd were in similar establishments all over the country.

Entry standards often weren't very tight. You could get in with hardly any official qualifications

> *"As long as you didn't fall behind with the rent, you could revel in romantic squalor (well, squalor anyway)"*

whatsoever – as Jeff did at Wimbledon. It was the same at Kingston where Keith Relf, Eric Clapton, Jimmy Page and folk guitarist John Renbourn honed their musical skills in an atmosphere of coloured dust, palette knives, hammer-and-chisel and lumpy impasto.

Inevitably, a concentration of art schools in that part of Surrey meant it teemed with so-called bohemians eking out livings or feeding off grants within back-to-back buildings, once the acme of elegance but now divided into studio flats that might be described by an estate agent as 'compact'. Their various states of disrepair were expressed to passers-by in peeling pillars, window ledges off-white with pigeon droppings, and rubbish sogging behind railings. A door-knocker's rapping thunder would shake a fresh avalanche of brittle plaster from mildewed walls in hallways where bare light bulbs were coated in dust.

It was understood – sometimes wrongly – that as long as you didn't fall behind with the rent, you could revel in romantic squalor (well, squalor anyway), get carried home drunk at seven in the morning, lie in until the street lights came on, leave crockery unwashed in the sink, and entertain intimates behind the closed door of your bedroom.

A popular uniform for both sexes of student was army-surplus duffle-coat draped with a long scarf; sunglasses even in a midnight power cut; Jesus sandals or desert boots; baggy sweater with holes in it; and carefully rumpled hair above a visage that effused melancholy and poor health. Your similarly paint-flecked corduroy strides looked as if they'd hung round the legs of a particularly revolting builder's labourer for three years.

How easy it is to forget that many of 1960s pop's tight-trousered lead vocalists or clenched-teeth guitarists may have once thus aspired to fine art, with music as simply an extra-mural pursuit for a dressed-down 'existentialist' with bum-fluff beard, a 'nothing matters' engrossment with self-immolation and death, and 'cool' defined less by Gene Vincent, or even Kerouac's Dean Moriarty, than by Amedeo Modigliani.

The idea of living like the improvident post-Impressionist – starving in a rat-infested garret, burning furniture against the cold of winter, and going to an early grave for his Art – may have held vague charm, but for most there was always the safety net of your tut-tutting mother's home cooking, the untaxing televisual comfort of *The Lone Ranger*, soft toilet tissue, a full tube of toothpaste, and soaking yourself in the hot scented water of an aqua-coloured bath before going to sleep in your own little room again.

It helped restore your nerve before going back to stepping over the debauchee face-down in a puddle of piss on the stairwell, and entering another round of fish-and-chip paper in the fireplace, sock-smelling frowsiness, overflowing ashtrays, and pooling loose change for a trip up the off-licence to see you and your colleagues through candle-lit palaver until dawn. All-night sessions would open with a debate about the transmigration of souls, degenerate into free-association 'poetry', and finally ego-massaging soliloquies about your life, your angst, and the masterpieces you were going to paint, the avant-garde films you were going to direct, the clever music you were going to make...

Always looking for new (and inexpensive) thrills, some students had also been introduced to the early 1960s equivalent of glue-sniffing. This entailed buying a Vicks inhaler from the chemist's shop and isolating the part of it that contained an excitant called Benzedrine. This you then ate. It was a tacky way of getting high, but that was the nearest you could easily get to sharing something with doomed musical icons whose credibility was enhanced by having some sort of addiction. The originator of Peggy Lee's 'Fever', Little Willie John, was an alcoholic who died in jail, and there were junkies galore to hold up as role models, from urban ghettos to Nashville.

Certain undergraduates would distance themselves from the others by listening unashamedly to the trashiest pop – in keeping with the newish Pop Art movement, scorned by the art establishment as a novelty. Ostensibly snooty about pop too, most of the rest were 'sent' by Thelonious Monk, Charlie 'Yardbird' Parker, Dave Brubeck, The Modern Jazz Quartet (the MJQ – of whom Keith Relf was an avid fan) and Meade 'Lux' (rather than Jerry Lee) Lewis.

"As well as idolising black jazz musicians, students of the day were also getting into Bob Dylan"

Other jazz albums strewn about student 'pads' embraced the orchestral euphoria of Count Basie and Duke Ellington; vocal daredevilry from Anita O'Day, Peggy Lee and Mel Tormé; the sensual fretting of Django Reinhardt, Charlie Christian and Wes Montgomery; and the controlled swing of Woody Herman, Lionel Hampton and Buddy Rich – every smart Alec's received idea of percussive splendour. More rousing was the blaring bebop of Parker, Charlie Mingus, the Jazz Messengers and Miles Davis, and the differing textural complexities of Roland Kirk and Ornette Coleman.

If one sure sign of 'maturity' was the dropping of buzz-words like 'Monk' and 'Brubeck' into late-night twaddle, another was attending students union dances in boaters or top hats, and a variety of hacked-about formal wear, drinking heavily of cider, and launching into vigorous steps that blended a type of skip-jiving with the Charleston in a curious galumphing motion to the fervent plinking and puffing of a 'trad' jazz band.

Outside college portals, trad jazz had revived to the extent that Chris Barber had notched up a Top Ten placing – but this was nothing compared to the pop success story of another trad 'dad', Mr Acker Bilk. This chin-bearded Somerset clarinettist was the new fad's Lonnie Donegan – judging by the vast number of trad bands bedecked in matching Roman togas, legal gowns-and-barrister wigs, Confederate army regimentals, or some other ridiculous variation on the bowler hats and striped waistcoats worn by Bilk and his Paramount Jazz Band. Already a pop star by any other name, Bilk just about walked the line within fickle collegiate circles.

As well as idolising mainly black jazz musicians (regarded as the 'genuine twisted voice of the underdog') students of the day were also getting into Bob Dylan – whose fame grew out of Greenwich Village, New York's vibrant beatnik district, where the civil rights movement would fuse with folk song to be labelled 'protest' by 1962, when Dylan signed to CBS Records. Paul Samwell-Smith, a weekend dropout on the periphery of the Kingston Art School crowd, was a big Dylan fan: but he also loved the blues – as did Keith Relf, Chris Dreja, Anthony Topham and Eric Clapton. They were still yet to link up, but from early adolescence all had been casually knowledgeable about the music that lay beneath and fluttered above skiffle's chewing-gum-flavoured veneer.

Yet this 'blues' was something the Surrey boys couldn't touch at first. It was peculiar to black American experience (though it has been argued that it had partly Gaelic roots, as discussed in Jim Wilkie's book *Blue Suede Brogans*), and obtainable on vinyl only after it had wended its way across the Atlantic to specialist outlets like Dobell's up Charing Cross Road and Carey's Swing Shop in Streatham, south London.

If the truth was told, blues was an unknown quantity throughout most of its land of origin too. In the years that preceded rock'n'roll, white radio listeners might tune in by accident to muffled bursts of what segregationalists heard as "screaming idiotic words and savage music on some negro-manned station" – and only the most free-spirited Caucasian teenager was to gravitate to juke joints in run-down districts of the bigger US cities to fraternise with the nation's most shunned sub-culture.

Blues, therefore, hovered as distant thunder in mainstream pop. Bessie Smith's first single, 1923's 'Down Hearted Blues', had shifted a million copies without a minute's airplay on white radio. Over a quarter of a century later, John Lee Hooker was selling records by the ton in Uncle Sam's 'race' or 'sepia' market without figuring at all in the pop Hot 100.

> *"Of all the blues entertainers who found favour with white bohemia, Hooker's credentials were perhaps the most impeccable"*

Of all the blues entertainers who found favour with white bohemia, Hooker's biographical credentials were perhaps the most impeccable. An upbringing in the same rural Mississippi town as Robert Johnson and Muddy Waters was followed by an adolescence spent in Memphis. Next came migration north, purchase of an electric guitar and discovery by a record company scout during a club residency in Black Bottom, a Detroit suburb.

Just as an insistent boogie undercurrent was the stylistic trademark linking Hooker's 1963 singles 'Boom Boom' and 'Dimples', so a bottleneck approach was the common thread between Elmore James – whose 'Rollin' And Tumblin' was to be another blues standard – and his mentor Robert Johnson, a pre-war bluesman tormented by an inferno of ectoplasmic monsters. The most obsessed of Johnson's exorcisms in this vein, 'Me And The Devil Blues', was taped in 1937, a few months before this remarkable youth's sudden death at the age of 24.

Thanks in part to later versions of his songs by the likes of the Stones, Cream and the late Jo Ann Kelly, critical awareness and reassessment of Johnson resulted in some people – such as noted pop pundit Charles Shaar Murray – regarding him as the greatest musician ever to have walked the planet. I wouldn't go that far, but I would urge anyone making a serious study of the blues to go first and last to Robert Johnson.

One major post-war blues voice was Aaron 'T-Bone' Walker, whose full-throated singing and stark six-string obligatos were echoed by Albert King. In turn, King's influence was felt by Eric Clapton – to be demonstrated most blatantly in Cream's resuscitation of Albert's 'Born Under A Bad Sign' in 1968. Howlin' Wolf also defined what are now clichés of the idiom after his earthier lyrics and guttural bass-baritone made profound impact during the resurgence of interest in the blues in Britain. Principal among Wolf's own influences during a Mississippi delta boyhood was that of his brother-in-law Rice Miller, better known as Sonny Boy Williamson, who taught Wolf to play harmonica (though not to be confused with the Sonny Boy Williamson who recorded 'Good Morning Little Schoolgirl' – he died in the late 1940s).

In 1948 Wolf became a full-time musician, backed by one of the first electric blues bands in the Deep South. Then in 1952 he moved to Chicago, nearly ten years after the arrival of fellow Mississippi bluesman Muddy Waters, who had also 'gone electric'. Though the Windy City left an ingrained mark on their respective styles, neither Waters nor Wolf would ever forget their down-home beginnings.

> *"Howlin' Wolf defined what are now clichés of the blues idiom with his earthy lyrics and guttural bass-baritone"*

The 1960s marked the most commercially fruitful chapter of both their careers, mostly thanks to their 'discovery' by the emerging beat groups and the British R&B scene. Waters' influential fistful of initially 'race' hits at home had included 'Rollin' Stone Blues', 'Hoochie Coochie Man', 'I Just Wanna Make Love To You' and 'I Got My Mojo Working'; and many of the singles Wolf released up to 1964 – among them 'Backdoor Man', 'Smokestack Lightning', 'Spoonful', 'Killing Floor' and 'Wang Dang Doodle' – would also surface as repertory fixtures for white groups as varied as The Rolling Stones, The Mojos, The Doors, Canned Heat, Love Sculpture, Ten Years After, Electric Flag... and, of course, the once and future Yardbirds, whose celebrated extrapolations of 'Smokestack Lightning' circa 1963 would spark off sometimes tedious long-term imitative patterns – as epitomised five years later by Cream's in-concert recording of 'Spoonful', a full 20 triple-forte minutes long.

Cream's Clapton, Bruce and Baker – like many other musicians who did well out of the post-psychedelic 'blues boom' of the late 1960s – had all cut their teeth in an earlier wave of British blues.

THE YARDBIRDS

This was a movement whose conception is usually dated from Mississippi songster Big Bill Broonzy's London debut (with his then-novel 12-string guitar) in September 1951 – though Lonnie Donegan suggests, "Before that, Josh White came over to England: I was there every night for every house for the whole week he was on at the Chiswick Empire."

White also recorded an influential version of the old folk-blues whorehouse ballad 'House Of The Rising Sun', which in turn became the magnum opus of The Animals – who, as The Alan Price Combo, had started out by knocking 'em dead at the Downbeat and plusher Club-A-Go-Go in Newcastle. (Frontman Eric Burdon, gripped by a ritualistic obsession beyond simple enthusiasm, was known to have scratched the word BLUES in his own blood across the cover of an exercise book he used for compiling lyrics.) Another blues hero of numerous British bands of the early 1960s was Chicago's Jimmy Reed. The Animals recorded his 'Bright Lights Big City', The Pretty Things did 'Big Boss Man', while The Yardbirds covered 'I Ain't Got You', and in 1966 recorded a self-penned homage in 'Like Jimmy Reed Again'.

Many of these US blues artists were originally introduced to the UK by some of this country's more open-minded jazz players: trad trumpeter Humphrey Lyttelton had been effusive in his praise for Reed, White and Muddy Waters as long ago as a New Musical Express interview in 1955. But Lyttelton was neither the first nor the most committed blues enthusiast within Britain's jazz community. As early as 1950, Manchester's Bogeda Jazz Club had presented a blues trio fronted by John Mayall, then a 17-year-old boogie-woogie pianist. Moreover, while Lyttelton, Ken Colyer and others may have arranged a few bookings for blues artists, it was Chris Barber who sank actual cash into the conservation of the form, after overseeing the Broonzy concert in 1951.

> *"Chris Barber's jazz band was the first to try 'I Got My Mojo Working', later the British blues crusade's anthem"*

Defying the likelihood of financial loss, Chris also underwrote round-Britain tours by Waters, Wolf, Williamson, Little Walter, multi-instrumental duo Sonny Terry and Brownie McGhee, Sister Rosetta Tharpe, Roosevelt Sykes, as well as several lesser names. In fact at that time a blues fan in Dublin or Bournemouth might have seen more of these artists than a counterpart in Seattle or New Jersey ever would – as many US blues practitioners had reached the evening of their lives without once performing professionally on their native soil.

It was at Barber's prompting too that, in 1958, the National Jazz Federation had acquired its own London shop-window in Oxford Street's Marquee club – which was still hosting a regular blues evening as late as 1966. Blues also infiltrated the Barber Jazz Band's post-Donegan output. Indeed, they were the first known domestic unit to try 'I Got My Mojo Working', which was to emerge as the growing British blues crusade's anthem.

Bypassing trad jazz and proceeding directly to the blues, Anthony Topham and his best friend Chris

Dreja spent an exploratory afternoon, during the unquiet dusk of their schooldays, sifting through the erudite collection of records in which Mr Topham Senior had immersed himself – as other heads of families might have done in, say, golf or do-it-yourself home improvements.

Dreja recalled: "Top's dad had all these great import blues records – Blind Lemon Jefferson, Robert Johnson, Mississippi Joe Calicott... It kept me awake for days on end. I went ballistic when I heard the electric sounds of Jimmy Reed. It wasn't regimented. It was pure emotion, feel. That was probably what shaped me forever – and partly what shaped The Yardbirds too."

Record-playing sessions evolved into attempts to reproduce the music on guitars and self-conscious voices perhaps yet to break. Amused by the memory, Chris recounted: "We'd bring our guitars into school or skive off to Bell's Music Shop in Surbiton where they had electric models. I was eventually able to buy a 15-watt Vox amp [in those days *Melody Maker* advertised amplifiers "with a ten-watt punch"] and a solid-body Watkins Rapier [electric guitar] – terrible instrument, but it looked flash enough for Eric Clapton to borrow so he could pose in front of the mirror with it.

"Top and I wanted a harmonica player and a drummer. We started with Robin Wayne – who was essentially a jazzer, but played harmonica. He was also asthmatic, like Keith [Relf] was, and we used to get the bus to his house in Ealing at dead of winter. Then someone suggested Jim McCarty as drummer – and he was the link to Paul Samwell-Smith and then Keith – who were then half of The Metropolitan Blues Quartet. And so we formed an all-electric group in 1963. The first booking we did was at the Railway Hotel in Harrow during a trad band's interval. They'd never heard anything like it."

CHAPTER 4

BOOM BOOM

"Everyone would laugh and say, 'Play some proper blues.' There wasn't much room for experiment."

JEFF BECK
ON HIS PREVIOUS GROUP, THE TRIDENTS

Rather than 'The Yardbirds', it may have made sense for the amalgam of Dreja, McCarty, Relf, Samwell-Smith and Topham to commence trading as The Metropolitan Blues Quintet (the MBQ). There were and would be plenty of R&B groups of that prosaic kidney: The Beaconsfield Rhythm & Blues Group, Big Blues (featuring Joe Cocker), The Mann-Hugg Blues Brothers, Blues By Six, Blue Sounds (from Leeds), The Blues Committee (Reading), the two Midlands versions of The Rhythm & Blues Group (one of which had Spencer Davis and Steve Winwood sharing lead vocals), and so on, ad nauseam.

Frontman Keith Relf on-stage

The patron saint of all of them was Blues Incorporated, the brainchild of two disgruntled Chris Barber sidemen, Cyril Davies and Alexis Korner, who'd been motivated to further the cause of R&B, irrespective of personal popularity or financial gain. This was just as well, because the first meeting of their Blues And Barrelhouse Club in a Soho pub in 1957 had drawn an audience of three.

Five years on, attendance figures were more heartening at the G Club, between a jeweller's and a teashop along Ealing Broadway. This was patronised instantly by zealots from London, the Home Counties and beyond, as devoted to R&B as other societies were to yachting, say, or numismatics. At later meetings, clientele would learn of other R&B venues, such as St Mary's Parish Hall, L'Auberge, the Vineyard Church House, the Craw Daddy, Eel Pie Island and the Crown – all dotted round Richmond, Kingston and Twickenham – and the weekly evening at the Marquee (by then moved to Wardour Street) conferred on Blues Incorporated by promoter Harold Pendleton.

As the G Club's house band, Blues Incorporated was primarily an instrumental unit, although it regularly featured the smoky growl of Alexis Korner himself and the harsher hollering of blond giant Long John Baldry – and a flux of additional vocalists drawn from the audience. Inevitably this led to a fair number of musical assassinations, but among the many who came forth this way were Paul Jones and Steve Marriott – pending respective tenures in Manfred Mann and The Small Faces – and, glistening with embarrassment, a London School of Economics undergraduate called Mick Jagger who, with another future Rolling Stone, drummer Charlie Watts, was to become a semi-permanent member in the loose set-up that was Blues Incorporated.

Some performers and listeners didn't confine themselves to the G Club and its kind, but infiltrated inner London watering holes like The Crazy Elephant, The Scene, The Roaring Twenties and, crucially, The Flamingo – self-proclaimed 'Swinging Club of Swinging London'; not to mention more exclusive niteries such as the Cromwellian, the Speakeasy, the Bag O' Nails *et al* – attractive to the 'in crowd' for their strict membership controls and tariffs too highly priced for the man-in-the-street.

> *"The patron saint of all R&B groups was Blues Incorporated, the brainchild of Cyril Davies and Alexis Korner"*

Yet from South Harrow to North Woolwich, none of these clubs was exactly the Harlem Apollo or Chicago's Big Squeeze (where Howlin' Wolf presided nightly), though they were as close as you could get in London, especially during sets by the better R&B longhairs – all Hohner Bluesvampers and 'Hoochie Coochie Man' – or the more uptown and versatile likes of Zoot Money's Big Roll Band, Georgie Fame & The Blue Flames, Herbie Goins & His Nightimers, Jimmy James & The Vagabonds, The Graham Bond Organisation, Carl Douglas & His Big Stampede, The Brian Auger Trinity, The Peddlers, or Julian Covay & The Machine.

All of these were 'group's groups', who usually meant little in the Top 40 but were admired for their stylistic tenacity and exacting standards, delivering styles as varied as West Indian bluebeat, the most low-down blues, early Tamla Motown – particularly the call-and-response panic of The Isley Brothers – and proto-jazz-rock (at least five years ahead of its time), all in the first hour alone of their set.

This was the musical meat of prototype mods, who recognised each other by a whim-conscious dress sense and a short-haired pseudo-suavity. Principally male, they were generally of a lower social caste than the aggressively unkempt bohemians heading for darkest Ealing after drying their increasingly shaggier hair to *Jimmy Reed At Carnegie Hall*, Bob Dylan's *Freewheelin'* – or perhaps just occasionally Blues Incorporated's *R&B From The Marquee*.

By the time this debut LP had been released in 1962, Blues Incorporated had split into two factions. Cyril Davies – preferring a narrower, Chicago-type interpretation of the music – was at loggerheads with Korner's 'everything from Leadbelly to Joey Dee and the Starliters'. With Long John Baldry, Davies quit Blues Incorporated to found a suitably purist club in Harrow-on-the-Hill. Another of Cyril's gripes concerned horns – forever associated with trad – and it's significant that neither brass nor woodwinds were in the scheme of things for any of the subsequent Rolling Stones, Kinks, Pretty Things, Small Faces and Yardbirds in the G Club throng.

No longer a Blues Incorporated splinter group by 1963, the Stones had gained a residency at the Craw Daddy, held on Sunday nights in the back room of Richmond's Station Hotel. Soon descending on the place in droves would be a nouvelle vague of 'youths' and, half a class up, 'young people' whose parents probably collected them afterwards in Morris Minor 'woody' estates. An ever-tighter jam of youngsters blocked the view for the dismayed longtime R&B addict. Massed round the front, clusters of girls in fishnet, suede and leather would melt if they grabbed the attention of Mick Jagger, with his grotesque beauty, and shiver with delight at Brian Jones's rare bashful grins.

Within months, the first screams were to reverberate for The Yardbirds too – especially frail Keith, who looked as if he needed mothering. See, you could deliver the most erudite R&B set in the world, sing like a nightingale or make a guitar talk, but if – like Cyril Davies, perspiring over his harmonica (as he was doing when he collapsed and died on-stage in 1964), or Alexis Korner, old enough to be your dad – you suffered from middle age, baldness or obesity, you'd never get more than a cult following.

With the Stones offering both credibility and rebel teen appeal, there was suddenly a lot of interest in R&B groups, and plenty of places for them to play. For The Yardbirds, a Friday night at the Craw Daddy would soon be netting £120 – five times the amount pocketed each by Keith and Paul for five days working as electrical engineers for Paul's father.

"There weren't so many bands about at that time," explains Paul, "and 120 quid didn't seem too surprising. You'd need about three or four hundred people paying seven-and-six [38p] to cover it." For Jim McCarty, though, earnings from the Yardbirds weren't quite enough – aside from the fact that, for parents with elbow-grease values, a boy joining a professional beat group was roughly the equivalent of a girl becoming a stripper. Any notion of making a living in show-business in general, let alone in rhythm & blues, wasn't taken seriously. But with a demanding day-job as a trainee financial analyst in the City, the strain was showing for Jim. This was a typical career option for a Hampton Grammar School leaver with so-so GCE grades, but his evenings were not being spent relaxing over an after-dinner crossword or watching TV.

Columns of figures swam before budgerigar eyes at the office on many occasions, when McCarty had only got to bed as the small hours chimed that morning. One compensation for living so far away from work was that he was generally able to secure a seat on the District line tube train before it filled to standing-room only in the morning rush hour. Yet the journey's banal chit-chat and body pressure, on top of residual tiredness, had him slouching despondently up to the offices, screwing himself up to go in.

Hardly able to think straight, he'd muddle through the day on automatic, greeting with a snarl colleagues who approached his desk. Not allowed to take off his suit jacket, even in summer, he turned pages, pondered figures, drafted letters, liaised on the telephone and swivelled on his chair to chuckle politely when a superior bantered about what the temps were like that week. Much of the time was spent watching out for nosier members of staff, and doing something 'normal' whenever one or other of them hoved into view, while he was using the telephone for Yardbirds business. Otherwise, Jim let his body relax and mind go numb with the listlessness of the completely bored. Taking exasperated stock, he promised himself that if found the courage to jack in this soul-destroying job, he'd never again set foot in the premises.

I wonder, in the offices and factories of Britain today, how many 50-somethings there are who now regret making the 'wise choice' of abandoning 1960s pop groups – especially if those groups later made it big. When Top Topham's double life burnt the candle to the middle, it was The Yardbirds that had to be sacrificed in the interests of higher education. Arriving at the same crossroads at the same time, Chris Dreja elected to plod a more treacherous path: "Unlike Top's parents, mine let me get on with it – but teachers thought me making my way as a musician was a mistake."

Things had begun to look up for The Yardbirds in spring 1963 – now with Eric Clapton on board – when they took over from the Stones at a Craw Daddy relocated to Richmond's Athletic Association club building. Just as far too many would profess to have been at Woodstock or have seen the Sex Pistols' early fiascos, so there would be a profound lack of retrospective honesty about attendance at wild Craw Daddy evenings, where the sweaty intensity grew by the minute as The Yardbirds seized 'Boom Boom', 'Smokestack Lightning', Muddy's 'I'm A Man', languid 'Got Love If You Want It' from Slim Harpo, and anything from Bo Diddley by the scruff of the neck and wrung the life out of them.

No question, the second edition Yardbirds was a howling success – but it still seemed fanciful to look very far ahead when there were so many other groups similarly battling even for encores. Yet as 1963 mutated into 1964, the slow pageant of sunrise soon began – and Jim McCarty's agonised decision to quit his day job was becoming easier to justify.

The Stones had already shown what was possible when a second 45, 'I Wanna Be Your Man', breached the Top 20 at the end of 1963 without them having to compromise their hirsute, motley image, as they'd done in order to plug 'Come On' on ITV's Thank Your Lucky Stars (Saturday's prime-time pop show). While 'I Wanna Be Your Man' had been composed by their new friends The Beatles, the Stones had stuck to their erudite R&B guns, and the new 45 was still discernible as the noise – not all of it beautiful – that was fermenting beneath low ceilings in dim-lit and often insalubrious bastions of R&B that were now pocking towns all over the country.

Greater London boasted by far the highest concentration of such venues, but The Yardbirds were also scrimmaging around the likes of the Wooden Bridge in Guildford, Andover's Copper Kettle R&B Club, the Ricky Tick upstairs at the Star & Garter in Windsor, St John's Ambulance Hall along Reading's Chatham Street – and, of course, Uncle Bonnie's Chinese Jazz Club in Brighton. Beyond the pale of the capital, they also invaded the likes of the Club-A-Go-Go – via a cultural exchange with The Animals – the CubiK ("Rochdale's Biggest R&B Club"), Swansea's R&B Cellar, Bluesville in a Sheffield pub, the Gamp in Edinburgh and, beneath the shadow of Birmingham Town Hall, Rhythm Unlimited – where The Spencer Davis Group held sway as The Yardbirds did at the Craw Daddy, or The Troggs at the Copper Kettle, and the more multi-faceted Downliners Sect (traceable back to a late 1950s outfit from Gunnersbury Grammar School) down at Studio 51.

In 1963 Studio 51 had a new guideline that enabled trad outfits and groups like the Sect, the Stones and The Yardbirds to share the same bill. As legend has it, it was here that Van Morrison, then in the rank-and-file of an itinerant Irish showband, saw The Downliners Sect perform and decided, "That's the sort of group I want to have…" Morrison was one of the few vocalists who could really hack it as blue-eyed bluesmen. Though the spirit was usually willing, and most could contend well enough with the feverish lechery, British voices were found wanting when they tried to extemporise from wolf-howl to close-miked sotto voce over a thuggish cloning of original arrangements of 'I Got My Mojo Working', 'Baby Please Don't Go', 'Smokestack Lightning' et al. Yet some – Morrison, Burdon, Winwood, Craine, Marriott, Rod Stewart, Joe Cocker – showed that you didn't have to come from the chain gang or the ghettos of southside Chicago to sound world-weary, cynical and knowing beyond your years.

In common with these contemporaries, Keith Relf was barely the Mannish Boy that Muddy Waters bragged about being, but was as agreeably devoid of vowel purity, plummy eloquence or nicety of intonation. Still, he wasn't up to corrupting his rather nasal mid-tenor to Burdon's ecstatic yell, bellyaching Cocker's depth of sound, Marriott's strangulated anguish, the natural coarseness of Morrison, or Stewart's lived-in rasp.

> *"Relf was barely the Mannish Boy that Muddy Waters had bragged about being, but was as agreeably devoid of vowel purity"*

Yet on the highest plane, it's not what you do, but who you are. Who wanted Keith Relf to be a fantastic singer when he was carving a niche of true individuality in perhaps the 20th century's most stylised form? It was his very lack of prescribed virtuosity that was a key element in Craw Daddy sessions that veered from stentorian vehemence to down-home warmth. This was also the ace up the sleeves of other British vocalists of the time who likewise reinforced an idiosyncratic appeal by warping a limited range and quirky delivery to their own ends (think of the Long John Silver burr of The Troggs' Reg Presley).

If you half-closed your eyes, with delicate suspension of logic, Relf, spotty Herbert though he was, also sounded as if he nearly meant it. Unburdened by the acoustic guitar that had dangled from his neck in the MBQ, Keith never sacrificed passion when walking a tightrope between the straining attack of The Pretty

Things' Phil May and the unslurred if slightly stilted clarity of The Zombies' Colin Blunstone. More 'authentic' than Colin and a little more technically proficient than Phil, Keith pushed a disjointed and narrow range well past its two middle octaves.

In context, the dominance of spontaneity over expertise through a muffled public address system was not unappealing – because, however inaudible without electronic assistance, Keith's often tortuous endowment still conveyed such exquisite brush strokes of enunciation and inflection that a fractional widening of vibrato during a sustained note could be as loaded as Joe Cocker's rawest wail.

Relf was also as recognised a master of blues harmonica as Cyril Davies, John Mayall, Brian Jones and The Downliners Sect's Ray Sone. Within the space of an instrumental chorus he slipped from suppressed lust through lazy insinuation to intimate torment – more comfortably than he could then manage as a singer – silencing Studio 51 drinkers like a mass bell in Madrid. (Trad jazz trumpeter Kenny Ball once expressed the jaded opinion that British R&B was "just rock'n'roll with a mouth-organ".)

> *"Duelling with Clapton's over-amplified eloquence, Relf was at the forefront of the rave-ups"*

Duelling with Clapton's over-amplified eloquence, Relf was at the forefront of the extended improvisations – known as 'rave-ups' – which The Yardbirds were daring long before the Stones' 'Goin' Home' filled 12 jammed minutes of 1966's *Aftermath* – although Van Morrison's freshly-formed Them evolved a similarly open-ended design that could run on and on and on when working split-shifts with The Wheels or The Mad Lads at Belfast's Club Rado.

In the meantime, Jeff Beck had formed Nightshift, after a spell with Screaming Lord Sutch & His Horde Of Savages (an outfit which also featured the likes of Jimmy Page and John Bonham at one time or another). With cascading tresses now splayed halfway down his back, and flickering across a surly, blemished complexion, Jeff's guitar-hero image was taking shape, but his domestic life was proving troublesome: incomprehension, lamentation and oppressive 'atmospheres' pervaded newly-married Jeff's partaking of tea-and-biscuits with elderly relations.

He'd started Nightshift with the drummer from Kerry Rapid's Blue Stars, after the Stones' behind-the-scenes pianist Ian Stewart had lent them relevant R&B albums – notably 1963's *Folk Festival Of The Blues*, an aural souvenir of a Chicago concert the previous summer showcasing Muddy Waters, Howlin' Wolf, Buddy Guy and Sonny Boy Williamson (introduced on the night as "Sonny Boy 'Nine Below Zero' Williamson") – in all, the cream of black urban blues.

To the chagrin of the rest of Nightshift, Jeff's time with Lord Sutch's unruly and excitingly anarchic outfit had left its mark: Jeff was prone to "going off on a tangent," as he put it. This was not appreciated: "Everyone would laugh and say, 'Play some proper blues.' There wasn't much room for experiment."

He was to be similarly frustrated in his next group, The Tridents, during a spell in 1963 as accompanists to former milkman Craig Douglas – a fading UK 'Bobby', but still perhaps the Isle of Wight's biggest contribution to British pop.

This lucrative if brief stint prompted The Tridents to approach Craig's record label, Fontana, with an acetate – which was rejected not for Jeff's tyro lead vocals but because "the guitar sounded distorted" – as well it might with Beck overdriving a new Stratocaster through one of the early Marshall amplifiers to actively create the effect. He was also tossing in leitmotifs that alternated Oriental-sounding exotica with the most hackneyed clichés of showbiz cabaret.

The boy deserved attention – and so did his Tridents now that, sans Craig Douglas, they were on a par with The Epitaphs, The Birds, Blues By Six, and like exponents of art school R&B who were chasing the Rolling Stones' tail. The Stones' heirs apparent, however, were clearly The Yardbirds, who – like the Spencer Davis Group, Blues Committee and others – had been buoyed further by opportunities to back venerable US bluesmen such as John Lee Hooker, Sonny Boy Williamson and Jimmy Reed (someone that, according to the Committee's Mike Cooper, was "drunk for breakfast").

These engagements weren't always easy. Only the most cursory rehearsal might be feasible before star and pick-up band trooped on to entertain with mutually familiar standards of the 'Boom Boom'/'Sweet Home Chicago' variety. Tainted by an inverted colour prejudice, the audience – generally dignified by scholars from the nearest university – blamed any errors on the group rather than the jet-lagged dotard fronting them. Lacking the required skin pigmentation and advanced age, what the hell did the town oiks on-stage with him know about having the blues?

"We rehearsed all of Sonny Boy Williamson's numbers," groans Jim McCarty, "but he'd always do them different when it came to the show. We were all a bit in awe of him. Keith just stood at the back somewhere, and the rest of us muddled through, never really knowing what Sonny Boy was going to do next."

The group backed Sonny Boy Williamson (whose harmonica contortions included playing the instrument with his nose) on the majority of dates during his UK tour in late 1963/early 1964, a tour organised by the British Jazz Federation's Giorgio Gomelsky – who also happened to be The Yardbirds' manager. They also reached a wider audience via an in-concert LP recorded during the tour. The highlight of the trek was at Birmingham Town Hall on Friday 28th February – a foggy night-of-nights where, bowler-hatted and vulture-like in posture, Williamson lorded it over a bill on which only The Spencer Davis Group represented the Second City. Their opening slot enabled Gomelsky and his assistants to adjust the PA system levels, the better to tape on a fancy Ampex reel-to-reel the more important artists who would be coming on later. Monitor speakers were unknown in 1964 so, hindered further by malfunctioning microphones, Davis and Steve Winwood, his young sidekick, bawled out songs going the rounds with myriad other R&B bands.

Admittedly it was well-received by partisan spectators numbering over a thousand, but the fidelity was still far from crystal-clear during The Yardbirds' spell on the boards without Williamson. Still, all's well that end's well, and none of the preceding acts had been so unnerved by technical problems that they couldn't pitch into the assembled cast's 'I Got My Mojo Working' finale.

The Yardbirds' payment for the thankless if prestigious task of backing Williamson was an all-in fee of maybe £40 per night – not a bad deal at a time when ten pounds was considered an adequate weekly wage for a young executive. As The Spencer Davis Group's Muff Winwood has put it, "You could make money when you were still a semi-pro musician. This meant you could take your time developing."

CHAPTER 5

GOT
TO HURRY

"Had we continued to play just blues, we would, in the end, have broken through anyway. But at the time we were desperate for a hit."

PAUL SAMWELL-SMITH

A sea-change in British pop was spearheaded back up in Jim McCarty's birthplace by local heroes The Beatles. A group that didn't have an obvious frontman, and who wrote its own songs, was a novel phenomenon then. As it happened, comparatively few Merseybeat exponents were to impress a grasping recording manager by also throwing in a stockpile of original material into which others dipped – exceptional in this respect were The Mojos, who had a Top Ten hit in March 1964; they also dubbed themselves "the Liverpool Yardbirds" due to a penchant for the brand of R&B

more likely to be heard in the Craw Daddy than the Cavern, where nearly everyone else was doin' the Hippy Hippy Shake with all o' their might.

Youth club outfits from Limerick to Lowestoft were now wearing collarless suits, shaking their fringes and going "Ooooo", and dropping words like "gear" into on-stage continuity. Other attempts by a wider world to cash in included a Merseybeat-flavoured inaugural A-side from The Kinks, and Eric Clapton and fellow guitarist Tom McGuinness briefly joining The Engineers who backed Casey Jones, a vocalist with a potentially breadwinning Scouse accent and a one-shot EMI single, 'One Way Ticket', released in July 1963.

"Introducing a home-made song at a live show was tantamount to announcing an intermission"

Though the ferry 'cross the Mersey was grounding on a mudbank by 1965, when even the likes of The Searchers, Billy J Kramer and Gerry & The Pacemakers could no longer guarantee a hit every time, the swing towards leaderless beat groups was complete – and the demarcation line between performer and jobbing tunesmith was eroded for all time.

The gift of a number by John Lennon and Paul McCartney became like a licence to print banknotes. It was after John and Paul completed 'I Wanna Be Your Man' virtually to order for the Stones (when watching them rehearse one afternoon in Studio 51) that Keith Richards and Mick Jagger made their first essays as songwriters. The two Beatles' inventiveness rubbed off too on the Kinks' Ray Davies, who penned the chart-topping 'You Really Got Me', followed by several more smashes in the same jerky vein to prove it hadn't been a fluke.

Meeting The Yardbirds backstage at the Hammersmith Odeon in later 1964, John Lennon recommended a 1962 item by US soul star Chuck Jackson, but he didn't proffer any of his own compositions – even though he and the other Beatles had seen for themselves The Yardbirds' Stones-like effect on the Craw Daddy mob, where a squeak of feedback had heralded the first episode of pulsating bass, crashing drums, Relf's vocal attack and surging harmonica, and Clapton and Dreja's guitar interaction, exacting customary submission from the minority there who hadn't wanted to like them.

Their first tinkerings with writing fragments of melody and rhyme aroused little enthusiasm, even as the ghost of a possible opening verse or a sketchy chorus smouldered into form. Most were dependant upon recurring R&B structures. 'Honey In Your Hips' was the only self-penned item with which The Yardbirds had bothered during their first studio session a year earlier. As everybody knew, introducing a home-made song at a live show was almost tantamount to announcing an intermission. Even the group's attempts at doing different non-originals from the hits of the day were considered bold.

To The Yardbirds' annoyance, both Manfred Mann and The High Numbers (before they reverted to their earlier name, The Who) were also performing 'Smokestack Lightning' on the boards, just as The Kinks were doing 'Got Love If You Want It', the obvious pattern for 'I'm The Face', The High Numbers' first single. R&B retreads on the Stones debut LP included another Slim Harpo item, 'I'm A King Bee', as well as Bo Diddley's 'Mona' and the ubiquitous 'Route 66'. Likewise, The Pretty Things and The Zombies had each seized upon Diddley's 'Road Runner', and The Mojos had cornered 'Spoonful'. Hard listening to 1961's *Muddy Waters At Newport* had resulted in recordings of 'Hoochie Coochie Man' by Dave Berry, Manfred Mann and, as inevitable as Valentino's reading of 'Kashmiri Song', Long John Baldry.

The duplicated repertoires – 'Help Me', 'Hoochie Coochie Man', 'I Got My Mojo Working' and all the others – went down a storm on the boards, but successful recordings were rare. (Ironically, at this time reissues of John Lee Hooker's leering 'Dimples' and Howlin' Wolf's eight-year-old 'Smokestack Lightning' were suddenly scoring better in the charts than the young white groups who were soon to displace them.)

There was only so much The Yardbirds could do to avoid lapsing into stylistic cliché and being consigned to the oblivion from which they were still surfacing. The group felt the vague unease of a specialist act in danger of missing the last flight to a higher commercial plateau.

In retrospect, Paul Samwell-Smith reflects that: "Had we continued to play just blues, we would, in the end, have broken through anyway. But at the time we really were desperate for a hit. Otherwise, we thought, you can't get up onto the next level. We'd have had to keep playing the Craw Daddy and all those provincial one-nighters. It's no use saying, 'We're a great blues band,' when there's only 3,000 people who have ever heard of you."

In a similar position to The Yardbirds, Manfred Mann had shown what was possible. Once an octet called The Mann-Hugg Blues Brothers, they'd enlisted Paul Jones and Tom McGuinness (on bass), slimmed down to five, and were using the less cumbersome nomenclature Manfred Mann when they were commissioned to come up with a new theme for *Ready Steady Go*, that liveliest of British TV pop series. What emerged was '54321', a catchy if self-mythologising opus that reached the Top Ten. A subsequent LP, 1964's *The Five Faces Of Manfred Mann*, consisted mostly of worthy work-outs of jazzy R&B which betrayed little hint that those responsible were operating ambiguously as a straight pop group on the same level as, say, Gerry & The Pacemakers.

Yet Manfred Mann weren't beyond crass publicity shots and stunts (like Jones being dragged into a barber's by his bandmates, or having his shirt ripped off by libidinous fans) – even though the group's 'intellectual' image appealed less to wearers of mini-skirts than girls who hid their figures inside tent-like jumpers borrowed from undergraduate boyfriends. After all, Jones had lasted a year at university, and Mann wore glasses (like Jim McCarty did in early Yardbirds photographs) plus a beatnik beard – and if that isn't intellectual, I don't know what is.

At the rowdier, punkier end of the R&B spectrum, The Pretty Things managed a Top Ten hit in late 1964 with 'Don't Bring Me Down' – a stop-start creation riven with beatnik slang: 'chick', 'man', 'dig', 'rave' – followed up by the thrash-and-rant of 'Honey I Need'. With their Rolling Stones connection (founding member Dick Taylor had been guitarist with the prototype Stones) and a demo of 'Route 66' as bartering tools, they'd been signed to Fontana after only their fourth paid booking by an A&R department pressured from above to find something to combat Decca's Stones. The fact that the Things were, "led by a sickening effigy of Mick Jagger" (Mike Cooper's description of singer Phil May) was all to the good.

Pretty Things tours were sometimes (literally) riotous affairs, and on the supporting bills, in among names like The Howlin' Wolves, The Dimples, The Bo Sneekers, The Smokestacks, The T-Bones, The Boll Weevils, The Primitives, The Authentics, and, gawd help us, The Little Boy Blues, were a couple of groups – The King Bees and The Mannish Boys – fronted by David Bowie when he still used the surname Jones.

Groups everywhere were tracing the Rolling Stones-Pretty Things scent by ditching stage suits and Beatle winsomeness for longer-haired taciturnity. A typical case was that of Burton-on-Trent's Atlantix, who played a farewell engagement before reforming the next week as Rhythm & Blues Incorporated.

New venues had also been springing up all over the country since 1963 in response to the beat group and R&B boom. In every nook and cranny throughout Britain, guts had been ripped from old factory premises, cellars cleared, bars extended and swimming pools boarded over to make space for some awful guitar combo, happy just to have a place to make its row for the many daft enough to pay to hear it.

That was the perspective of most established parochial agencies providing such entertainment. They saw themselves as no more than bookers. Certainly they had little interest in the career development of their clients, particularly beat groups, who were sold like tins of beans – with no guarantee of money back if they tasted funny. Take care of the pennies and the lads can take care of themselves.

Younger entrepreneurs, on the other hand, did not regard the group craze as so transient. Neither did they undervalue their own apprehension and love of pop. At the Craw Daddy and his other clubs, Giorgio Gomelsky booked acts that tended to be at least competent. He was also using whatever willingness and energy could do to advance the cause of The Yardbirds, who had melted into his managerial caress following his loss of The Rolling Stones to flamboyant Andrew Loog Oldham. For Giorgio, that had been the price of directions around the sly quagmires of the music business.

Perhaps more so than Oldham, Gomelsky was to prove useful when he chose to get involved in the creative activities of his charges. He presumed, for instance, to produce The Yardbirds' recording sessions, and be more than just a shadowy figure behind publicity and merchandising. Mixing thrift with a hands-on approach, it was Giorgio himself who sent out the letters and tapes, filed the cuttings, wrote the press handouts and made the telephone calls.

Not only that but he helped with unloading the equipment, parleyed with promoters and counted heads when the group was on a percentage. In every kind of in situ hassle ("the contract's not worth the paper it's written on, and your group's in breach of it anyway"), he kept his tenacious cool, clinging to his dignity and outfacing the most vehement shouting and swearing. Though full of "if you'll pardon my correction…" and "excuse me, but five minutes ago you said…", he was capable of striking a bellicose stance himself when necessary, while spewing out dizzying arrays of supporting facts and figures at a second's notice.

Gomelsky may have graduated from the old school of British show-business management, but he was not inclined to work according to the lodged conventions of his kind. Convinced of something incredible taking place in the Craw Daddy, he understood what it actually was better than some of his 1970s counterparts would when looking for a New Sex Pistols. Learning his craft, he – like Pistols svengali Malcolm McLaren – would make disturbing blunders, but Gomelsky believed so wholeheartedly in The Yardbirds' talent that he wasn't above standing outside the venue on the pavement and barking the show to passers-by. Could you imagine Brian Epstein doing that for The Beatles?

It was through knowing Epstein that Giorgio pulled strings to secure The Yardbirds ten minutes on the lower end of the bill during The Beatles' 1964 scream-rent Christmas season at the Hammersmith Odeon. This was a pivotal event of sorts, though the rave-ups that had made them the toast of the Craw Daddy had to be curtailed as they went the distance against the ear-stinging decibels of someone else's audience.

When this disputable moment of glory passed, it was back to normality. Keith Relf's plumber father's overloaded van would pull up outside a hall in High Street, England. From the vehicle, an unexpectedly large number of shadowy human shapes would emerge, numb from bearing amplifiers and drums on their laps. They'd hobble from the neon of early evening streetlamps towards the venue's front steps. A janitor would answer their banging, but not help lug the careworn equipment into the darkened auditorium with its draughty essence of disinfectant and echo of tobacco, food and alcohol intake from that afternoon's wedding reception. It's been raining all day, there's something good on television, and the local newspaper's on strike – so the sum total of the advertising is a sign outside with 'No Weirdies, Beatniks or Coloureds admitted' along the bottom.

However acclaimed they were at the Craw Daddy, The Yardbirds were essentially still scrabbling around the same as also-rans of Mannish Boys and Boll Weevils kidney. Every chart entry by the Stones or Animals was countered by up to a dozen flops by such acts, for whom artistic consolidation rather than development was the watchword. The executive attitude seemed to be: "Who needs market positioning research? All we have to do is grab as many peas from the same pod as we can, see which of them catches on and cash in quick. None of these dozy little twerps last long anyway, so why waste resources trying to prove otherwise?"

The Yardbirds had already been rejected by Decca, after they'd been summoned to RG Jones Studios in Morden in December 1963 by one of the label's junior recording managers, Mike Vernon. To

> *"Gomelsky wasn't above standing outside the venue on the pavement and barking the show to passers-by"*

intrigue someone like Vernon was a feather in any aspiring R&B group's cap. For a start, he knew what he was talking about – he and his brother compiled *R&B Monthly*, probably the first fanzine of its kind in Britain. An art school drop-out, Mike had entered Decca on the ground floor: "I was the general runaround making tea." He served his apprenticeship to the strains of Mantovani and satirist Paddy Roberts, and his first production was an LP by Texas-born pianist Curtis Jones, who – like another Vernon charge, Champion Jack Dupree – had made Britain his home.

As well as these bona fide US practitioners, Mike searched out blues-derived British talent. Among his early discoveries were The Graham Bond Organisation, The Artwoods and, shortly after their Sonny Boy Williamson jaunt, The Yardbirds (who'd also recommended The Spencer Davis Group to him). Vernon also signed Rod Stewart to a solo deal with Decca, and later launched Peter Green's Fleetwood Mac on his own Blue Horizon label.

In 1963 Decca were still trying to live down the fact that they allowed The Beatles to slide from their then-unconcerned clutches the previous year. As a result the firm began saturating itself with beat groups in the hope that one of them might take off like their rejected Scouse suppliants had when signed by arch-rival EMI, to teeth-gnashing effect. Yet for all Mike's championing of The Yardbirds, only his A&R superiors on their customary Tuesday morning 'supplement meeting' could say yea or nay about the group's market viability on disc – and just as they would with The Spencer Davis Group and The Who a month later, the Decca quorum decided that The Yardbirds' four-track demo wasn't quite right for teenagers: "We know these things, Mike."

At the post-mortem, the artists listened quietly as Vernon and Gomelsky hit the roof. Bitterly, the two dissected Decca's salaried time-servers and their short-sightedness and cloth-eared ignorance. No men of vision left, that's the trouble. Even if he had to dial his index finger to a stub, Giorgio was going to get his Yardbirds signed to another label, and sell so many millions that their faces would peer at Decca from every record shop window in Europe.

The outraged Giorgio didn't prove true to his word overnight. Nothing The Yardbirds presented on tape to EMI leapt out as an unmistakable smash hit either – but one of their subsidiaries at the time, Columbia (who were also "interested" in The Downliners Sect), was prepared to cast a 45 adrift on the vinyl oceans after The Yardbirds acquitted themselves well enough for first-timers behind closed doors at the firm's Olympic Studios in Barnes.

Their straightforward arrangement of Billy Boy Arnold's 'I Wish You Would' – with a strong, maybe too strong B-side in 'A Certain Girl' (featuring Gomelsky's own basso profundo on the "what's her name? I can't tell you, no" hookline) – spread itself thickly enough in sales terms over the next few months for EMI to hold on, hoping they'd strike luckier with a second effort. I mean, The Yardbirds could very easily end up as big as The Mojos, couldn't they?

> *"Decca decided that The Yardbirds' four-track demo wasn't quite right for teenagers: 'We know these things' "*

The most tangible benefit of being described as "EMI Recording Artists" on posters was a broadening catchment area of work – so much so that The Yardbirds were able to compare notes with other proficient units who had likewise broken free of parochial orbits. On terms of fluctuating equality when their paths crossed in dressing room or transport cafe, they could brag about imminent tours of outlandish countries and the surefire certainty of opening for the Stones at the Albert Hall, behaving as if this was still a possibility long after the trail had gone cold (if it had ever existed in the first place).

Though shared with scores of other groups on-stage, the Yardbirds' second A-side 'Good Morning Little Schoolgirl' made a better impression on the charts. Aided by press photos taken outside Twickenham Girls Grammar, it'd had a clear run up to Number 44 by November 1964, and may have progressed further had not a solo Rod Stewart entered the race that month with a slower version of the same number (ironically on Decca), filtered through his unmistakable rasping baritone.

There was also the matter of Relf's health. "Keith was always a bit poorly as a result of his chronic asthma," explains Paul Samwell-Smith. "If anything was physically demanding, he would get breathless. Whenever there was real stress too, Keith's asthma would play up." At times, if engagements couldn't be cancelled, stand-ins were called upon – often Mick O'Neill of The Authentics (burly, saturnine and Irish: no biological duplicate for Keith but nonetheless an adequate understudy) or even Mike Vernon.

To capitalise on this thwarted venture to the chart interior, it was proposed that the issue of an atmospheric 'live' LP, recorded on the cheap, might serve as a holding operation prior to a third single. Georgie Fame was talking about doing one from the Flamingo, a stone's-throw from the Marquee where Gomelsky had already immortalised a Yardbird bash in March 1964. The overall sound wasn't brilliant, but it was a marked improvement on the Birmingham Town Hall tape – group and audience were much more as one, and everybody involved seemed to be having fun on it.

The idea appeared sensible to Chris Dreja: "One of the virtues of The Yardbirds was the amazing onstage energy – the 'rave-ups'. It came from the heart and our excitement with the music." Away from the sterilising exactitudes of the studio, *Five Live Yardbirds* had a just-sufficiently ramshackle lucidity engendered perhaps by pre-performance anxiety about making mistakes that might be preserved forever on vinyl.

With the bespectacled figure of Keith's father at stage left, holding a boom mike like a Watusi spear, The Yardbirds powered through what was somehow a requiem for their incubation in the underground security of the clubs. There's often much false bonhomie during such exercises, but a kind of committed gaiety from a genuinely uproarious crowd lent an inspirational framework to a streamlined but representative set by an *au naturel* Yardbirds, sweating off half-a-stone each, and playing together as they wouldn't for much longer.

Today, *Five Live Yardbirds* stands up still as more than a mere period documentary. Kicking off with thunderous huzzas as the group is introduced one by one, a galvanising squiggle of lead guitar plunges them into 'Too Much Monkey Business' and a less speedy demolition of 'Got Love If You Want It'. The spooning out of further R&B elixir continues as Clapton and Relf advance with the grace of fencing masters on a free-for-all 'Smokestack Lightning', in which the tension piles up to boiling point until Samwell-Smith's lurching run-down signals the re-entry of the see-saw riff that brings the house down.

By contrast, there's Keith holding himself in check to emote the exquisite dirge that is 'Five Long Years'. Then it's on to a bravura 'Louise' from the John Lee Hooker songbook – with an off-key coda that I'm convinced was deliberate – and a crescendoing 'I'm A Man'.

Riding roughshod over tempo refinements, complicated dynamic shifts, or indeed anything that needed thinking about, some verse-chorus transitions were cluttered, and certain numbers were a fraction too bombastic – but so what? Casually-strewn errors were brushed aside like matchsticks during ovation-earning rave-ups conducted by instinct and eye-contact, with the jigging multitude willing the players on: worrying when they flagged, cheering when they rallied, and glowing when, by the time The Yardbirds resolved into the 'Here 'Tis' finale (the third Bo Diddley excursion of the night), they'd long been home and dry.

Clapping onlookers assumed the role of backing chorale, augmenting the rhythm section, and almost taking over the show (as during The Isley Brothers' 'Respectable') – almost but not quite. The Yardbirds remained the stars, guarding that fragile status with the passionate venom of a six-year-old with a new bike.

CHAPTER 6

FOR YOUR LOVE

*"You could never get him to tune up ...
he'd bend the strings. He never really
played chords – just all bendy notes – but
he never once played out of tune."*

KEITH RELF, ON JEFF BECK

Melody Maker's 'Pop 50' for January 1965 showed The Rolling Stones in retreat from Number One with an unrevised arrangement of Howlin' Wolf's 'Little Red Rooster', colliding on the way down with a definitive 'Baby Please Don't Go' by Van Morrison's Them – whose unkempt belligerence was in keeping with that of the other 'hairy monsters' of the day, detested by adults but applauded by the weekend hipster who saw them as an 'uncommercial' antidote to the audibly grinning Beatles.

At this point there still wasn't much to choose between The Yardbirds and a

New guitarist Jeff Beck, March 1965–November 1966

group like The Downliners Sect, who had also selected R&B warhorses for their *Nite In Great Newport Street* EP – an attempt to capture their diverting stage act at Studio 51 – and whose first album was as rife with Bo Diddley and Chuck Berry covers as many of their contemporaries. The Sect did enjoy a brief Number One hit in Sweden, but the failure of their 45s at home rouses both sympathy and speculation about how different their fate might have been had they put themselves in the way of a song like 'For Your Love' before the Yardbirds.

'For Your Love' was composed in the changing room of a men's clothing shop where one of British pop's great enigmas then worked. The originator of smashes, home and abroad, for The Hollies, Herman's Hermits, Dave Berry, Freddie & The Dreamers and Wayne Fontana as well as The Yardbirds, Manchester's Graham Gouldman was oddly unable to get far with his own groups, The Whirlwinds and then The Mockingbirds – whose 1964 version of 'For Your Love' had been turned down by Columbia (though a US-only solo version by Gouldman was issued on RCA in 1968).

> *"The Yardbirds nailed their colours to the mod mast, until the cult faded circa 1966"*

At first, Gouldman's manager Harvey Lisberg pondered sending the number to The Beatles – but as Graham himself would muse with a laugh, "They were doing all right in the songwriting department… but he still mentioned the idea to a publisher friend, who suggested that instead it should be offered to The Yardbirds as they were looking to break away from pure R&B and become more commercial."

Most of the group were, anyway…

After the Marquee LP, The Yardbirds' next move depended upon so many variables. In broad terms the way forward was either building up an image as the Stones had done – working up an overwhelming grassroots following by playing every toilet in the country over and over again – or recording a fantastic single.

You might also have to demean yourself with gormless PR ploys – like Manfred Mann outside the barber's, or The Primitives actually submitting to having their girlish tresses shorn to short-back-and-sides on a TV chat show one Sunday evening. More essential was keeping on the right side of the powers behind *Ready Steady Go*, as well as pirate radio programme presenters, among them Simon Dee, John Peel, and the former singer with Bournemouth's Tony Blackburn & The Rovers – a group whose lead guitarist was Al Stewart. (By coincidence, Blackburn and Stewart were each later to cover a song from 1966's *Yardbirds* LP.) To this end, it helped if you seemed to belong to the most dandified and citified of Britain's two main youth sub-cultures.

With Eric Clapton's crew-cut and Italian-suit, and Keith Relf's later capitulation to a back-combed bouffant, The Yardbirds nailed their colours to the mod mast, until the cult faded circa 1966. Always trailing furthest behind was Paul Samwell-Smith: "I was happy to follow… dyeing my jeans and making them flare at the bottom when the others had moved on."

Paul always felt the odd-one-out as a performer too: "I was always so bad on-stage. I hated being there because I couldn't move like the others could. Keith as singer and the lead guitarists would be at the front getting the screams, and Jim, Chris and I would work away at the back. I'd have liked to have wiggled my hips and thrown myself about the stage, but I couldn't do it."

Paul came into his own in the studio – but it was also there that he was most at odds with Clapton, who resented the increasing control of the group's destiny by a bass guitarist who later admitted, "I behaved very badly towards Eric most of the time. I was not easy to work with, and he was in the group for different reasons to me."

Even before Eric had joined The Yardbirds, there'd been the axiomatic 'musical differences' with Samwell-Smith, who recalls: "When The Metropolitan Blues Quartet first played at Kingston Jazz Cellar, Eric was in the audience. He came up to me at the end of our session in which I'd taken a couple of guitar solos. 'I tell you what,' he said, 'do me a favour: don't play any more solos.' I appreciated what he said. He was just a bit brutal and rather put me off continuing to play guitar."

Between ourselves, for all their shared ordeals and jubilations, Eric never cared that much for Paul as a person. But the two were in complete agreement on the subject of the blues, and Samwell-Smith on bass was to prove an agile foil to Clapton – having "copied the technique of Cyril Davies's bass player, Ricky Fenson" (whose stage-name was an amalgam of 'Fender' and 'Gibson' – he'd used his real name, Ricky Brown, when he was with Lord Sutch).

"I never thought my playing was great, especially when I used to watch bass guitarists like Ricky who knew much more than I did about chromatic scales and things like that. That really intimidated me, so I just played what I felt, intuitively. It was never very clever musically – there were others who could say, 'Well, that's a diminished seventh there, which means you have to do this...' Their knowledge and skill was amazing, but my attitude about it was different, and for whatever reason, people were impressed."

Artistically, Paul was more like Eric than the guitarist would have ever liked to imagine. But disagreements between them came to a head after The Mockingbirds' tape of 'For Your Love' was threaded onto Giorgio Gomelsky's machine. Unconvinced of its suitability as a third A-side, Giorgio abdicated his *de facto* producer's chair to Samwell-Smith.

So it was that, while The Yardbirds themselves piled in for the arresting nine-bar tempo change that was the bridge section, the record began and ended with session players on bongos, bowed double-bass and what one reviewer was to call the "sexy" harpsichord (played in block triplets by Brian Auger), which had more resonance than the blander piano as it plucked rather than struck the strings.

For its deviation from conventional beat instrumentation alone, Paul's was an imaginative, even eccentric arrangement. While bongo-pattering was associated with the clichéd 'party sequence' that dates a type of 'modern' continental flick made over and over again in the early 1960s, the harpsichord's impact on pop had hitherto been blunted by the fine line between an ear-catching extraneousness and its association with the late Middle Ages when it was first manufactured. Mostly it had been employed either as a gimmick (eg Jerry Lee Lewis' 1964 reading of 'Rockin' Pneumonia And The Boogie-Woogie Flu') or to convey an olde tyme flavour – as on Jimmie Rodgers' 'English Country Garden', a Top Ten hit in 1962.

If there was any justice in the world, 'For Your Love' was going to inflict at least as much chart damage as 'English Country Garden', despite Clapton's dislike of "messing about" with harpsichords, bongos and double-basses. It wasn't that Eric didn't want a hit – he just wanted to do it with a different kind of song. As he recounted later: "When we did the Beatles' Christmas show, we really began to feel the lack of a hit. We'd be on for 20 minutes or half an hour, and either you were very entertaining or you did your hits. A lot of times the 'rave-up' bit got us through, and a lot of times it didn't. It became very clear that if the group was going to survive and make money, it would have to be on a popular basis. We couldn't go back to the clubs, because everyone had seen what fun it would be to be famous."

Apparently Clapton wanted to release an Otis Redding song: "I thought it would make a great single because it was still R&B and soul, and we could do it really funky." But the obvious commercial appeal of 'For Your Love' won the day. Eric was "very disappointed, disillusioned by that."

"He hated 'For Your Love'," reckons Samwell-Smith, "because he thought we were selling out to market pressures – which we were." Clapton once said his basic attraction to the blues, as played by someone like Howlin' Wolf, was that "it was primitive". Now, with 'For Your Love', The Yardbirds were clearly an R&B outfit in transition to (in pirate disc-jockey's parlance) a "chartbound sound".

It had been decided that, on-stage, a seated Keith was to tap bongos gripped between his knees, and the harpsichord was to be approximated by a 12-string guitar clanged near its bridge for maximum metallic effect. This was Eric's job – though not for very long. Before 'For Your Love' had entered the charts at Number 32 on 20th March 1965 (12 placings higher than 'Good Morning Little Schoolgirl' at its apogee) Clapton – who by his own admission had become "withdrawn... and intolerable" – had been asked to leave, and was preparing for a tenure with John Mayall's Bluesbreakers, while The Yardbirds were sniffing round for another lead guitarist.

Jimmy Page was their first choice. Middlesex born and bred, he'd appeared on ITV's *Search For Stars* talent contest at 14, and had chosen to make a living on the stage – until, "One day somebody asked me if I'd like to play on a record. That led to other offers and suddenly there were more than I could cope with, often as many as four or five a week."

Unwilling to face another moonlight mile in the company of either Lord Sutch's Savages or Neil Christian's Crusaders, Jimmy chose this more comfortable professional sphere where you didn't have to like what you did, but if you were sufficiently versatile you could work near home in the employ of whoever called the shots, with no extra time or favours done.

Outside the context of work, Page's tastes ran to Kingston Art School student John Renbourn and his sometime musical partner Bert Jansch, folk club behemoths esteemed by better-known players such as George Harrison. Both had huge followings from the kind of guitar enthusiast who'd sit in the front row watching their fingers. Jimmy too was learning from the pair – to the extent that he was to adapt Jansch's version of the traditional 'She Moved Through The Fair' as 'White Summer', a showstopper when Page finally joined The Yardbirds 18 months later.

In the meantime, already one of the brightest stars in the London session firmament, Jimmy was fresh from being loud and clear on both 'Silhouettes' by Herman's Hermits and 'I Can't Explain' – the hit that made The Who the toast of would-be mods – when he declined the initial Yardbirds' offer in 1965. He had his head screwed on, and wasn't so dazzled by the beat boom to think that its groups were immortal. But he recommended Jeff Beck as an alternative. A reliable studio stand-in whenever Jimmy was indisposed, Jeff was still fronting The Tridents, who, as club booking calendars imply, had plenty to do on the London R&B circuit. Beck himself recalled: "The Tridents had built a great following. But there was no way I could exist – they weren't paying me anything. And I got a free suit when I joined The Yardbirds..."

After a deputation from The Yardbirds looked in at a Tridents' headlining spot at The 100 Club, an audition in the Marquee a few afternoons later was a mere formality. Noticing albums by The Four Seasons, The Beach Boys and Julie London in Jeff's Balham flat, his new *confreres* concluded correctly that he was less committed to the blues than Clapton had been, and therefore more adaptable.

Furthermore, displaying eclecticism and unpredictability in compatible amounts, Beck's solos and *obligatos* were constructed to integrate with the melodic and lyrical intent of a given piece. This approach seemed more attractively unfussed to anyone attuned to the more obvious aesthetics of a song, rather than a reaction principally to underlying chord sequences with high-velocity flash – as dispensed by Clapton on, say, 'A Certain Girl', in which his break has almost a separate life from the rest of the number.

Yet Beck was as capable of severe dissonance as serene melody, being both more experimental and more direct in style than either Clapton or any of the mainstream pop guitarists like George Harrison. Now a master of both fretboard and feedback, he was winding on slackened extra-light strings for novel legato effect. "You could never get him to tune up," Keith Relf was to notice. "He'd go on stage with his guitar totally out of tune and bend the strings. He never really played chords – just all bendy notes – but he never once played out of tune."

> *"According to Mike Vernon, Jeff's arrival in The Yardbirds was the best thing that ever happened to them"*

Beck was also to be a visual asset to The Yardbirds, especially on-stage. As he put it, "I would feel myself leaning forward, legs all apart, lunging with the guitar towards the audience like a boxer." Already within his archive of party tricks were the idea of leaving the guitar squealing against the speaker as he prowled the stage, and turning round abruptly to play it on the back of his neck, above his head or in the small of his back. For a crowning bit of swagger, he might then use a microphone stand or edge of an amplifier to create the careen of a bottleneck.

Teenage guitarist Brian May (a decade before Queen) had been a Yardbirds fan and Craw Daddy regular since the Clapton days, and he was amazed at what Beck would do: "I remember seeing him put the guitar down, make it feedback, and play a whole tune without even touching the fingerboard." The way Jeff himself remembers those halcyon days: "There were no two nights the same. Everybody loved it. We tried to weld this experimentation onto the format of a pop song – that's where the Yardbird style developed." According to Mike Vernon, "Jeff's arrival in The Yardbirds was the best thing that ever happened to them." This was borne out too by his gameness when taking part in a banal promotional 'For Your Love' film short, clanking around in a suit of armour. He also agreed to sport a shorter haircut and wear mod clothes.

As it would always be, most fans, even if fickle in affections towards individual members, found it in them to maintain loyalty to The Yardbirds as a whole. A few, however, voiced objections to the changeling during his maiden engagement – a Radio Caroline presentation in Croydon on 5th March. "I got these idiots shouting out, 'Where's Eric?'," Jeff grimaces. "So my first public announcement with The Yardbirds was, 'Don't be so fucking rude. Don't you read the music papers? Eric's left.'"

Thus it came to pass that Jeff Beck was handed his Yardbirds boarding-pass on point of take-off. During its second week in the charts, 'For Your Love' shot up to Number 13. Throughout the fortnight that followed it was to nestle among 'Silhouettes', 'I Can't Explain', Unit Four Plus Two's 'Concrete And Clay' and the first singles-chart entries by Tom Jones, Bob Dylan and Donovan, as well as the latest from the Stones, The Supremes, Them, Gene Pitney, The Beatles, The Searchers and Cliff Richard.

Could anyone not empathise with the Surrey lads' mortification when, before the disc slipped suddenly to Number 18 and then out, only Cliff's weepy 'The Minute You're Gone' hindered their passage to Number One – though, as was the case with Roy Orbison's 'Only The Lonely' and The Troggs' 'Wild Thing' before and after them, some lists had 'For Your Love' at the top on aggregate.

"There were now engagements in venues with tiered seating and dressing-room mirrors bordered by light bulbs"

Never mind, while the men-of-the-moment were yet to transcend scruffy jive hives with makeshift stages, at least they were no longer being paid in loose change. And there were now engagements in venues with tiered seating and dressing room mirrors bordered by light bulbs (not all of them working), and after-hours relaxation in the ten or so fashionable metropolitan clubs, some of which were already starting to feature visual projections soon to be given the attributive adjective 'psychedelic'.

Just one hit was the price of admission, however short-lived, to this pop elite with its informal sense of solidarity that dissolved competitiveness into much the same kind of camaraderie as there had been back in the Craw Daddy or Studio 51. The cardinal sin, of course, was to show any insecurities. Visible desperation was too nasty a reminder of the impermanence of fame and wealth, even in what was then "a bit of a cottage industry," as Dick Taylor of The Pretty Things called it. "There was no sense of career development. We thought we'd last maybe two or three years. We never felt we were in the entertainment industry as such." Pariahs in polite society, the Things had whetted the appetites of adolescent North America and its exploiters to such a pitch that a freak carnival of greater magnitude than that of the Stones the previous year was hungrily awaited. Yet the opportunity was lost through managerial indecision and faint hearts... Er, it's a big place, America, isn't it?

Initially The Yardbirds followed the same blocked pathway to the US as the Things: a tour was negotiated and postponed; advertisements were designed for trade journals, and snippets of film screened there before the group were tied-up in fibres of red-tape by immigration authorities who refused visas and generally obstructed entry for this latest bunch of Limey longhairs wishing to propagate their filth in Uncle Sam's fair land.

But at the same time as the domestic success of 'For Your Love', the single had a nine-week harrying of the *Billboard* Top 40, not to mention slicing as a wire through cheese into the hit parades of every other territory in the free world. America could wait while there were trips pending *sur le continent*. These included appearances on French television, typified by a stint before the cameras in Paris for a variety show in which a miming Yardbirds were less prominent than jugglers, acrobats and lines of choreographed chorus girls.

On their home-town turf The Yardbirds were still able to frequent pubs without being required to listen to starstruck drivellings. The local-boys-made-good were taking celebrity in their stride. Heads might turn when Paul halted his old Morris 1000 at a zebra crossing along Kew Road, but he didn't attract the beginnings of a crowd. Even when Keith ambled from the newsagents near his parents' sleepy street, no more than a few children might swoop to see the smile and wave as the singer who'd been on *Top Of The Pops* hurried indoors.

A Yardbird's leisure time was brief in those days, but sundown might bring on an onset of high spirits, and he would long to share these with more than South-Western Hotel drinkers, who were always ready to take him down a peg or two if he got too full of himself just because he had sold a million gramophone records.

CHAPTER 7

THE TRAIN KEPT A-ROLLIN'

"I've always been quite happy as a backroom boy. I like to be behind the ideas without necessarily being the one performing them."

CHRIS DREJA

Perhaps despite themselves, The Yardbirds were pop stars now – and to the cold-shouldering blues bigot down at the 100 Club they were now in the same league as The Honeycombs and Herman's Hermits. 'Heart Full Of Soul', another Graham Gouldman song, sold almost but not quite as well as 'For Your Love', but still tore up charts across the globe. Triumph followed triumph, and a period of prolific creativity was commensurate with vast increases in The Yardbirds' booking fees and royalty statements. This two-year golden age was evinced more insidiously by the irritation and at the same

Chris Dreja, originally rhythm guitarist, switched to bass in 1966

time flattery of seeing artists from The Beatles and the Stones downwards borrowing their musical ideas – from guitar feedback to exotic instrumentation such as sitar and dulcimer.

There wasn't, however, much that was new about either the group's marketing methods or their rise to fame. Like that oft-seen movie sequence of dates being ripped off a calendar to a background of clips, it had been: working the clubs ... record deal ... *Ready Steady Go* ... the ballrooms ... week-by-week climb of first hit into the Top Ten ... *Top Of The Pops* ... wild scenes on the boards and off ... police cordons and helmets rolling in the gutter ... hundreds of clamorous fans chasing the getaway car...

Sucked into a vortex of events, places and situations that hadn't belonged even to speculation a few months earlier, The Yardbirds might not have been particularly bewildered if the tour bus had drawn up outside an auditorium on Mars.

Over the next two years, the five were to turn up at 'a theatre near you' at nearly every point on the compass throughout the Commonwealth and Europe – Italy, France, Singapore, New Zealand, Norway, Germany – but commercial accolades in these climes were trifling compared to the heftier financial potential in the most important territory of all. After The Beatles' and then The Dave Clark Five's conquest of North America, further demand for UK pop precipitated what has passed into myth as the 'British Invasion', when two-thirds of *Billboard*'s Hot 100 was British in origin. Despite undercutting by countless incumbent soundalikes, nearly all of the kingdom's major pop acts – and some minor ones – made headway in the uncharted States. While the Stones' US breakthrough wasn't as immediate as expected, an encouraging precedent for The Yardbirds had been Manfred Mann's fat 1964 in which they had placed respective nonsense titles 'Do Wah Diddy Diddy' and 'Sha La La' high in the US Top 20.

> "In America they either thought we were The Beatles, or else we got spat on"

'For Your Love' had come to rest at US Number Six during the week in May 1965 when Wayne Fontana & The Mindbenders, Freddie & The Dreamers and Herman's Hermits monopolised the first three positions. "Britain hasn't been so influential in American affairs since 1775," ran one Billboard editorial.

Perhaps smelling perishable commodities, US record labels rush-released as much Limey product as the traffic would allow – hence only a six-week gap between two Dave Clark Five LPs. The same company, Epic, also issued the summer's *For Your Love*, a Yardbirds album with Beck seated at a harpsichord on the front cover, and its contents padded with The Hit, its flip, the previous two singles and their B-sides, and further makeweight tracks of diverse vintage, two with Clapton that were never to see the light of day at home for decades. Hot on its heels came December's *Having A Rave Up With The Yardbirds*, with half of *Five Live Yardbirds* occupying Side Two (plus a lengthy version of the Vibrations' 'My Girl Sloopy' – the Yardbirds worst cover).

North America was only kept waiting until September for the group in the flesh. As well as the administrative problems, Giorgio Gomelsky had been deliberating whether it was politic to commit them to such a venture when their domestic standing might be damaged by their absence. (The Honeycombs had made that mistake.) But after weeks of virtual inactivity, a telephone call from Gomelsky banished his clients' recreational sloth, and the Great Adventure began.

The reception at New York's Kennedy Airport was muted compared to The Beatles' tumultuous arrival 18 months earlier. After disembarkation and long corridors of light and shadow, The Yardbirds were greeted not by a unison banshee wail from thousands of teenagers on the upper terraces, but a handful of staff from the agency that had arranged the trip. (This included a lady who was so dismayed by the adolescent spots exploding on some of the group's faces that she suggested immediate applications of lacto-calamine lotion before they faced the press.)

At towns further west, though, even in the graveyard hours, they were to be confronted by hordes of hot-eyed girls, albeit still unsure which Yardbird was which, due to the outfit's comparative facelessness and lack of collective identity in that grey area between Herman's Hermits conservatism and Rolling Stones outrage. "Either they thought we were The Beatles," reflects Jim McCarty, "or else we got spat on."

Sometimes they'd be lugging their baggage towards airport escalators as cameras clicked like typewriters, and stick-mikes were thrust towards their mouths in the hope that another unreconstructed British beat group would crack back at the now stock questions about long hair and mini-skirts with a Beatle-esque pot-pourri of zaniness, unsentimentality, unblinking self-assurance and the poker-faced what-are-you-laughing-at way they told 'em. But nothing notably droll or even significant was reported fresh from the lips of an overwhelmed and most unbrash Yardbirds during these and other episodes of wry shallowness – like the many radio interviews, often before cock-crow on out-of-the-way regional stations, dominated by yapping disc-jockeys with lurid *noms de turntable*.

Beyond rustic backwaters, it was also cool for the hippest of the hip to dig the group. When they returned to New York for a show, it's said that Andy Warhol, US pioneer of Pop Art, was sneaked in because, as he apparently put it, "I wanted to be in the presence of The Yardbirds."

Because of visa constraints, media obligations had also filled the outward leg of the US itinerary more than actual Yardbirds performances. But, for the group, the highlight of the visit – more eagerly awaited than the few concerts they were allowed to play, and even more than a slot on the nationally networked *Hullabaloo*, the US's *Ready Steady Go* – was a hush-hush session at Chicago's Chess Studios, once a never-never land to English schoolboys confessing the blues in the privacy of their own homes.

In a sense the Windy City itself was like everywhere else they'd been in the US: a contradiction of familiar mystery. A Woolworth's reared up in North Clark Street, scene of the St Valentine's Day Massacre; Coca-Cola tasted just the same, and pizza was the city's answer to fish-and-chips. Yet the sights and sounds in the streets were so diverting that you could spend hours ambling within a mile of Chess – it became clear, for instance, that Chicago blues lived on largely in the efforts of its buskers, usually some scruff lilting an unaccompanied and never-ending 'Baby What You Want Me To Do'.

Inside the hallowed Chess address of 2120 South Michigan Avenue, the Stones had taped their first UK Number One, 'It's All Over Now', under the auspices of the same house team that had forged the definitive works of Waters, Wolf, Diddley and Berry. Now The Yardbirds were there to put down another go at Bo's 'I'm A Man' as a spin-off 45 for *Having A Rave-Up*, and would be back again in December to tease 'Shapes Of Things' from nothing more than a riff.

The backing track to its B-side, 'You're A Better Man Than I', as well as that to 'The Train Kept A-Rollin', had already been recorded down below the Mason-Dixon line in an untidy river port as thoroughly steeped in blues as Chicago. Sun studios – Sam Phillips' legendary one-storey complex – still stood next to a used-car lot on the junction of Union and Marshall Avenues in Memphis. Albeit much-modernised at the time (it was later restored to something like its original glory), Sun has always been venerated as the wellspring of recordings by the likes of Wolf and Sonny Boy, for leasing to Chess, and for the process whereby Elvis, Jerry Lee Lewis, Carl Perkins, Roy Orbison and Johnny Cash had been conditioned for what lay ahead.

> *"The Yardbirds was a wonderfully democratic band – everybody's contribution was recognised"*

Knowing that the rough edge and excitement of Sun's early output had been manufactured in this studio – about the same size as the average hotel bedroom – The Yardbirds were putty in Phillips' hands. Apart, that is, from an irresolute Relf, who could endure only so many 'fantastic' playbacks of the backing to 'You're A Better Man Than I', and whose moonshine-fuelled pitching was so suspect that his lead vocals had to be overdubbed in New York, just hours before the group flew back home, where later they trudged around British theatres – some half-empty – with Manfred Mann (whose Mike Hugg had written 'You're A Better Man…').

Despite such dispiriting assignments, and the then-imperceptible storm clouds gathering between factions within The Yardbirds, the operation was running as smoothly as it ever would. The double A-side 'Still I'm Sad' and 'Evil Hearted You' had tramped what was becoming a well-trodden path into the Top Ten in Britain, and everyone from principals to road crew seemed to be functioning well enough according to capacity.

"The Yardbirds was a wonderfully democratic band," opines Chris Dreja. "Everybody's contribution was recognised. Paul was the most musical member, in the purest sense. Jim was a fair songwriter. Keith was an interesting lyricist – though I wrote the words to 'Lost Women'. Can you imagine Muddy Waters singing, 'You can hardly call it humane'? We were the sum of the parts as opposed to one guy presenting five numbers as a *fait accompli*."

Dreja was the group's most hidden talent. However little you were aware of him on stage, you'd have missed him if he hadn't been there. One of nature's sidemen, he was solidly at the heart of the music, ministering to overall effect on rhythm guitar or wielding maracas, and possessing a voice reliable enough for harmonies.

"There've been occasions when I've been forced into playing lead guitar through absences or walk-outs," he would disclose, "but it wasn't my natural field. Riffs, rhythm, jamming, energy: that's where I come from – and I've always been quite happy as a backroom boy. I like to be behind the ideas without necessarily being the one performing them."

Some of these ideas would be in readier states of completion than others: sometimes the most detailed demos, or music without lyrics, or vice-versa, or just nebulous fragments computed in the brain. On the journey around the world, McCarty, Relf and Samwell-Smith – and to a lesser degree Dreja and Beck – couldn't help but get together in differing combinations to construct songs from only a title or melodic phrase. As much part of touring luggage as spare underwear was a transistorised reel-to-reel tape deck – forerunner of the cassette recorder – on which to note shards of inspiration that may have cut a Yardbird during an elevator ascent to his hotel suite, or when fastening a thoughtful economy-class seat-belt, or sinking into a velvet-blue oblivion with a notepad and biro beside the bed.

Because space restrictions and the laugh-a-minute ambience of package tours circumscribed serious in-transit revision and elaboration of individual doodles, Yardbirds numbers grew most often from standing over, say, Paul or Chris at the piano, and listening intently as a sketchy chorus ripened and expanded. Then some of the others – even Giorgio or Simon Napier-Ball, the manager who replaced him in 1966 – would sling in rhyming couplets, chord changes and twists to the plot, as Keith and Jim paced up and down the carpet, bedevilled with an impulse that might have manifested itself at some inconvenient moment on their travels. Either that or they'd be staring into space... thinking of a drum pattern.

"We all muddle in together," explains Samwell-Smith in Runyonese present-tense. "Somebody comes up with a riff and then someone else writes the words, but then it's worked on so much by the band. A good example is that Jeff didn't get a composing credit for 'Shapes Of Things' when he really should have done, just for the way he developed it when the song was being formed. Keith had this idea for a riff, and I definitely wrote most of the lyrics, but the riff and the lyrics aren't really what 'Shapes Of Things' is about. It's a lot more than that."

As Jeff himself later put it: "I didn't write – all I did was wait for them to come up with these threadbare songs and then make something of them."

To Simon Napier-Bell, his new charges' recording methodology appeared slap-dash and last-minute – like a painter dabbing at a hanging canvas minutes before the gallery opens. There were instances of them walking into a studio with hardly anything prepared, even with a ticking clock and a pound-sign hanging over every fretful quaver. From particles of a would-be song, traces of pattern might only be discernible after what seemed like interminable unshaven and red-eyed centuries of false starts and scrapped takes, and started shining through with increasing clarity as the studio clock dictated short-cuts and the ditching of more and more clutter.

"We'd start with a basic rhythm and bass pattern," elucidates Jim, "and then sort of build it up."

> *"Jeff didn't get a composing credit for 'Shapes Of Things' when he really should have done, just for the way he developed it"*

While the instrumental track was being organised, or some tedious mechanical process going on in the control room, someone – usually Keith – might have been elsewhere collating the words.

Originals, if laughably derivative at times, had been penned since the Clapton days, but it wasn't until the near-suicidal nocturne 'Still I'm Sad' that any were risked as A-sides, and The Yardbirds truly found their feet as composers. It's debatable, all the same, if pieces such as 'Still I'm Sad' would have been envisaged in a pop context without the earlier – sometimes ill-fated – accomplishments of a group like The Zombies. The minor-key introspection of Rod Argent's 1964 classic 'She's Not There' – though it drew inspiration from a John Lee Hooker album track – was the antithesis of the blueswailing aggression of their R&B peers, yet the paradox of enjoyable melancholy was to be a feature of some later Yardbirds work; not only 'Still I'm Sad', but 'Turn Into Earth' and 1967's 'Only The Black Rose'.

With internal sources of new material and their own publishing concerns, a lot of these blasted young guitar groups had given the traditional 'tin-pan-alley'-based music industry a nasty turn – yet as late as 1966 even Lennon and McCartney were still being damned with faint praise by the *Sunday Times* as "reasonably good 'amateur' composers".

When The Hollies' own 'We're Through' seized up three places short of its 1964 predecessor's peak of Number Four, cautious EMI ordained a return to 'professional' songs for the next six 45s. And the same firm was only prepared to chance its arm with 'Still I'm Sad' – in which a moaning unison headwind causes trees to flay a moon in a falling sky – if it was coupled with 'Evil-Hearted You', another Graham Gouldman *meisterwerk* with a formulaic 'For Your Love' tempo change.

In the 18 months since his resignation from The Yardbirds, Eric Clapton had achieved an exalted status – almost that of a deity, after "Clapton Is God" had been scrawled in the Marquee's gents toilet, but also "best guitarist in the country", as Steve Winwood described him, following the issue of *Blues Breakers*, Clapton's *piece de resistance* under the aegis of John Mayall. This wasn't always seen as an obvious sequence of events. According to the late Vivian Stanshall, then mainstay of The Bonzo Dog Doo-Dah Band: "When he was a Yardbird, no one had been under the impression that Eric was about to become a world-class musician."

There was a brief group reunion of sorts: one evening in 1966 Clapton, all friends again, had 'sat in' with The Yardbirds at The Marquee. During his time as one of Mayall's Bluesbreakers, Clapton also featured in The Powerhouse, a one-shot sextet convened by Paul Jones, with Steve Winwood and bass guitarist Jack Bruce, for 30 uneven minutes of recording in an otherwise deserted Marquee. In fact it was through the Bluesbreakers that Clapton first played with both Bruce and Ginger Baker, with whom he was to form Cream before 1966 was out.

Eric was initially happy to see The Bluesbreakers as his salvation – a blues haven – but his time working under John Mayall wasn't always easy. A former Royal Engineer, Mayall may have commanded respect for his painstaking vocational dedication and disciplined enforcement of his own order, but wouldn't tolerate intemperance – and if he caught you with drugs, God help you. This regime didn't suit everybody, and Clapton had enjoyed a two-month absence without leave on a hedonistic odyssey to Greece with five pals.

Though admirable young men in many ways, a lot of Swingin' Sixties musicians – and not just the longhairs – had their quota of young men's vices, and time that hung heavy between soundcheck and performance wasn't necessarily killed with chess tournaments and tea-and-biscuits. I know it's distasteful to mention such things but alas it's true: mobbed by libidinous admirers not much younger than himself, a bachelor Yardbird with no steady girlfriend may have been tempted to pick and choose from unsteady ones who were practised at evading the most stringent security barricades to impose themselves on famous groups. A natural prudity forbids me from going into detail, except to say that newly-divorced Jeff Beck in particular was, apparently, a Lothario on the road – for as well as requests for autographs, he received more invitations than most to partake in casual dalliances with glad-eyed young ladies in the romantic seclusion of, say, a backstage broom cupboard.

As *omerta* is to the Mafia, a vow of silence among bands of roving minstrels persists concerning outlawed drugs as well as illicit sex. Quoted in a 1966 edition of the *Daily Express*, Keith Relf protested that drugs were no more rife in pop than they were among the general public – although amphetamines had been the subject of Bo Diddley's song 'Pills' years before pop stars and drugs became as commonly related as politicians and sleaze in newspaper headlines.

The drug habit may have been inherited from such dissimilar older musicians as Charlie Parker and Johnny Cash, and others who may have turned to chemical stimulants in order to keep the Dracula hours of their profession. The major recreational drug in the mid-1960s, however, was marijuana. It served too as a herbal handmaiden to creativity – especially when certain pop figures started thinking there was more to life than cranking out the same 30-minutes' worth of stale, unheard noise night after night.

> *"Keith Relf told the* Daily Express *that drugs were no more rife in pop than they were among the general public"*

Paul Samwell-Smith was one who'd begun seriously questioning his career path, weighing up the cash benefits of being forever on the move with The Yardbirds against his own self-picture as an artist. But he at least had a Plan B to fall back on: his career as a record producer had jolted into quivering action almost a year before he was to quit the concert stage, seemingly forever.

His first commission had been in autumn 1965 – a Mockingbirds single, 'You Stole My Love'. Head-to-head at the mixing desk with Giorgio Gomelsky, Paul's comprehensive logging of the minutiae of technological studio-work since The Country Gentlemen's try-out at Abbey Road had bred in him the self-assertion to issue jargon-ridden instructions through the talkback, and make learned recommendations to the engineer about equalisation, vari-speeding, bounce-downs and spatial separation.

Since the 'For Your Love' date, Paul had ascertained what he could *in situ*. Now, as if it was the most natural thing in the world, he was apportioning tracks, short-listing devices and effects, and furrowing his brow over stereo panning and the degree of echo on Graham Gouldman's lead vocal.

While he was still a Yardbird, Paul's work in this field was sporadic, and the next such job wasn't until the following spring – when the act in question was none other than Keith Relf. "I was keen to do some more producing, and Keith wanted to do something in his own right, as opposed to being singer with The Yardbirds," Paul explains.

About once a month, from the middle of 1966, the music press would report a key member of some group or other attempting a solo single. Keith's 'Mr Zero', however, attained the dubious distinction of peaking at Number 50 during its first week in the shops, and then falling backwards. The logic behind this choice as an A-side was that it was composed by Bob Lind, a then-trendy folk singer from Baltimore, whose winsome 'Elusive Butterfly' (to which Jim McCarty was to allude in his *Roger The Engineer* sleeve-notes) had just tied at Number Five with a UK cover by middle-of-the-road Val Doonican. As demonstrated by versions of other Lind songs by such notables as Cher, Marianne Faithfull, Nancy Sinatra and even Adam Faith, he'd caught on with those who preferred his 'poetic' gentleness to harsher Bob Dylan – especially now Bob had buried his most recent songs in alienating surreality and amplification.

"Keith wasn't that struck by Bob Lind," reckons Jim McCarty, "but Paul liked him. Actually, we had a party round at Paul's parents' home for him one day, and it was really strange: Bob Lind and all these Hollywood people in this suburban house."

> *"Giorgio wanted us to be the first English band to do the* San Remo Song Festival...*"*

Keith Relf's next – and self-written – attempt at solo stardom, 'Shapes In My Mind', would be lost to the archives of oblivion before the year was out. A couple of trivia items of note here: a promotional copy of a Relf disc entitled 'Make Me Break This Spell', with a date (November 25th) scrawled on it, fetched a vast amount in a German auction in 1982. It was exactly the same recording as 'Shapes In My Mind' – the wrong title was assumed from a line in the first verse. Its B-side, a harmonica-led instrumental called 'Blue Sands', was attributed to Keith, but was actually by The Outsiders, a unit hired by Simon Napier Bell. (By the way, we can also lay to rest here the myth that Keith used the pseudonym 'Keith Dangerfield' on a single called 'No Life Child' – not true. Nor did the group issue any discs under the name 'Philamore Lincoln'. And our Jim McCarty is not the gentleman who recorded with Jimi Hendrix and The Amboy Dukes, featuring Ted Nugent.)

In subdued but expressive manner, 'Shapes In My Mind' was plugged in-person on *Ready Steady Go*, and there came requests by *Fabulous* and other teen magazines for photo sessions featuring Keith alone, and even a pop annual that was to profile him without a single mention of The Yardbirds. Possessing the most visual fascination (certainly before Jeff Beck joined), Relf hadn't been unfamiliar with approaches to cast aside the group. McCarty remembers: "In the Marquee in the early days a couple of quite sharky-type agents came down, and they wanted to sign Keith as a solo singer – but he really wasn't interested."

Relf may in fact have pondered the wisdom of spurning this offer on an afternoon in January 1966 when The Yardbirds found themselves as far from Howlin' Wolf as any Marquee customer could ever have imagined... "Giorgio had a lot of contacts in Europe," explains Jim McCarty; "he was a very continental guy: Swiss mother, Russian father, educated in Italy, spoke several languages. He wanted us to be the first English band to do the *San Remo Song Festival*…"

So, through Gomelsky's most ill-conceived tactic as manager, The Yardbirds were booked for a function which, while not quite plumbing the bing-bang-biddley-bang depths of the *Eurovision Song Contest* (a vital date on the calendar for the *cognoscenti* of kitsch), did attract an audience of pearly cleavages and twirled moustachios for whom the main events of the day were the intermissions, with their see-and-be-seen gossip and flagoned cocktails like melted crayons, and who expected to hear easily assimilable melodies with hooklines like snatches of kindergarten babble.

Going far beyond the self-humiliation they'd had to endure in a comedy sketch on *Hullabaloo*, The Yardbirds squeezed themselves into formal attire for their appearance on the San Remo casino stage, where Relf was to mouth the syllables of 'Questa Volta' – a number repeated by the country's own Bobby Solo, who at least sounded like he understood what he was singing.

"Bobby was Italy's answer to Elvis Presley," McCarty adds, somewhat abashed, "and he'd won *San Remo* every year he'd taken part." Other participants included quasi-operatic Domenico Modugno – omnipresent at almost every such extravaganza on the mid-European calendar; Germany's swashbuckling Fred Bertelmann ('The Laughing Vagabond'); and Gene Pitney, the US balladeer who, other than Roy Orbison and the remote Elvis, had come to command the most devoted European following of any American pop star of the 1960s. For his dentist's drill tenor, defiantly short hair, besuited garb and artistic consistency – 'squareness' some might say – Pitney, like Modugno and Bertelmann, was idolised by older consumers who'd been disenfranchised by beat groups.

The Yardbirds' presence was, therefore, as profoundly disturbing as Gandhi bowling for a pig at a vicarage fête. All the same, containing their exasperation with the mess in which Gomelsky had landed them, the five went the distance with a cold accomplishment that belied their ordained song's saccharine quality. Keith tried to make a show of it, even taking a bow at the end – but roundabout persuasion had given way to naked pleas from Giorgio for Jeff Beck to tread the boards for 'Questa Volta'. Defiance, hesitation and final acceptance had chased across Jeff's countenance, though even when he got as far as the wings there'd been no guarantee he wasn't going to bolt at the last second…

CHAPTER 8

TOO MUCH MONKEY BUSINESS

*"I'm not an easy person anyway ... and I
was starting to snap at everybody. I knew
there had to be something better in life –
and there was."*

PAUL SAMWELL-SMITH

Throughout their recording career the Yardbirds stuck, more or less, with a conventional guitars-bass-drums format. True, there'd been a harpsichord on 'For Your Love', but though a sitarist had been hired for 'Heart Full Of Soul' in 1965, such ostentation had been disregarded after Jeff Beck's guitar tone exhaled what was in pop terms a more pungent breath of the Orient – albeit with a sub-flavouring of a blackboard-scratching saxophone effect, probably achieved with a foot-operated fuzz-box, all the rage in 1965 after one was used on the Stones' 'Satisfaction'. As Beck describes

Samwell-Smith left the band to become a producer in June 1966

his own sonic adventures: "I was happy making silly noises," Beck laughed. "I'd get carried away. I'd slacken off the bottom two guitar strings and press them against the pickup and play a kind of sitar thing, with wobbles."

It was reported that during the *Revolver* sessions The Beatles had commanded an underling to go out and buy *Aftermath*, the new – and all-original – Rolling Stones LP. As well as the improved quality of Jagger and Richards' songwriting, *Aftermath* was admired for Brian Jones's stitching of quaint instrumentation into the overall fabric, exemplified by the sitar *ostinato* on 'Mother's Little Helper', and the dulcimer chords on the 'medieval' 'Lady Jane', respective takes on what had been pre-empted by The Yardbirds on 'Heart Full Of Soul' and, after a fashion, 'Still I'm Sad'.

A few weeks after 'Heart Full Of Soul' hit the UK Number Two (it made the US Top Ten later in 1965), The Kinks showed they were even less afraid of commercial risks by releasing 'See My Friend' –

"It was primarily thanks to The Yardbirds and The Kinks that non-European sounds became more than a trace element in pop"

a track which The Who's Pete Townshend has called "the first reasonable use of the drone – far, far better than anything The Beatles did, and far, far earlier."

Several months before George Harrison first dabbled with the sitar on 'Norwegian Wood', it was primarily thanks to both The Yardbirds and The Kinks that non-European sounds, if not musical theories, became more than a trace element in pop. 'Heart Full Of Soul' and 'See My Friends' were also among the first audacious creaks of a door that was to open wider on a treasury of what would be termed 'world music'.

From these caskets, Malcolm McLaren, Adam & The Ants, Peter Gabriel and other post-punk cultural burglars helped themselves in the 1980s, as did the likes of Kula Shaker in the 1990s – demonstrating that the East still held as much allure for Western pop as it did in 1965 when The Yardbirds were metamorphosing – on vinyl anyway – into something infinitely more arresting than the 12-bar blues band they once were. Blueswailing ferocity now deferred to studied artistic progression.

Yet amid the bedlam of the stage, while the 'new music' could be reproduced only as far as guesswork and eye contact would allow, it was largely lost on audiences that had bought tickets for a tribal gathering rather than a hushed recital. In the days before programmable desks, graphic equalisers, megawatt PAs and even stage monitors, Jim McCarty punished his kit without electronic assistance while the guitarists' amplifiers were less a sound than a presence. Virtually gulping the microphone, Keith would strain against the horrendous barrage of screaming girls.

Though 'Still I'm Sad' was dropped from the stage repertoire after less than a decent interval, it can be seen as influential: better late than never, The Herd's monkish lower register cantillatings a la 'Still I'm Sad' (which had featured a muffled 'amen' unscripted on the fade) were to underline 'From The Underworld' and 'Paradise Lost' in 1967. The group's musical departures had a wider impact too: "a typical Yardbirds tempo change" was noted by an *NME* reviewer of 'Psychotic Reaction' by San Jose's Count Five, and this jarring selling-point was to be elaborated by The Pink Floyd (eg 'Astronomy Domine'), Zoot Money's new Dantalion's Chariot ('Madman Running Through The Fields') and, later, King Crimson and Yes.

As well as 'For Your Love' and 'Evil-Hearted You', a tempo change cropped up on 'Shapes Of Things' – a track that also made a feature of guitar feedback howl, something that might simply have been an aggravating hazard to groups like The Dave Clark Five or The Honeycombs. But The Yardbirds – and The Kinks, and then The Who and The Creation – had never dismissed guitar feedback as such: instead they pursued it as a deliberate contrivance, and a method of sustaining notes and reinforcing harmonics. With no instructional *Play In A Day* published for feedback, Jeff Beck, Dave Davies, Pete Townshend and Eddie Phillips were in virgin territory, and had learned what they could from trial-and-error.

When The Beatles' had begun the recording of 1964's 'I Feel Fine' with a feeding-back guitar it echoed the in-concert use of feedback by The Yardbirds and The Kinks. Rendering the circle unbroken, The Kinks would reiterate the 'I Feel Fine' intro on 'I Need You', a 1965 flip-side, while the following year's 'Shapes Of Things' and 'You're A Better Man Than I' were perhaps the best examples of Jeff Beck's lubrication of The Yardbirds' output with feedback.

It was prominent too on 'Shame', a 1966 B-side by Dave Dee, Dozy, Beaky, Mick & Tich – an outfit used as an example of 1960s junk culture in a 1990s BBC TV documentary, *When Art Went Pop*. This may evoke a howl of derision from the programme's facetious commentator, but I happen to think that Dave Dee & co were a very interesting group. Actually, I wonder sometimes how their career might have gone had they chosen a less ridiculous name – say 'The Yardbirds'.

Fans of either group appeared to be blind to underlying similarities: both made use of quasi-symphonic dynamics, and as The Yardbirds had investigated raga and Gregorian chant, so Dee's bunch had superimposed accelerando (and a Greek bouzouki) on the risqué 'Bend It', and a Russian *czardas* rhythm on 'Okay!'. In retrospect, the chasm between 'Still I'm Sad' and 'The Legend Of Xanadu' is far from unbreachable.

But, then as now, there were music lovers who believed that the more arduous the effort needed to 'appreciate' something, the more 'artistic' it must be – thus magnifying the gap between themselves and the common herd. Yet however much such snobs might have refuted the suggestion, The Yardbirds had become, by 1966, as much hard-sell entertainers as Dave Dee, Dozy, Beaky, Mick & Tich, and their blood-brothers The Troggs.

The main difference lay in the image – assumed or otherwise – that attracted consumers of either. While none of them wore swot spectacles onstage, as did two of Manfred Mann, or contained "the first Bachelor of Arts to top the charts" like The Spencer Davis Group, The Yardbirds continued to get by on the 'intellectual' ticket – even though there had been nothing intellectual about 'My Girl Sloopy' or 'Questa Volta', unless regarded as Dadaist for their calculated mindlessness.

Unlike Dave Dee et al, The Yardbirds were at least attempting to explore lyrical possibilities beyond boy-meets-girl. Rather than the more narrative quarry The Kinks had been stalking since their first flush of hits, Yardbirds' lyrics tended to hinge on less immediately graspable topics than those outlined in the likes of 'A Well Respected Man', 'Sunny Afternoon' and 'Waterloo Sunset'.

Bob Dylan's pervasive appeal was also obvious. Both The Kinks and The Yardbirds performed his 'Most Likely You'll Go Your Way (And I'll Go Mine)' in concert, while other similarly-placed groups dipping into Dylan's discursive songbook included Them and Manfred Mann (whom the bloke himself reckoned were the most effective interpreters of his work). An absorption of Dylan's lyrical approach could be identified too in early work by The Beatles (eg 'I'm A Loser'), the Stones ('Get Off Of My Cloud'), and The Downliners Sect in 'Bad Storm Coming', a euphemism for impending nuclear holocaust.

Although not so overtly anti-war, the more abstract 'Shapes Of Things' could itself be seen as a searing indictment of The Society In Which We Live – but though The Yardbirds could write, and Keith Relf articulate, the most oblique metaphysics without pretension, there were no serious analyses of their librettos as there were for those of Dylan. And there were occasions when The Yardbirds (and Dylan too) could be suspected of leaning on pretty-but-meaningless syllables and negative symbolism as pseudo-cryptic disguises for what were essentially banal – and even completely void – perceptions. Try 'Glimpses' on the *Little Games* LP.

All the same, while not in the royalties-earnings bracket of The Beatles or The Stones, The Yardbirds could argue that, with 'Shapes Of Things' and 'Over Under Sideways Down' in Top 20s on both sides of the Atlantic – and with the occasional cover version of one of their tracks, such as Manfred Mann's instrumental 'Still I'm Sad', and 'Turn Into Earth' on the B-side of Al Stewart's debut single, or 'I Can't Make Your Way' by Paul & Barry Ryan – they were among Britain's most commercial songwriters.

> *"The Yardbirds' eponymous studio LP was declared a 'mini-*Revolver*' by a* New Musical Express *pundit"*

While they may not have soundtracked the mid-1960s to anything like the same degree as the Stones or Beatles, The Yardbirds' eponymous studio LP (also called *Roger The Engineer*, after the cover artwork) was declared "a mini-Revolver" by a *New Musical Express* pundit. Such praise was all the more deserved because The Yardbirds' recording budget was always limited, unlike that of The Beatles, who'd turned out to be as sound an investment for EMI as Elvis was for RCA.

As it was, although The Yardbirds were granted only a block-booked a few days to record their album – from plug-in to final mix – during 1966's rainy summer, any extension may actually have detracted from the proceedings' spontaneity and endearing imperfections. Rather than the weeks often spent on one track by The Beatles in those days, no gadgetry and superimposition intruded upon the Yardbirds grit; no over-premeditated vocal allowed to float effortlessly on layers of treated sound.

Disappointingly, the *Yardbirds* LP's zenith during an eight-week stay in the album charts was Number 20 – and it maintained steady if unremarkable sales. All this was rather a comedown in the light of heftier market attainments in the preceding months. Regardless of this, *Yardbirds* was a masterpiece of imagination and invention, with everyone involved firing on all artistic cylinders.

While the album ventured into areas that had the most shadowy link to their R&B core, *Yardbirds'* opening track 'Lost Women' came closest to recapturing the *Five Live Yardbirds* power, which in its full flowering could exact 'hey-yeah' submission from the most ill-disposed audience.

A "disgusted" Eric Clapton had confided to a journalist's tape recorder that he had introduced his former group to an opus by Snooky Pryor, another of Chicago R&B's lesser lights, from which the 'Lost Women' riff had been lifted. A more blatant if less effective theft was Elmore James's 'Dust My Broom' – itself derived from any number of Robert Johnson's rural stumblings – as the melodic basis for 'The Nazz Are Blue', as 'I Ain't Got You' was for its words. 'The Nazz Are Blue' was also the first time Jeff Beck-as-lead singer had been heard on disc.

Though one spin alone wasn't enough to comprehend trifles like the mock-Scottish pentatonic touch in the final seconds of 'What Do You Want', the fact that the majority of tracks highlighted a lead guitar tour de force to some degree (especially the 'Jeff's Boogie' instrumental dredged up from his Tridents days) was actually a contributory factor in The Yardbirds' eventual self-destruction.

Indeed, however unknowingly, Beck had already started his solo career via 'Beck's Bolero', taped with an *ad hoc* crew that included Jimmy Page and session bass player John Paul Jones, a few weeks before the Yardbirds sessions. Jeff still lists this 'Beck's Bolero' as one of his all-time favourites, claiming, "The riff in the middle was the first heavy metal riff ever – and I wrote it." (He recalls performing a live version with Jimi Hendrix on lead guitar, but unfortunately it seems no one committed it to tape.)

> "Yardbirds *was a masterpiece of imagination and invention, with everyone involved firing on all artistic cylinders*"

Artistic tensions had practically become the norm for The Yardbirds by this time – in fact, Simon Napier-Bell decided during these recordings that "you might lose the underlying creative element" if you didn't let the scum of internal dissent surface. Certain Yardbirds, for instance, did not subscribe to the maxim that if a thing's worth doing, it's worth doing pedantically: Paul Samwell-Smith was not one of those. "As much as time, the restrictions were to do with the four-track machine," he would later protest, "and we only had the one four-track machine. We couldn't bounce across."

With Paul in charge of the hurried meticulousness, it didn't improve fraying tempers elsewhere to be kept hanging about during, say, the guiro overdub to 'He's Always There' or some complicated tweaking at the desk. The combination of boredom and a cash-haemorrhaging urgency raised pulse rates to such a height of vexation and cross-purpose that those on the periphery would slope off for an embarrassed coffee break until the contretemps subsided to simmering huffs – lent palpable form on one occasion in Jeff's perversely monotonal solo in 'The Nazz Are Blue'.

The diverging paths of various Yardbirds' later careers were already visible: as belligerently alive as Beck's refinement of his 'Heart Full Of Soul' sitar simulation were Relf's counterbalancing lead vocals on the infectious 'Over Under Sideways Down' (with 'Rock Around The Clock' its apparent point of origin); other tracks were as much an anticipation of the pastoral lyricism and acoustic determination of post-Yardbirds projects such as Renaissance and Stairway as they were of Beck's own louder future ventures.

> *"The Yardbirds concert itinerary was such that if they weren't on an aeroplane, they'd be waiting for one"*

Although he even throbbed bass whenever Paul was too busy in the control room, Jeff's guitar was entirely absent on the deceptively placid 'Farewell' – an instance of "the self-destructive streak that ran throughout Keith's work," as Samwell-Smith puts it – "throughout his entire life, for that matter." It was described as "a sick nursery rhyme" in the *NME*.

Some Yardbirds items defied succinct description: among them 'Ever Since The World Began' – divided evenly between dirge and Latin-American samba; Dreja's 'Hot House Of Omagararshid' – palpitating with wobble-board; and the elegiac 'Turn Into Earth' – one of my eternal favourites, and the brainchild of Samwell-Smith (with help from his then-wife, Rosie), who now saw production and songwriting as a more viable proposition than raising riots on tour with the group.

In 1966, The Yardbirds' concert itinerary was such that if they weren't on an aeroplane, they'd be in a departure lounge, waiting for the next one to jet them from, say, Heathrow to Chicago's O'Hare airport, with the ease of daily commuters on the morning train from Surbiton to Waterloo.

At home they were more inclined to hurtle through the countryside to "a sleazy club in Dumfries, changing in a coal cellar", prior to another bout of the small-talk that always supervened in the van when late-night radio went off the air, at times replaced by a fatigued silence, with just the road roaring in their ears.

Travel across Britain didn't broaden the mind necessarily, and the group often couldn't even find on a map some of the places last month's *Melody Maker* gig guide said they'd played. Scarborough, Huddersfield, Middlesborough... outlines dissolved simply because The Yardbirds generally arrived and left by night. Like insects, they could see only their immediate environment; most contacts with any given town's street life occurred only during the moments it took to cross from kerb to venue doorway in early evening lamplight.

In a typical fortnight they might zig-zag from The Birdcage in Portsmouth and to the Majestic up in Newcastle Upon Tyne, then back down to Windsor's Ricky Tick, to five nights in Scotland. On the way, they had to fit in recording the basic track of 'Still I'm Sad' back at Olympic Studios in London.

Supposed 'rest days' were pocked with interviews, shopping excursions for new equipment, and photo calls. With the creation of a publishing receptacle for their compositions, there were also closetings with accountants and solicitors, and playing company directors amid mumbo-jumbo about franchises, merchandising and estimates containing phrases like 'tax concession', 'capital expenditure' and 'convertible debenture' that reminded Jim of when he worked in the City.

Simon Napier-Bell was particularly disquieted by The Yardbirds' worries that they'd recoup little more than golden memories when their time was up. Between Simon and the group there would never be the open-handed conviviality that they'd enjoyed with Giorgio Gomelsky. Indeed, discontent was being expressed with increasing frequency – first subtly and then less courteously – as Napier-Bell fielded circular and sometimes half-understood cross-examinations, usually conducted by the tenacious Paul Samwell-Smith, about where this percentage had gone or why so-and-so had been paid that much.

"How expensive can five guys with three amps doing 350 gigs a year be?" demanded financial trouble-shooter Mark St John when disentangling the mazy finances of The Yardbirds (and The Pretty Things) 30 years later. "You can only eat so many plates of egg-and-chips and drink so many glasses of beer… most of the time all you're doing is pouring petrol into the van and moving from place to place."

Bickering helped consume the miles: "Paul versus Jeff; then Keith versus Paul; then Jeff versus Keith," observed Jim McCarty. "Chris and I were in the middle all the time. We never fell out with anyone."

Other aggravations drip-dripped from outside via, let's say, an appointed tour manager who couldn't stand silence, having to fill every unforgiving minute with 60 seconds of drivel. When he wasn't either talking himself or trying to get others to talk, he'd be humming, whistling or making other noises with his mouth. You'd come close to snapping when, for instance, you were having a shave and he'd be outside the bathroom remarking on items from the newspaper and inviting your comments. Finally you'd explode when, desperate for some peace and quiet, after a day of both him and yak-yak-yakking to disc-jockeys, journalists and so forth, you go to your hotel suite for a lie-down – but he follows you in, leans against the chest-of-drawers, and asks in his drawling voice if you'd seen anything of Mick Jagger lately. When you finally got around to dumping your luggage in the hallway at home, weary from another time-zone, you'd feel in need of post-traumatic counselling.

> *"We gigged virtually every day for four years … Paul became disillusioned – it all became a bit uncivilised for him"*

"From 1964 we gigged virtually every day for four years," estimates Chris Dreja. "*Roger The Engineer* was recorded in less than a week, writing it in the studio. None of it was even pre-rehearsed. Paul became disillusioned – it all became a bit uncivilised for him."

After growing to manhood in the hothouse of the beat boom, Paul was becoming sick of it being taken for granted that he existed solely to vend entertainment to folk at all points of the compass. It was a typical journeyman musician's lot, but Paul was recalling too many drained moments when he'd put down some challenging book he'd scarcely peeked at since a given string of bookings began, and glowered from his hotel room in this Crest or that Trust House, sun-blanked spectacle lenses flashing like a heliograph over the concrete desolation of the car park. Was this all there was? A Ramada in Scotland was just like a Holiday Inn in Toronto. If it's Tuesday, it must be Rotterdam.

Let's tarry for a while on The Yardbirds' tour bus. You're suffering from a headache, an eye-crossing cough and a certain queasiness after that last plateful of overpriced lard-and-chips, hours of torpid warmth ago in a nameless service station on the *autobahn*... Now you are on a flight to a soundcheck somewhere in Scandinavia. Devoid of will, you could soundcheck forever. After the show – and contrary to sensationalised reports in the tabloids – you're more likely to go for an exhausted pint than indulge in anything resembling either Satyricon or a BBC mock-up of an imagined pop group's drugs-and-sex debauch, replete with pushers, tarts and loud-mouthed showbiz periphery almost smothering the post-gig blues jam on an improvised stage.

In tomorrow's dressing room, the support band's obnoxious saxophonist piddles down the washbasin, and you wander off to the wings where equipment changeovers are keeping the second house in Skovde waiting. The stagehands loaf about, eating pork pies and smoking. Isolated in the midst of it, what was there left to enjoy about such a debasing job in which, like them, you couldn't wait until knocking-off time?

But Paul Samwell-Smith still maintained some pride and concern about the music – which only served to deject him further. It wasn't merely fear of deteriorating as a stage performer that haunted him when he finally got to bed. There was also the disturbing psychological undertow that, according to superstition and the laws of averages, there was bound to be a serious accident sooner or later – as there'd be in October 1966 for Johnny Kidd, killed in a crash on the M1 motorway straight after an engagement in Preston, Lancashire. Over in the States, the way to go was by air, like Buddy Holly, Patsy Cline and Jim Reeves.

> *"Samwell-Smith still maintained some pride and concern about the music – which only served to deject him further"*

Closer to home, other acts' days appeared to be numbered – albeit in less absolute terms. It seemed that every week brought a potentially injurious schism in some hit parade group or other: the rowdy style of The Kinks' opening cache of hits was reflected in disorderly behaviour on the road – The Yardbirds were among witnesses to an onstage brawl in Cardiff that resulted in hospital treatment for Dave Davies and rumours of disbandment; Manfred Mann took formal leave of Paul Jones at the Marquee; Wayne Fontana parted from his Mindbenders; Them were without X-factor Van Morrison following a mismanaged US tour; Alan Price had scored his second Top 20 entry as an ex-Animal and Steve Winwood was in the process of forming Traffic because he could no longer hide his real or pretend embarrassment whenever any of The Spencer Davis Group's early 45s shook the record-player at parties.

Emitting an almost palpable aura of self-loathing as he slouched on with a face like a Croydon winter, Paul Samwell-Smith's last straw was on Saturday 18th June 1966 at an Oxford college ball where Keith Relf contrived to appear roaring drunk at the microphone. Into the bargain, the vocalist had injured himself in his backstage delirium. "The Hollies were doing all this karate stuff," recalls Jim McCarty, grinning, "and they'd got Keith to do it on a chair. I think he broke his fingers."

There'd been other occasions when Relf had had a skinful, and had managed to get a grip at showtime. But he'd never been as far gone as he was now. Pain could have honed his singing to razor-sharp poignancy but, muzzy with liquor, he chose instead to confront the crowd with belching, swearing, and stumbling about aimlessly before sinking to the floor.

"He couldn't stand up," groans Paul. "I actually had to sing some numbers just to try and keep the thing going. Jeff sang too. Under previous circumstances, we'd say, 'Don't do that again, Keith, because it was awful,' but I'd had enough of years and years of getting out of the van. There'd been only two occasions when we stayed in one place: the Beatles Hammersmith season – which meant I could actually live at home for two weeks – and five days in Hollywood, which was super because we could arrive at the theatre, plug in and play. It also meant we could almost develop relationships with people there.

"What got to me was driving 200 miles, setting up the gear, soundchecking and all that… You can do it for 30 days, 60 days even, that's fine: but you can't keep it up for seven years. It's pathetic to make a group try. Then you get a day off. Fantastic – except you have to go to Soho Square for photos in the morning.

"And who made money from The Yardbirds? Where was it? I had a new car that I was still paying for, and a tax bill that was owing. I'm not an easy person anyway – certainly the most awkward member of the group to an outsider – and I was starting to snap at everybody. I knew there must be something better in life – and there was."

In the aftermath of Oxford, Paul marshalled his words and dared the speech that he'd been agonising over for months. The cards were on the table, and within a week an announcement was made to interested press that Jimmy Page was the new Yardbird.

CHAPTER 9

PSYCHO DAISIES

"Once I was back on-stage again ...
I found I was covering new ground ...
I was doing new things."

JIMMY PAGE

Though able to continue in a recognisable form and still pull unexpected artistic strokes, The Yardbirds never really recovered from Paul's departure, just a month before the issue of their eponymous album in time for 1966's Christmas sell-in. When needles slid into respective pre-release grooves, a surprising number of critiques, if patronising at times, testified to the presence of more intrinsic virtues than had been expected of participants in a branch of entertainment where sales figures and numbers of bums-on-seats were arbiters of success. The immediate impact of

Jimmy Page joined in June 1966, first on bass, then reverting to guitar

THE YARDBIRDS

Yardbirds and other musical events occurring between 'For Your Love' and the Oxford showdown had been deeper than suggested by the raw data of a smattering of chart entries. Upping the standard by which the most unassuming beat group could judge itself, The Yardbirds – although finished as UK Top 40 entrants by autumn 1966 – would be able to cling on in North America via grassroots support and their influence on Anglophile 'garage bands' with names like The Shadows Of Knight, The Seeds, Thirteenth Floor Elevators and ? & The Mysterians. These had crawled from the sub-cultural woodwork throughout the continent after they'd been able to grow out their crew-cuts and seize upon whatever aspects of the new Limey idioms they found most comfortable.

The Yardbirds had outfitted Count Five with the vestments of musical personality that had just propelled 'Psychotic Reaction' into the US Top Ten. A more sincere form of flattery was a ghastly 'For Your Love' that was an inexplicable regional hit in the Deep South for Charles Christy & His Crystals, pride of Fort Worth. From the same city, The Cynics weighed in with 'You're A Better Man Than I'. In every state in the Union, it seemed, you'd find further local acts ripping chapters from The Yardbirds book, albeit mostly with a pronounced easier-to-play pre-'For Your Love' bias.

Those that moulded themselves most lucratively to Yardbirds specifications were to include Alice Cooper – then soberly-attired and mop-topped Vince & The Spiders – Todd Rundgren's Nazz, The Raspberries (once The Choir, who were to warm-up for The Yardbirds in Ohio), The Box Tops (whose 'Cry Like A Baby' hit in 1968 featured an electric sitar), and Johnny Winter. Steppenwolf, traffickers of as potent a concoction of both hard rock and psychedelia, began in Toronto as Sparrow and, as it was with The Yardbirds, mainstays of their blues repertoire remained in the set until they gave up the ghost.

Over in New York, The Velvet Underground had paid no such Craw Daddy-like R&B dues. All the same, they prized the impromptu as much as The Yardbirds, and underlined some numbers not with bass guitar but a noisy electronic drone that made a melodrama of what was merely implicit in the Yardbirds-Kinks singles. Rejected as 'decadent' by a West Coast media bedazzled by flower-power, The Velvet Underground's stunning debut album in late 1966 lulled listeners with the lovey-dovey orthodoxy of 'Sunday Morning' before diving headlong into a hacking paean to drug dependency, 'I'm Waiting For The Man' – which was to join 'Most Likely You'll Go Your Way' in an ailing Yardbirds' stage set.

> *"Keith was fighting to be heard against the flat-out blast of the guitarists' increasingly more splendid amplifiers"*

After Samwell-Smith had quit as a player and Page joined the line-up it was proclaimed – incorrectly – in the *NME* that the group would henceforth be known as 'Keith Relf And The Yardbirds'. Vacillating between despondent chagrin and guarded enthusiasm about the future of a world-famous act with its heart ripped out, Keith, leader or not, was fighting to be heard against the flat-out blast of the guitarists' increasingly more splendid amplifiers – Beck's "musical utopia as far as The Yardbirds go" – and Jim's now miked-up rataplans. The singer's minutes of pure enjoyment on-stage became increasingly rare; and the old sweetness he'd once invested in the slow numbers deferred more and more to stone-cold technique, with the exasperating realisation that, while The Yardbirds were able to fill US stadiums, the audience went just as ape over straggling lines of bum notes as it did over the most startling solos.

Nowadays the five's hard-won musicianship was not being desecrated by screaming hysteria as much as a ceaseless barrage of stamping, whistling and discomforted snarls from everyone with same-priced tickets grappling for a clearer view. If they either couldn't get one or weren't bothered anyway, the occasion became an excuse for a social gathering, an opportunity to purchase soft drugs in the toilets, and get stoned while the matchstick figures on stage half-a-mile away became a gradually more distant noise.

Those for whom Yardbirds had been the Word Made Vinyl in the comfort of their own homes were doomed to disappointment. The absence from the set of 'Turn Into Earth', 'I Can't Make Your Way' or, from further back, 'Five Long Years' was symptomatic of the piquant ironies of old becoming brutalised by high-decibel diddle-iddle-iddling – especially after Jimmy Page reverted from bass to a more customary role as co-lead guitarist.

> *"An advantage of Paul leaving was that it freed us to explore other areas – music with more muscle"*

"An advantage of Paul leaving in 1966," argued Chris Dreja, "was that it freed us to explore other areas – music with more muscle. I switched to bass, keeping it fairly simple. A lot of the lines had been established already, but some were crazy when we linked one number to the next."

For Jimmy, the top session guitarist, it was the first time he'd actually "stood up and played" since the days of Sutch's Savages and Christian's Crusaders. "I was becoming very stale," he confessed at the time. "Once I was back on stage again, even though I was playing bass, I was thinking in terms of a guitar, and I found I was covering new ground. As soon as I got back on the six-stringer after my bass-playing I found I was doing new things."

One of the engagements that featured Page transitionally on bass took place at a Kent ballroom where young fan Richard MacKay vanished into the seafront night afterwards, lost in wonder. "The whole evening was magic, though the audience hardly moved," he'd recall. "The band used to complain about the lack of response, but it was their own fault – they shouldn't have played like musical gods."

It was this event that inspired Richard to begin the first of many scrapbooks that chronicled the goings-on of both the group and its ex-members, which led eventually to him launching the *Yardbirds World* fanzine. Hundreds of hours of hard listening to the records were less to do with pleasure than with being addicted, as surely as someone else can be to heroin. Long before the advent of memorabilia auctions, vintage record shops and the first edition of *Record Collector* in 1979, Richard was haunting jumble sales, and scouring Kent for any emporium bearing the sign 'junk', 'second-hand' or 'bric-a-brac' in an obsessive search for Yardbirds artefacts.

I went through exactly the same phase: as a 16-year-old, heart pounding in anticipation, I would squeeze between hags blocking access to a pile of scratched singles at a jumble sale stall. On a day-trip to Boulogne, I discovered that foreign pressings made exactly the same sound, but there were visual differences – and not simply that they were issued with picture sleeves. Take 'Shapes of Things': in some European territories, EMI-Columbia was in the final months of using its old logo – with the company name in large capital letters across the top of the label, and an additional '45' prefix at the start of the catalogue number. The new one stuck to the same fundamental design, except it was printed in a more compact typeface. This was most noticeable on the song title. Another feature is that "McCarty" is misspelt in the composing credits. Weird, eh?

> *"We were on the threshold of this new thing. The Yardbirds were the first psychedelic band"*

As an excitable schoolboy from a country town in Hampshire – where I was a complete misfit – I had no direct contact (any more than Richard did) with a Yardbirds almost permanently in America. Our function then was just to absorb the signals as they came, and make dignified excuses for the higher percentage of artistic nullities that followed 'Happenings Ten Years Time Ago'.

Yet of this period, Jeff Beck would later reflect: "We were on the threshold of this new thing. The Yardbirds were the first psychedelic band." When they were in beat groups, certain musicians may have entreated God only as a sort of divine pimp, but now some had already become pseudo-mystics responsible for self-consciously 'strange' discs like 'Happenings Ten Years Time Ago' and The Pretty Things' 'Defecting Grey' – which put the tin lids on their makers' respective chart careers. Of the two, 'Defecting Grey', despite an aesthetic brilliance, was the most wilfully uncommercial, lacking as it did a discernable melody as it darted from section to spliced-together section. Slightly more successful, 'Happenings Ten Years Time Ago' still foundered at Number 43 in the UK, 30 in the States.

With a keener weather eye on the Top 40, Jim McCarty elucidated that, "If you didn't have a hit single, you were a fading band." Catching if not *the* mood, then *a* mood of late 1966, 'Happenings Ten Years Time Ago' should have scored higher positions than it did. Even for those opposed or insensible to shifts in musical consciousness at the time, its attractive mid-tempo tune, vigorously lyrical expression – when you could make out the words – and a tough riff rode roughshod over the oscillations, police sirens and Jeff's shreds of speech (based on a conversation with a doctor at a Hammersmith Special Clinic).

Although an acquired taste, it was theoretically as much a pop record as Jim Reeves' 'Distant Drums' (at Number One when 'Happenings Ten Years Time Ago' was expiring) – in the sense that Russ Conway and Thelonious Monk were both pianists. But if pop, like jazz, can be polarised in particular styles, Reeves was strictly 'trad' while The Yardbirds roamed the most distant reaches of the avant-garde.

It's easy to forget that in 1966/67 easy-listening was represented as much as psychedelia – as instanced by 'Release Me', crooner Engelbert Humperdinck's chart debut, keeping The Beatles' 'Penny Lane'/'Strawberry Fields Forever' from Number One in March 1967. Unreconstructed pop was still very much alive too. On the horizon were the likes of Love Affair, The Equals – and Marmalade, who had once been as mind-expanding as the best of them, and were still prone to launching into iconoclastic psychedelia on-stage, just as square Roy Orbison had accidentally earned the brief approbation of the blossoming hippie sub-culture with 'There Won't Be Many Coming Home', seen as a donation to the anti-Vietnam war effort.

Headlining over The Yardbirds on a 1967 tour of Australia, Roy and his musicians would shake baffled heads in the wings during the group's spell on the boards; and Jim McCarty's concentration wandered when the star turn just "seemed to be doing all his old hits in chronological order". The Yardbirds and Orbison nonetheless parted cordially, and Roy presented Jimmy Page with some Fender guitar accessories from Nashville.

But by then such dragnet packages had really had their day, and the divide between 'rock' and 'pop' was becoming such that mismatched pairings of Yardbirds-Orbison persuasion were no longer mutually beneficial. Another prime example was the one going the rounds in Britain consisting of Engelbert Humperdinck, The Walker Brothers, singer-songwriter Cat Stevens, and the show-stealing Jimi Hendrix Experience, whose leader was the darling of London's pop elite.

Like Jeff Beck – and The Pink Floyd's Syd Barrett – Hendrix was prone to risky improvisations that escaped key and bar-line restrictions. (Dick Taylor remembers meeting Hendrix around this time, "chatting to Jimi in some crowded dressing room as he tinkered on his Stratocaster – and I kept losing the thread of the conversation because he was just as amazing musically on an unamplified electric guitar as he was with one plugged into a 200-watt stack".)

> *"The guitar interaction between Beck and Page was becoming compulsively exquisite"*

Decisively, Hendrix was admired at a time when a deeper respect for instrumental proficiency was surfacing – outlines were dissolving between rock and jazz, and bands like The Sam Gopal Dream, The Soft Machine and The Nice thrived on 'meaningful' interplay.

In The Yardbirds, the guitar interaction between Beck and Page was becoming compulsively exquisite. From the beginning, the concept of one of them simply cementing the other's runs with subordinate chord-slashing hadn't been a consideration: over Dreja's low throb, the two anticipated and attended to each other's idiosyncrasies and stylistic clichés, producing transcendental moments on the boards that would look impossible if transcribed.

There was as much mutual admiration as there was rivalry between the various high-profile guitarists at the time: among those who wished that they were either in a position to or had the nerve to be as dangerous as Beck and Page was Eric Clapton – now in Cream with Jack Bruce and Ginger Baker. Far from being dismissive of the man who'd replaced him in the Yardbirds, Clapton admitted at the time to feeling in some ways inferior to Beck, saying: "Jeff is more of a musician than I am. I do things the longest way round… but Jeff knows exactly what he wants and how to get it."

Beck, in turn, considered Clapton "Britain's best blues guitarist", but he particularly admired Hendrix, with whom he shared a more risk-taking approach: "I just hadn't the guts to come out and do it so flamboyantly," Jeff would later lament. "I'm too withdrawn a character. I bitterly regret not having exploited my style a bit more, because there was a lot of stuff he [Hendrix] actually got from me – which he admitted. Some of the little licks he did came from Yardbirds records."

> *"I'm too withdrawn a character. I bitterly regret not having exploited my style a bit more"*

To be copied thus was pleasing to someone in a different (rather than lower) league to Hendrix as pop hurried next through its 'classical period'. With *Sgt Pepper's Lonely Hearts Club Band*'s expensive and syncretic precedent, record companies found themselves underwriting concept albums, rock operas and the like – The Who's *Tommy* and The Pretty Things' *SF Sorrow* are two which spring to mind. (Incidentally The Pretty Things' move from Fontana to EMI had guaranteed an artistic freedom that was to be denied The Yardbirds after the group's 'Happenings Ten Years Time Ago' single failed to live up to market expectations.)

It was a time of musical expansion, crossover and experimentation – in many senses. As well as awareness of post-serialist composers such as Cage, Berio and Stockhausen, and the unorthodox tonalities of avant-garde jazz blasting from newly-fitted car stereos, much of the new pop had been forged too from drug experience beyond mere pills and reefers.

Not yet versed in hip jargon, the BBC passed The Small Faces' 'Here Comes The Nice', which dealt with the dazzling effects of amphetamine sulphate, although just plain 'Heroin' by The Velvet Underground hadn't a hope of a solitary Light Programme (soon to be Radio One) airing, and the Corporation frowned on The Byrds' 'Eight Miles High' and Beatles tracks like 'Tomorrow Never Knows' and 'Lucy In The Sky With Diamonds'.

The 'us and them' estrangement intensified when John, George, Paul and Ringo were among the celebrities advocating the legalisation of marijuana. Breaking box-offices records with Cream in the

US, Eric Clapton was arrested on a narcotics charge. 'Dropping acid' had become so prevalent that Dave Dee felt the need to insist to *Melody Maker* that, as far as he and his clean-minded lads were concerned, LSD still stood for pounds, shillings and pence.

The Yardbirds had known of lately-outlawed lysergic acid diethylamide since 1965. "Keith and I were turning on all the time," admitted Jim McCarty, "and more or less dropped out of a normal existence." The Pretty Things had fairly blatant titles like 'Trippin'' and 'LSD', while a more subtle approach was taken by Eric Burdon & The Animals on 'A Girl Named Sandoz' (the place where the stuff was originally manufactured).

With 'San Francisco Nights', Burdon's outfit also paid tribute to the psychedelic storm centre where berserkers with eyes like catherine-wheels cavorted beneath flickering strobes, ectoplasmic light projections and further audio-visual aids that simulated acid experience. These 'flower children' were part-and-parcel of a perpetual small-change of hangers-on that were able to contrive access to The Yardbirds during a third US tour, and proffer the ingratiating tabs of LSD and 'tokes' of marijuana that passed as common currency among many bands and artists at the time.

The Yardbirds, see, were now a band (not a 'group' any more) that catered for hippies, either in a cross-legged trance or 'idiot dancing' with psyches boggled by paranormal sensations. The effects of LSD varied from person to person, from trip to trip: sometimes it was comparable to a mystic purging, akin to an extreme religious experience; on other occasions a fantastic voyage to untold heights of creativity might 'come down' in a nonsensical frenzy.

One day Jim McCarty surfaced from an acid-induced quagmire of horror, and imaginary phantoms so engulfed him that his condition necessitated his replacement for the opening engagements of a US tour. This was not as regrettable as the non-appearances of Jeff Beck for most of the previous visit – which included the month-long *Dick Clark Caravan Of Stars*.

This coast-to-coast endurance tester – whose tour management and staff seemed to regard 'pop stars' as personally objectionable commodities to be bought, consumed and replaced when of no further use – was characterised by terrible all-night journeys in an uneasy doze. If you were lucky, you might seize the first opportunity to shave in a week just prior to going through the hot and bothered motions, usually for customers puzzled by all this marijuana-smoking musical crap.

"The Yardbirds were now a band that catered for hippies, with psyches boggled by paranormal sensations"

Often The Yardbirds would deliver their four-song set twice in one evening at 'round robin' venues in Mid-Western 3000-seaters, 100 miles apart, sandwiched between Brian Hyland – a fallen Bobby making a Hot 100 comeback – and, pandering as blatantly to assumed customer desires, Gary Lewis & His Playboys, direct from the Top 20 with 'My Heart's Symphony'.

"It was the worst tour I'd ever been on, as far as fatigue is concerned," Jimmy Page would conclude. "We didn't know where we were or what we were doing." A Yardbirds beyond sleep and kept awake by hunger would collide with microphone stands and stumble over wires as stage-lights came on to a scene not exactly welcoming. Instead of the band coming belligerently alive with casually cataclysmic opening bars, there'd just be thuds, electronic crackles and savage oaths censored by unintended ear-splitting feedback while the guitarists searched for their own or someone else's input.

Hastily fed and superficially rested, a rueful but light-hearted mood might persist afterwards for a few fiery-eyed miles among the grubby human cargo hurtling from state to state in a dilapidated Greyhound bus, maybe three oil changes from the breaker's yard. But it wouldn't last. "The bus was supposed to have air-conditioning," scowled Jeff Beck, "but didn't seem to. And all the American groups with us on the bus played their guitars non-stop, and they were always singing. Can you imagine? Cooped up on a stuffy bus with everyone around you singing Beatle songs in an American accent?"

A stoic cynicism would sour to moody discontent, cliff-hanging silences and sullen exchanges. Someone would go too far, and slanging matches would explode like shrapnel and continue on arrival backstage, audible in the galleries, even as the compere unzipped his scripted grin and launched into wonderful-to-be-here vapourings.

> *"Having two guitarists was no longer a great idea ... Jeff felt – justifiably – that his space was being invaded"*

Jeff's behaviour was particularly disconcerting. "Having two guitarists was no longer a great idea," noticed Chris Dreja. "It had become so undisciplined, and Jeff felt – justifiably – that his space was being invaded."

Jimmy Page was to recall: "One time in the dressing room, Beck had his guitar up over his head, about to bring it down on Keith Relf, but instead smashed it to the floor. Relf looked at him with total astonishment, and Beck said, 'Why did you make me do that?'."

"I was quite messed up," Jeff said later. "At 21, I was really on my last legs. I just couldn't handle it." He recalled one particularly infamous on-stage incident: "We were playing this place in Tucson, Arizona, this warehouse full of people. Imagine the Marquee Club in the middle of the Arizona desert. I had this piggy-back amp set-up – a Vox Beatle thing, if you'll pardon the expression – and I'd just gone crazy, did my act, smashed the amp, pushed it over. The amp top went through the window and was dangling down outside, swinging about. The thing that saved someone's life down below was the fact that it had a locking plug."

Close to a nervous breakdown, Jeff – not for the first time – dragged himself to the nearest airport, and slipped smoothly away into the skies and out of an intolerable existence. This time he initially pleaded inflamed tonsils – and, indeed, had every appearance of being ill. He was, he said, intending to seek treatment straight away, and hopefully rejoin the *Caravan Of Stars* as soon as he was fit. But Beck was to be sacked *in absentia* after it came to his colleagues' ears that he had been seen roistering in Los Angeles night spots, quite openly squiring the film starlet who'd been the muse for 'Psycho Daisies', the group's most recent B-side.

This and 'Happenings Ten Years Time Ago' were the only Yardbirds releases to feature both Page and Beck, apart from one track ('Stroll On') on the soundtrack album of Michelangelo Antonioni's arty *Blowup* movie, in which they also made a cameo appearance. Slightly antiquated in 1967, and 'modern' enough to seem dated now, this portrayal of the euphoric, anything-goes (some would say nihilistic) spirit of Swinging London was a slow-moving two hours without much of a plot – though Vanessa Redgrave removed her bra, and pubic hair (Jane Birkin's) was seen by UK movie-goers for the first time. Jeff Beck also smashed up a guitar, Pete Townshend-style, as The Yardbirds delivered a thinly-disguised 'Train Kept A-Rolling' to unnerving stares from what looked like a gigantic photograph of a silent and undemonstrative audience – rather like the one in Kent where Richard MacKay saw the Yardbirds play "like musical gods", before they turned out to be all-too-human somewhere in America.

CHAPTER 10

FAREWELL

"The Yardbirds had split into two factions. Jimmy and I saw a future for the four-piece, and Jim and Keith had got more ethereal, melodic and delicate"

CHRIS DREJA

The Yardbirds did not replace Jeff Beck, favouring instead the simpler expedient of continuing as a four-piece. By now, records had become adjuncts to earnings from incessant touring. They'd realised that going down well on the boards wasn't an accurate barometer of market standing. As singing and playing instruments was their only saleable trade, The Yardbirds seemed to be in the same endless-highway dilemma as the olde-tyme rockers or black bluesmen of a pre-Beatle age. It looked like the writing was on the wall when their single 'Little Games' eluded the UK Top 40 even more

Keith Relf was an enigmatic if occasionally erratic performer

emphatically than 'Happenings Ten Years Time Ago'. More so than The Who and The Kinks – who also couldn't take Top 40 entries for granted as 1967 wore on – it was deemed necessary for The Yardbirds to strike a more potentially lucrative balance between art and commerce. As the quality of their own originals was becoming erratic, this meant relying once more on outside help for made-to-measure efforts such as the bolt-upright 'Little Games' and 'No Excess Baggage' (from the team responsible for The Animals' chartbusting 'It's My Life'). The understanding was that, sooner or later, another song as good as 'Heart Full Of Soul' or 'Evil-Hearted You' would come their way.

Look at Manfred Mann. Their chart fortunes, in Britain at least, remained unaltered – albeit as a hard-sell mainstream pop act by this time – via tasteful selection and interpretation of external compositions. This knack was particularly evident on 'Ha Ha Said The Clown', at Number Four in spring 1967. When it was clear that it wasn't going to do the same in the States, in stepped The Yardbirds – as an illustration of the extremes to which they were prepared to resort – enjoying slightly more luck in July with their inferior US-only cover of the track.

In Britain, The Yardbirds were no longer contenders, and they'd become too tired, indolent and out-of-touch to do much about it. Somehow, it was already over. Their virtue all but gone, what mattered most as 1968 got under way was raking in as much loot with the least effort possible by accommodating thousands in one go in the US baseball parks and exposition centres, with which no venue at home could yet compare.

En route, the group – sorry, band – issued a few disinclined records solely for the US market, on which the actual presence of some Yardbirds personnel, now past caring, remains in doubt. It provoked no friction when McCarty and Dreja, for instance, were replaced on 'Ten Little Indians' by session players after the desperate enlistment (at Jimmy Page's urging) of console whizz-kid Mickie Most – "a protagonist in our downfall," as Jim McCarty labels him.

> *"The Yardbirds were no longer contenders, and they'd become too tired, indolent and out-of-touch to do anything about it"*

Since his first efforts with The Animals and then The Nashville Teens, Most had also brought Herman's Hermits, Lulu and Donovan to international chart stardom. Theoretically, he was just what The Yardbirds needed; but whispered misgivings – like diners becoming increasingly unhappy about service in a restaurant – waxed to bold complaint with the appearance of *Little Games*, an LP not thought worthy of release in Britain but adequate for North America, where there were still fans sufficiently uncritical to digest frankly sub-standard produce – which even Page was to regard later as "horrible".

Permitting only a little more elaboration than Paul Samwell-Smith, Most dashed off *Little Games* as a testament less to quality than to market pragmatism. It wasn't as cynical as The Dave Clark Five's US albums – throwaway patchworks of tracks, short on needle-time and padded with unoriginal 'originals', groove-consuming instrumentals and makeweight copies of smashes by rivals. Yet 'Drinking Muddy Water' was its namesake's 'Rollin' And Tumblin', just as 'Stealing Stealing' was precisely that – a theft of a jugband blues from the 1920s on which Epic hadn't the honesty to stick the abbreviation 'arr' (for 'arranged by') in front of the 'K Relf/J Page/J McCarty/Ereja (sic)' on the record label's composing credits.

As was common practice in the States, the album was hung on a single (the title track), although this had fizzled out at Number 51 in the Hot 100. Treasured by most only in retrospect, *Little Games* wasn't top-rate, but it was enjoyable enough and more rounded an entity than it might have been. Of course it was to be lost in the shadow of *Yardbirds*, a hard yardstick for any group; particularly if you looked at the compositions *per se* on *Little Games*, imagining them reduced to the acid test of just voice and piano, stripped of their wah-wah guitar ('Smile On Me'), electronically-warped voice and Creation-type bowed guitar ('Glimpses'), McCarty's mimicking of a trumpet ('Little Soldier Boy'), and backwards percussion ('Only The Black Rose').

> *"Treasured by most only in retrospect,* Little Games *wasn't great, but it was enjoyable enough"*

Those that stood tallest were Page's 'White Summer' party-piece – with Jimmy on an acoustic par with Manitas de Plata; 'Smile On Me' – fanning dull embers of the old fire, like 'Think About It', the final B-side; and the subdued ghostliness of Relf's 'Only The Black Rose' .

Stately 'Glimpses' – tinged with both 'Happenings Ten Years Time Ago' and a more buoyant take on 'Still I'm Sad' – today offers a general evocation of psychedelic times past, while 'Tinker Tailor Soldier Sailor' (though more the meat of Herman's Hermits) and 'Little Soldier Boy' epitomise pop's gingerbread castle hour as surely as 'Hole In My Shoe' by Traffic, The Rolling Stones' 'Dandelion' and 'Gnome' from Syd Barrett's Pink Floyd.

The Yardbirds were to travel further down that road with 'Ten Little Indians', the penultimate 45 left in them. It had dripped from the pen of Brooklyn-born Harry Nilsson, whose brace of RCA albums, *Pandemonium Puppet Show* and *Aerial Ballet*, were fixtures on the record-players of London's innermost in-crowd. Among the many covers these garnered was '1941' by a Billy J Kramer without a hope in hell of making the charts again. 'Ten Little Indians' – more 'Who Killed Cock Robin' (and 'Little Soldier Boy') than 'Mary Had A Little Lamb' – didn't do much for The Yardbirds either.

Even less of an impression was made by the detested, 'Jennifer Eccles'-esque 'Goodnight Sweet Josephine' – written by Tony Hazzard, the man who'd given Manfred Mann 'Ha Ha Said The Clown', and excluded from The Yardbirds' stage act even prior to its fall from Number 127 in the States.

And that, as far as the record-buying public was concerned, was just about that. The Yardbirds had had a relatively long run, all things considered and, if it was important to them, could die easy in the knowledge that most parochial rivals had never even been to America or been on *Top Of The Pops*.

THE YARDBIRDS

The Yardbirds were seldom seen in Britain. America seemed a land of greater opportunity than the one in which the conservative *NME*'s 'Alley Cat' tittle-tattler had crowed, "This year, Yardbirds absent from Top 30." In the States they were has-beens too – even so, members of local garage bands still trooped backstage after every show to pay their respects to celebrated living artefacts of the 'British Invasion': you know, the guys who did 'For Your Love'. The four were becoming used to young North Americans clustering round them like friendly if over-attentive wolfhounds, even the most garrulous of whom would suddenly fall into an awestruck silence, as if The Yardbirds weren't quite real.

They were, however, a Yardbirds dying on their feet, about to tape a so-so concert no better or worse than any other they'd given during the dinning weeks of their last overseas journey. The venue was a half-empty New York cinema, which had all the tell-tale signs of having known better days: the dust on the carpet, the padded wallpaper peeling off here and there, the depressed forbearance of the staff. It was the same "funny gig" where a few weeks later Reg Presley of The Troggs remembers "a lot of hippies turned up for us and The Who, and they put a light show on before us". Doctored with supplementary audience noise (actually from a bullfight) and newly-discovered guitar god Jimmy Page mixed to the fore, *Live Yardbirds!* was locked away to lie largely forgotten – though it was given a brief release in the early 1970s in an unsuccessful attempt to cash in on Page's fame with Led Zeppelin.

After the honouring of remaining commitments in North America, the flight back to London was an opportunity for continuous thought, as anti-climax flooded already overloaded minds, and individual Yardbirds wrestled with professional and personal stock-taking.

The Yardbirds had been overtaken on so many more fronts since The Pretty Things' *SF Sorrow*, Beatles *Sgt Pepper*, the Stones' *Satanic Majesties*, The Floyd's *Piper At The Gates Of Dawn*, Cream's *Disraeli Gears*, the list went on and heart-sinkingly on...

While they'd been rehearsing in a north London scout hut in 1966, Cream had initially expressed the intention to work Home Counties clubland as a blues trio – but they weren't so humble now, with *Disraeli Gears* and its 'Sunshine Of Your Love' spin-off 45 selling a million copies each. By early 1968 they'd removed themselves to grander and more impersonal showcases, where American collegiate youth seemed fair game to buy anything British labelled 'heavy', 'progressive' or – surely taking coals to Newcastle – 'blues'. These always seemed to involve "endless, meaningless solos," a bemused Eric Clapton would reflect. "We were not indulging ourselves so much as our audience... because that's what they wanted."

Looking back, Eric could see the flaws in the trio: "We didn't really have a band with Cream. We rarely played as an ensemble – we were three virtuosos, all of us soloing all the time. I was flying high on an ego trip. Then we got our first bad review, which said how boring and repetitious our performance had been. And it was true… We'd been flying with blinkers for so long, we weren't aware of the changes that were taking place musically. New people were coming up and growing, and we were repeating ourselves…"

Among the 'new people' back home were Fleetwood Mac, Jethro Tull, Ten Years After, Love Sculpture, and The Climax Chicago Blues Band, derived from Hipster Image and The Gospel Truth, Stafford units of Yardbirds-Downliners Sect vintage. Had they so desired, Dreja, McCarty, Relf and Page could have regained some lost ground during this period, the beginning of the late 1960s 'blues boom', which would turn Fleetwood Mac, Ten Years After and Jethro Tull into pop stars while letting them retain artistic individuality – and, also like The Yardbirds, absorb many other musical idioms.

> *"The Yardbirds could easily have reached out to nascent headbangers rather than wooing the introverted adolescent diarist"*

To The Yardbirds' further potential advantage, 'power trios' were the thing then too; most of them harking back to the one-guitar-bass-drums test cases like Johnny Kidd & The Pirates and The Big Three – though any muted cleverness or restraint that Cream, the *après-Tommy* Who, Rory Gallagher's Taste and even Black Sabbath might have displayed in the studio was lost to heads-down-no-nonsense rock. Now as gut-wrenching in their way as any of them – on stage at least – The Yardbirds could easily have reached out to nascent headbangers via blues-plagiarised sound-pictures of Genghis Khan carnage, rather than a stealthier wooing of the introverted adolescent diarist who preferred becoming pleasantly melancholy to 'Only The Black Rose'.

Distanced through their omnipresence in North America, The Yardbirds were on the periphery of the late 1960s post flower-power scene in Britain – unlike, say, The Pretty Things, whose bread-and-butter depended by then principally on one-nighters on the 'alternative' circuit, as typified by their engagement at a Goldsmith College sit-in at the request of Germaine Greer, then a professor of English there, and hanging around with Tyrannosaurus Rex, Mick Farren & His Social Deviants, Family, Eire Apparent, The Edgar Broughton Band, Hawkwind and similar denizens of the hippy community centred round Ladbroke Grove. These entertainers were all fixtures at the free concerts that pocked the agit-prop culture's social calendar.

The Yardbirds, however, were still thought cool enough for studio sessions on radio's *Top Gear*, in which John Peel, if not as "beautiful" as he'd been in 1967, still inserted 20-minute ragas between the usual progressive rock fare. Such infrequent appearances just about kept them before the ears of this market, but they were in danger of being otherwise forgotten at home.

Ironically it was a time when record labels began committing more of their budgets to 'albums' (no longer 'LPs') and 'bodies of works' by artistes entering realms far distant from their beat group bedrock, rather than simply expecting hit single after hit single. But this policy came too late for The Yardbirds, for whom *Little Games* was to be their final LP before the Sixties stopped Swinging – just as *Goodbye* was for Cream, whose calculated disbandment in 1968 stampeded Eric Clapton and Ginger Baker into Blind Faith with Steve Winwood and one of Family.

A letter to *Melody Maker* predicted "almost Beatle status" for Blind Faith, before this 'supergroup' threw in the towel after a free concert in Hyde Park, one patchy album and a troubled US tour. Thirty years later, when the Blind Faith album was reissued on CD, padded out with some hitherto unreleased jams and doodlings, Clapton revealed to *Rolling Stone* magazine: "At the time I thought these were magnificent things we were doing, just jamming away. But I was a kid. The only personality I had was within my fingers… When we didn't have a song, I'd just think, 'Let's get stoned'. Which we did when we didn't know what we were doing."

By this time Jeff Beck was asserting his claim to be crowned as heavy rock's boss guitarist. There'd actually been little sign that Jeff had this in him during the immediate months that followed his departure from The Yardbirds when, he says, "I didn't even touch my guitar – and when I came to play again, I was hopeless."

> *"Jeff Beck was asserting his claim to be crowned as heavy rock's boss guitarist"*

Trusting Jimmy Page's judgement, Jeff too had placed his immediate destiny in Mickie Most's hands – but, unlike The Yardbirds, he had made the Top 20 once more. Treated by Most as Most treated Herman's Hermits, Beck had succumbed to a spot on *Top Of The Pops* in May 1967 when his 'Hi Ho Silver Lining' was introduced by presenter Jimmy Savile, who also kindly plugged its B-side, 'Beck's Bolero' – the one Jeff taped when still a Yardbird. Jeff had felt obliged to dress up in clothes that were a little bit daft, and interject a topical soccer reference ("Up the Spurs!") during his 'live' singing and mimed guitar picking on 'Hi Ho Silver Lining'.

"I was a star again," affirmed Jeff. "I didn't dislike the tune, but playing my style across a song like that didn't make it." He also felt his vocal on the track "sounded like a Boy Scout". Be that as it may, this first A-side under his own name had shut down a heavily-publicised (and almost identical) version by The Attack. Maddeningly catchy, Beck's 'Hi Ho Silver Lining' was to re-enter the charts when it was re-issued in both 1972 and 1982, and endure as a singalong finale on a par with 'You'll Never Walk Alone' for all manner of acts on the 1960s revival/nostalgia circuit.

Then as now, Beck was as unproud of 'Hi Ho Silver Lining' as Graham Nash was of 'Jennifer Eccles', and The Yardbirds of 'Goodnight Sweet Josephine'. He said as much during a saloon bar encounter with Rod Stewart, at the time yet to touch the brittle fabric of fame. Perhaps because Jeff was honest in not over-justifying himself, Stewart decided "to help him out. I mean, for a guitar player like him to come out with a thing like 'Hi Ho Silver Lining' was a crime." So it was that the philanthropic Rod shared lead vocals on Beck's more plausible second single, 'Tallyman' (by Graham Gouldman) – not as massive a hit as 'Hi Ho…', but a hit all the same.

But Stewart was only a detached – and probably appalled – spectator with no stake in 'Love Is Blue (L'Amour Est Bleu)', composed by Andre Popp, a middle-aged orchestra leader who cut a suave figure at international awards ceremonies when nominated for some lush film score or easy-listening arrangement. Just as slushy, with violins and choral refrain, Jeff's 'Love Is Blue' was the last of his hat-trick of Top 40 entries. Of similar kidney to the contemporaneous 'Classical Gas', a Grammy-winning instrumental from Texan guitarist Mason Williams, Beck's 'Love Is Blue' peaked at Number 23, eleven positions behind a version by Paul Mauriat & His Orchestra, but shutting down Paris Conservatoire-trained Franck Pourcel's more nonchalantly proficient treatment of this gauntlet that Luxembourg had thrown down in 1967's *Eurovision Song Contest*.

"I didn't say anything, just left it to Mickie," muttered Jeff. He was thus a fine one to proffer unheeded 'Advice to The Yardbirds' in a *Disc* questionnaire as 'Love Is Blue' touched its commercial apex. Rubbing salt in the wound, Beck, on the rebound from 'Hi Ho Silver Lining', had, with Stewart and a pick-up combo, joined a UK tour headed by Roy Orbison and The Small Faces – but their performance on opening night had been so bedevilled with problems that they were paid off.

From the despair of artistic misadventures that might have destroyed a less strong-minded musician, Beck had rallied by conducting exhaustive auditions in a central London rehearsal complex for a new band in which, ideally, "everyone was in accord with everyone else." Not comfortable with an established outfit, he was headhunting unaffiliated individuals: a short-list was to boil down to Rod Stewart, drummer Mickey Waller (another Long John Baldry sideman), pianist Nicky Hopkins and, cajoled into transferring to bass, Ron Wood, fresh from serving The Creation on their farewell trek around Holland and Germany.

On 14th June 1968, this Jeff Beck Group made an outstanding United States concert debut. "The audience," reported the *New York Times*, "were standing and cheering. Beck and his band deal in the blues mostly, but with an urgency and sweep that is hard to resist. Their dialogues were lean and laconic, and had the verbal ping-pong of a Pinter play. The climaxes were primal, bringing the 'Big Beat' of the English rock school forward."

Creating much the same effect throughout a six-week trek, Beck was sounded out – to no avail – by Frank Zappa about

> *"At the New York stop, Jimi Hendrix had been genuinely delighted to sit in with the Jeff Beck Group"*

replacing him on stage with The Mothers of Invention so that he (Zappa) could devote more time to composition and record production. At the New York stop, Jimi Hendrix, at a loose end, had been genuinely delighted to sit in with the Group.

Significantly, none of Jeff's three 45s had been considered for a set that included 'Shapes Of Things', which was revamped for the Group's first album, *Truth* -- a diverting mixture of mostly workmanlike originals, casseroled blues and oddities like 'Greensleeves' and 'Ol Man River'. Despite a rubbishing in *Rolling Stone*, *Truth* rose with almost mathematical precision to Number 15 in the *Billboard* list.

By this point, in mid-1968, Jimmy Page's increasing say in The Yardbirds' ebbing fortunes had enabled them to crawl wretchedly on, even after they'd proved incapable of major commercial or artistic recovery. "By then, The Yardbirds had split into two factions," recalls Chris Dreja. "Jimmy and I saw a future for the four-piece, and Jim and Keith had got more ethereal, melodic and delicate. There was a thread between that and Jim's new age music, but it lacked excitement for me – though I was to help Jim and Keith form Renaissance, and assist on demos for one of Jim's later bands, Shoot."

Supported by the otherwise unsung Lynton Grae Sound, The Yardbirds downed tools as a working band on 7th July 1968, a drizzling Sunday evening. In the inauspicious setting of Luton Technical College, they'd run through this final evensong any old how; Keith forgetting words and Chris fluffing one or two bass runs as Jimmy tried to make a show of it.

> *"The Yardbirds downed tools as a working band on 7th July 1968, a drizzling Sunday evening in Luton"*

McCarty and Relf's tentative preparations for the end had embraced two sessions at Abbey Road under the eye of Paul Samwell-Smith, with whom the hatchet – if it had ever existed – had been buried. Since the Oxford debacle, Paul's vinyl output had been intermittent – thwarted completely at one point by a spell in hospital with pancreatitis amid press hearsay that he was about to start a new group with Graham Gouldman and guitarist Hilton Valentine, late of The Animals. A less credible, though brief, liaison with Barry Mason, Engelbert Humperdinck's tunesmith, came to a low-profile twin peak with a Mason 45 ('Over The Hills And Far Away'), and 'Seek And Find', a joint composition closer to 'Shapes Of Things' than 'The Last Waltz'.

As a bass player, Samwell-Smith had been put to use on many intriguing record dates, such as one for the LP *McGough & McGear*, on which two-thirds of Scaffold, the Liverpudlian mixed-media trio, were accompanied by Paul, Jimi Hendrix, and the violinist mother of producer Peter Asher, once half of Peter & Gordon, the beat boom's most successful duo. Asher also invited Samwell-Smith, Jeff Beck and Paul McCartney (on drums) to assist with his production of a Paul Jones single – for which they were paid the standard Musicians' Union rate by EMI's accounts department.

It was in the same studio that three-fifths of the old firm had been back again when Samwell-Smith had overseen 'Henry's Coming Home', the first – and last – single by Jim McCarty and Keith Relf as Together. If you own a copy, you could be talking money, according to the *Record Collector Price Guide*. I found mine entirely by chance on a market stall in London. I knew nothing about its release. Only '(Relf McCarty)' (sic) beneath the titles, 'Henry's Coming Home' and 'Love Mum And Dad', and 'Produced by Paul Samwell-Smith' betrayed any clue as to who Together might be. I needed a minute or two to recover from the shock. This was only The Yardbirds by another name... So why hadn't there been anything about this in any of the music papers, which I studied then as a stockbroker would a Dow Jones index? Could it be I'd just coughed up a florin (10p) for the mail-out that an inattentive music journalist had cleared away along with all the other supplicatory flotsam-and-jetsam that washed up around his typewriter every week? Why hadn't EMI made more of it instead of just tossing it negligently onto the commercial waters, where it stood as much chance of being a hit as a message in a bottle has of reaching its addressee? The nerve. The bloody nerve...

In a crammed railway carriage on the way home, I kept taking the record from my tie-dye hippy shoulder-bag and looking at it – noting that it also read, "Arranged and conducted by Tony Meehan" – and continued to do so as I walked homewards in the pallor of twilight. Within seconds of negotiating the front door, I was upstairs in my bedroom, thrusting 'Henry's Coming Home' onto the Dansette. It span away in a blur, but 'Love Mum And Dad' (presumed to be the B-side from its matrix number) was quite an articulate speech of the heart – about inner-city isolation being preferable to an adolescence of small-town dreariness and a perpetual domestic 'atmosphere' – with which I could identify as I traced a guitar in the vapour of a window and wondered why my mother didn't understand...

Of course, the other side of the coin in every sense was the perkier 'Henry's Coming Home'. Laden with 'Wonderful Land' strings, staccato brass and b-b-ba-ba-bas (like The Troggs' 'With A Girl Like You'), the prodigal returns, pining for the mellow rural sunshine where he started rather than coping with a plainer present in the big city. Instead of his old home town looking the same when he stepped down from the train, Henry was more like the chap in the cabaret standard, 'When The World Was Young (All The Apple Trees)', in his sentimentality about a pastoral past where there's always nothing doing. If lacking the bucolic detail, 'Henry's Coming Home' – and 'Love Mum And Dad' – also relied on heavy acoustic overspill, conspicuous in the fingering of Jon Mark, a guitarist who had previously shared stages with Marianne Faithfull.

> *"Together might have had the potential to win a non-headbanging following like that of Pentangle"*

Overall, the playing on the record was polished, the production lush, Keith in supple voice, and both songs full of promise for better things to come... But as what? A Peter & Gordon for the 1970s? 'Rock' was but a trace element in Together. Had 'Henry's Coming Home' sold sufficient for Keith and Jim to hold on hoping, Together might have had greater potential to win a non-headbanging following like that of Pentangle – described by one journalist as "the missing link between folk, jazz, blues and pop" – and the other leading modern folk-rock outfits, such as The Incredible String Band, Fairport Convention, Eclection and Lindisfarne.

As the seasons turned from gold to marble for The Yardbirds, double acts seemed to be thriving. Peter & Gordon were long over, but drummer Pete York and singing keyboard *wunderkind* Eddie

Hardin had left The Spencer Davis Group in October to team up as "the smallest big band in the world" – and, courtesy of saturation airplay on *Top Gear*, Tyrannosaurus Rex were impinging on both the singles and album charts with a sound centred on pattering congas behind the guitar and querulous tenor of Marc Bolan, once creative pivot of psychedelic John's Children – an act that Simon-Napier Bell had attempted to nurture as a second Yardbirds after he'd surrendered his management of the original one to former wrestler Peter Grant in 1966.

The late Peter's strapping build, combative skills and knack of staring out of countenance the most intransigent ditherers over agreed fees – "dreadful misunderstanding, Mr Grant, sir... never forgive myself" – had been reassuring assets in the more unrefined engagements where The Yardbirds worked. His strengths were to be tested more thoroughly and not found wanting when he took charge of Led Zeppelin on The Yardbirds' demise.

Chris Dreja had participated in discussions about the proposed new version of the band, when, as he puts it, "Jimmy was hot for The Yardbirds to carry on. I even went up to Birmingham with him and Peter Grant to audition Robert Plant and John Bonham, but I wasn't interested in becoming a jobbing musician with strangers, and had made a conscious decision that I was going to go into freelance photography. It was such a foil being in this semi-artistic environment where you had complete control, pretty much."

> *"Jimmy was hot for The Yardbirds to carry on, but I wasn't interested in becoming a jobbing musician with strangers"*

During the Yardbirds-Led Zeppelin interregnum, Jimmy Page had occupied himself constructively by nodding towards Pentangle with his 'White Summer' on a BBC2 series hosted by folk chanteuse Julie Felix, and keeping the wolf further from the door as a hired hand, cropping up on television and in prestigious auditoriums backing the likes of Cliff Richard, Roy Orbison, The Everly Brothers, Engelbert Humperdinck, and in the studio on the likes of 1968's *No Introduction Necessary* by Keith David de Groot – a vocalist who vanished instantly from the pages of history. Issued by Spark (a label of no great merit) this album was intended to catch the general drift of late-1960s pop thanks to its embrace of both rock'n'roll revival and – given Keith David's big-name accompanists – the emerging trend of the 'super session'.

That most smug of all pop cliques was epitomised in December 1968 by A N Other, an *ad hoc* quintet with John Lennon, Eric Clapton, Yoko Ono, Keith Richards and Jimi Hendrix's drummer Mitch Mitchell, who made their only appearance on the BBC-commissioned *Rolling Stones Rock 'N' Roll Circus*. A month prior to this spectacular, Clapton had been part of a less glamorous all-day function in a Staines warehouse, where some of the ablest musical technicians of two continents dissolved outlines between rock and jazz. Among those captured on seldom-seen film were Steve Stills, Roland Kirk and Jack Bruce – who, with two other participants, saxophonist Dick Heckstall-Smith and drummer Jon Hiseman, would cut a one-shot jazz album the following year.

The clouds had parted on the gods at play a few weeks earlier when a stellar cast was assembled to underpin windmill-armed Joe Cocker's funereal-paced 'With A Little Help From My Friends' – set to wrench Mary Hopkin's 'Those Were The Days' from Number One in November 1968 – and its associated LP. Constituting one illustrious amalgam were Jimmy Page, Clem Cattini (who played drums on The Yardbirds' 'Ten Little Indians', as well as Jeff Beck's 'Love Is Blue'), Nicky Hopkins – and John Paul Jones. As well as pumping the bass, Jones was now known in the business as a reliable keyboard player – as exemplified on The Downliners Sect's 'Waiting In Heaven Somewhere' and The Washington DCs 'Seek And Find' – and for more general talents as an arranger and studio director. And since he'd been involved in most of The Yardbirds' post-Beck singles, he was an obvious choice for Page's new band, Led Zeppelin – initially remaining as The Yardbirds for September dates in Scandinavia and a couple more back in Britain in October, before the name-change later that month and, in spring 1969, for the new group's album debut, *Led Zeppelin*.

Mere weeks prior to the formation of this ultimate heavy metal band, the sunken orchestra who were sight-reading one evening at London's Talk Of The Town nightspot had contained Jimmy Page, John Paul Jones… and drummer Clem Cattini. "In a roundabout way," Clem would later reflect, "I turned down the job with Zeppelin. I now had a family, and I thought – wrongly – that I'd found my niche as a session drummer. Peter Grant twice rang me and asked me out to lunch to discuss a new project. As I was working three sessions a day, seven days a week, I hadn't a lot of time, so I left it. Two years after Zeppelin had really made it big, I said to Peter, 'That lunch date, was it to do with…?' He just nodded."

CHAPTER 11

LINE OF LEAST
RESISTANCE

*"The Yardbirds allowed me to improvise a
lot in live performance and I started
building a textbook of ideas that I
eventually used in Zeppelin."*

JIMMY PAGE

Together's career didn't plummet, simply because it never left the ground. 'Henry's Coming Home' and, especially, 'Love Mum And Dad' were therefore appreciated only in retrospect (by those who may or may not have heard them). Had the single been issued just a few months later, it might have been lumped with a downbeat genre known either as 'self-rock' (if you enjoyed it) or 'drip-rock' (if, like *Melody Maker*'s Allan Jones in a scathing article, you didn't). No Mick Jaggerings were necessary. All you had to do was park your bulk on a stool – either with a guitar or in front of a piano – whinge ploddingly 'beautiful' melodies to lyrics that would make some people ashamed to be human, and not forget to emit a small, sad smile every now and then.

All this was commensurate with the doldrums that followed 1969's mud-squelching *Woodstock Music And Arts Fair*, viewed from a distance of decades as the climax of flower-power culture. In an age as devoid as it could be of whatever makes pop fun, most of the lesser drip-rockers had all the personal magnetism of sacks of potatoes, and a supine cheesecloth-and-denim application to both recording and stage presentation. The royal couple were solemn James Taylor and twee Melanie; the national anthem Simon & Garfunkel's piteous 'Bridge Over Troubled Water', and the house band Crosby, Stills and Nash, who were to be supplemented by the high-pitched quavering of Neil Young, a drip-rock colossus.

In 1971, Young's 'Southern Man' got what it deserved in a version by The Dave Clark Five. Other old campaigners, like the now leaderless Dozy, Beaky, Mick & Tich and The Tremeloes, also developed an unprecedented introspection, catching this aspect of early 1970s rock more admirably in clever four-part harmony on predominantly acoustic numbers with 'laid-back' tempos, seemingly obligatory swirls of steel guitar – and the band all sporting facial hair.

Led Zeppelin grew a beard apiece too, and their music was to be marked with an occasionally openly pastoral outlook, as epitomised by Robert Plant's duets with folky Sandy Denny in 1971 on the band's fourth album. An element of this had been there from the beginning. Just as 'White Summer' had been a highlight of The Yardbirds' final *Top Gear* session in March 1968, so it was in Led Zeppelin's 15 months later.

Both groups also rehearsed 'Flames' by Elmer Gantry's Velvet Opera and Howlin' Wolf's 'How Many More Years' (rewritten as 'How Many More Times'), and performed 'Dazed And Confused', 'The Train Kept A-Rollin'', and, an early Zeppelin encore, 'For Your Love'. As Chris Dreja confirms: "Jimmy took many ideas that we'd been working on in the last 18 months of The Yardbirds for what became Led Zeppelin." Page would agree: "The Yardbirds allowed me to improvise a lot in live performance and I started building a textbook of ideas that I eventually used in Zeppelin." More than a touch of The Jeff Beck Group's *Truth* album prevailed too on 1969's *Led Zeppelin* – and there was even a pinch of *No Introduction Necessary* in there as well.

> *"Jimmy took many ideas we'd been working on in the last 18 months of The Yardbirds for what became Led Zeppelin"*

Just as sturdy and unoriginal were other heavy metallurgists who popped up on both sides of the Atlantic with almost the same frequency as beat groups had around 1964. The hit song of 1970 was 'All Right Now' by Free, *protégés* of Alexis Korner. Its similarity to Jagger and Richards' 'Honky Tonk Women' provoked *Music Echo* to cite Free as "The New Stones" – though, if simply for their dependency on old blues forms, so were a new Spencer Davis Group at 1972's *Lincoln Festival*.

Higher on the same bill were Canned Heat, whose flux of transient personnel included Stourbridge's Stan Webb from Chicken Shack, signed to Mike Vernon's Blue Horizon. On the same specialist label, Top Topham recovered scrapings of a lost inheritance with cameos on albums by Duster Bennett, Gordon Smith – blues boom cult celebrities – and Chicken Shack's Christine Perfect, as well as recording his own *Ascension Heights*.

There but for fortune might have gone Eric Clapton, had Topham not left The Yardbirds. As it was, after the high-profile break-up of Blind Faith at the end of 1969 – marking the peak of his guitar divinity – Clapton down-shifted and financed a European trek by support band Delaney & Bonnie & Friends, with himself as lead guitarist. He also appeared on-stage with John Lennon's Plastic Ono Band, having already had a hand in their 'Cold Turkey' single earlier in the year – an ironic title, as it turned out, since Eric was only a few months away from a descent into his own heroin abyss.

By 1970 Clapton was rich enough to be above tour-album-tour sandwiches, and could wait until he felt like making a new record. His eponymous solo album had sold well enough, but an attempt to integrate himself into a group again was short-lived. His Derek & The Dominoes was, in theory, a sturdy outfit, chosen from both talented friends – like Dave Mason, formerly of Traffic – and the most voguish Los Angeles 'supersidemen', mostly former Friends of Delaney & Bonnie. Yet neither he nor they could accomplish what any of his old groups, for all their casually-strewn errors, had committed to tape instinctively, and the band fell apart during sessions for 1970's *Layla And Other Assorted Love Songs*. "The band was getting very loaded," Clapton has said, "doing way too much dope. It broke down halfway through because of the paranoia and the tension."

Heroin condemned Clapton to self-imposed house arrest "for about two-and-a-half years" in his country retreat near the Surrey village of Ewhurst. "One day I found I was doing it [heroin] like a routine." Lethargic hours between fixes were passed asleep or in front of the television, nourished by fast food. When able to tear himself away from the *News In Welsh* or *The Epilogue*, he might fiddle with his guitar a bit before slipping back to monosodium glutamate and optical chewing-gum.

> "The essence of the Concert For Bangladesh *was Harrison and the thrillingly unrehearsed Clapton on duelling guitars*"

Eric made no long-term plans. How could he? Yet in August 1971, as an avowal of his regard for George Harrison (for whom he'd provided guest guitar in the studio on 'While My Guitar Gently Weeps' and the *Wonderwall* soundtrack back in 1968, as well as the more recent *All Things Must Pass*) – and perhaps in part due to his coveting of the former Beatle's wife, muse for the celebrated 'Layla' – he hauled himself tardily from his pit for the *Concert For Bangladesh*, a landmark on pop's journey to respectability. Many found the essence of the show to be Harrison and the thrillingly unrehearsed Clapton on duelling guitars during 'While My Guitar Gently Weeps', one of the few 'blowing' numbers.

Within days, Clapton would relapse into a continued withdrawal from his profession, prolonged beyond 1974's overblown 'comeback' concert with famous pals at London's Rainbow Theatre. The Who's Pete Townshend had been approached by Lord Harlech, anxious father of Clapton's then-girlfriend, "to see whether I would help Eric put a band together for a concert for one of Harlech's charities. To be honest, the only problem I saw was that Eric had been out of the scene for a long time."

The fans loved it, but to many – including me – the Rainbow show was a consummation of all the supergroup arrogance epitomised by Blind Faith, and Harrison's flabby *All Things Must Pass* triple-album, and carried like an Olympic torch into the later 1970s, where Clapton's previous reputation was sufficient to sell the likes of *There's One In Every Crowd* and *No Reason To Cry* – lacklustre albums in which dispiriting slickness and close-miked lethargy, laced with occasional drollness, testified to a mollycoddled but empty existence.

To certain perverse devotees, it was Clapton's misfortune to live on after shedding the greater part of his artistic load. Perhaps he should have been killed in 1966 in the same car crash as Johnny Kidd, ie a few weeks after recording *Bluesbreakers*. At one point, Eric himself might have agreed: "Dying from drugs didn't seem to be a terrible thing. When Jimi Hendrix died, I cried all day because he'd left me behind, but as I grow older, death becomes something I don't choose to step towards too soon." As a late 1960s myth rather than the mere mortal who couldn't cope easily with pop stardom, Eric was built to last.

For different reasons, Jeff Beck sometimes walked a precarious artistic line too. I bought *Cosa Nostra Beck-Ola*, the LP after *Truth*, almost for old time's sake, when it surfaced in some second-hand circumstance – though I didn't get round to giving it a spin until it'd been in my possession for maybe years.

"The only problem I saw was that Eric had been out of the scene for a long time"

To be more brutally honest, I've never made the time to absorb Jeff's music very deeply since 'Love Is Blue'. Actually, I quite liked 'Love Is Blue', but I'm nothing if not vulgar – though vulgar in a different way, thank God, to the fellow I once saw inserting his head into a yawning speaker bin to receive the full mega-blast of Beck's guitar.

Though he was by then tarred with a heavy metal brush, Jeff soon came to despise the form. His expression of this exacerbated internal ructions within The Jeff Beck Group. Rod Stewart has claimed he "couldn't take all the aggression and unfriendliness that developed. It was getting too ridiculous for words. Jeff would stay at the Hilton, and the rest of us at Hotel-Third-On-The-Bill round the corner. Do you know that in the two-and-a-half years I was with Beck, I never once looked him in the eye?"

Stewart famously left to launch The Faces with fellow sacked Beck sideman Ron Wood. Just as malcontented, Nicky Hopkins took a dim view of the maverick guitarist "constantly cancelling out tours. We'd wake up one morning in the States and find he'd left the night before and was back in England."

There were, however, odd twinklings of levity – such as when, responding to a sardonic request at the Marquee, the Group struck up a deadpan rendition of Frank Sinatra's 'Strangers In The Night'. Nonetheless, as the atmosphere of personal discord thickened, Jeff – no born organiser – sought scapegoats: "I had a really rough time trying to equal my playing with The Yardbirds, because I didn't have anybody as creative as those people."

> *"I had a really rough time trying to equal my playing with The Yardbirds, because I didn't have anybody as creative as them"*

In 1969 The Jeff Beck Group were supported by Vanilla Fudge in New York. Described in *International Times* as "molten lead on vinyl", the Fudge had enjoyed only one big hit – a rude 1967 awakening of The Supremes' 'You Keep Me Hanging On' – but had abided for a further three years with releases in much the same melodramatic, slowed-down style – all weighty 'holy organ', deliberated drum rolls and pseudo-Oriental guitar riffs rolling like treacle over cinematic arrangements of 'Eleanor Rigby', Donovan's 'Season Of The Witch' and the late Curtis Mayfield's quasi-gospel 'People Get Ready', one of Beck's lifelong preferences.

The Fudge had become fairly demoralised by this time, but a mutual admiration society was formed that night in New York, and when the Fudge gave up the ghost a fortnight later, bass guitarist Tim Bogert and drummer Carmine Appice rang Beck – who says he, "nearly fainted on the floor" – in his Detroit motel room to propose joining forces in a new group. This was thwarted, however, by Jeff's car accident near Maidstone, Kent, in December, which resulted in a fractured skull that, to all intents and purposes, put him out of action for almost the next two years.

While recuperating, he managed sessions for Pete Brown (Jack Bruce's singing lyricist), and for Screaming Lord Sutch – the resulting *Lord Sutch And His Heavy Friends*, despite featuring former Sutch employees and acquaintances like Jimmy Page, John Bonham, Noel Redding, Mitch Mitchell and Nicky Hopkins, as well as Beck, was designated as the "worst rock album ever made" in a 1999 poll among Britain's more unimaginative radio presenters.

Chris Dreja, meanwhile, in his new career as a photographer, shot the back cover image for the first Led Zeppelin album. "I shot a lot of stuff for Zeppelin," says Chris. "Being a musician helped me to switch comfortably from one career to the next. Friends in photography who used to come and watch The Yardbirds advised me to go to New York – where I was based for three years, and I found myself in dangerous situations like Detroit and Watts, doing picture stories for magazines.

"In 1971, Peter Grant rang to invite my wife and I to a Led Zeppelin concert at Madison Square Garden. They had a mega-watt PA, literally moving the concrete in front of 50,000 people. Having not been to many such events since The Yardbirds, it completely freaked me out – we had used just amplifiers and the house PA with no monitors. But it wasn't uncomfortable. There was no angst about what might have been for me."

Prior to leaving England, Chris had been in the process of forming a casual combo to let off steam at weekends. Its stylistic determination was splashed with a vivid hue of the countrified rock heard in licensed premises which, from the early 1970s, had transformed themselves into parodies of either Wild West saloons or truckers' roadhouses. Likely inclusions in the set were 'Sunday Morning Coming Down', 'Okie From Muskogee', 'Crystal Chandelier' and other items that, if they hadn't made the charts, were as well known as many that had.

"Chris's band contained a guy called BJ Cole on slide guitar and John Hawken on keyboards," says Jim McCarty. "Chris knew we were forming Renaissance, and suggested them." Cole wasn't suitable, but ex-Nashville Teen Hawken was, and got involved in a pooling of resources by Jim, Keith Relf and, reeled in as producer, Paul Samwell-Smith. Another great find was Louis Cennamo, a virtuoso bass player who had been in The Herd and The Chicago Line Blues Band as well as marking time with sessions – such as Al Stewart's 'Turn Into Earth' and James Taylor's maiden album – before joining the pit orchestra in the West End production of the 'hippy' musical *Hair*.

Renaissance's icing on the cake, though, was former maid-of-all-work for The Yardbirds Fan Club, Jane Relf – Keith's sister – whose clear soprano was worthy of a Sandy Denny or Jacqui McShee from Pentangle. With no previous experience of singing professionally, Jane had been living in Cornwall, but during a visit home, "Keith said what they were doing, and talked about having a girl in the group. I said, 'Well, don't forget me.' It was just a joke, although I wanted to. Keith then came down to Cornwall, and said, 'OK, you're on'."

With breathtaking chorale from Keith, Jane and Jim, the frame of reference on a promising debut album, *Renaissance* – with 'Produced by Paul Samwell-Smith' in lettering almost as large on the label as the name of the group – embraced folk, *musique concrete*, Missa Luba jungle mass (on the 'Bullet' finale), a tang of Frank Zappa at the beginning of 'Wanderer', and the post-serialist tonalities of such as Penderecki and Ligeti, particularly on the coda of 'Bullet'. It seems milder now, but in 1970 this was as unnerving – in a spookier way – as the screech-out that closed The Velvet Underground's 'European Son'.

> *"Hardly pop, the most pungent aftertaste of Renaissance was 'classical interpretations'"*

Hardly pop, the most pungent aftertaste of *Renaissance* was what the sleeve credits called "classical interpretations/riffs" – meaning Cennamo and especially Hawken's extrapolations on McCarty and Relf's "basic melodies and lyrics". Indeed, keyboards were as conspicuous in Renaissance as Eric Clapton's guitar had been in Cream's sprawling improvisations on 1968's *Live At The Fillmore*. Yet, for me, there was none of the same "how much longer?" exasperation and glancing at the watch with Renaissance – even as 'Bullet' approached the quarter-hour mark, and 'Kings And Queens' stretched into its tenth tightly-arranged minute, interspersed with cunning dynamic shifts and couplets with obscurely supernatural overtones which, if not significantly 'poetic', sidestepped bombastic rhetoric.

Tangential to the general post-*Woodstock* drift of ham-fisted heavy metal, supergroups and precious singer-songwriters, much of the clean, self-assured breadth of musical and lyrical expression on the album was down to Samwell-Smith, who made effective use of up-to-date equipment and techniques that had been unavailable at the time of *Yardbirds*, when 'What Do You Want', 'He's Always There' et al had been in the bag in two takes – no arguments and on to the next number.

Paul elected to use very little augmentation of the basic personnel on *Renaissance*. Nonetheless, despite a commendable paucity of gratuitous frills, aggravatingly familiar musical themes abounded on virtually every track: Chopin, Debussy, Byrd, William Lawes and, in 'Innocence', almost-but-not-quite Beethoven's 'Moonlight Sonata'. While Hawken was responsible for these, Cennamo's bass solo in 'Bullet' could be mistaken for flamenco guitar, and Relf proved no slouch on acoustic six-string – so much so that when Renaissance supported John Mayall in Helsinki in 1970, the man who'd once opined that The Yardbirds were "appalling" arrived, either by accident or design, with only a bass player, and persuaded Keith and Jim to make up numbers, in every sense of the phrase.

> *"Samwell-Smith made effective use of equipment and techniques unavailable at the time of* Yardbirds*"*

The closest Renaissance came to a rave-up was 'Bullet' – particularly in concert. Certain passages could not be reproduced outside the studio, so it became a vehicle for an on-stage extension of Relf's murky harmonica solo, as well as McCarty commanding the stage alone under his own voodoo spell for exhilarating minutes on end of round-the-kit cross-patterns and ringing cymbals.

Whether on the boards or on disc, it was often the sound of Renaissance at any given moment that counted, as opposed to separate pieces – though the stark essences of either 'Wanderer' or 'Kings And Queens' could have been developed more to become as viable a proposition as a loss-leader single as 'Island' – which, with Jane Relf to the fore, worked sensually rather than intellectually in its evocative of warm latitudes and an ocean daybreak from the quarterdeck. 'Island' was the item chosen to shop-window Renaissance on a cheap sampler album issued by the company – also called Island – to which the quintet had been signed in Britain, where the album crawled to Number 60. Released on Elektra in the States, it became more of a student bedsit fixture, after a slog round the continent and a full-page *Rolling Stone* advertisement stressing that the quintet had "risen from the ashes of The Yardbirds".

Renaissance was to notch up its biggest British seller, 1977's *A Song For All Seasons*, in the wake of a Top Ten entry for its 'Northern Lights' single. By then, though, any Yardbirds connection had long dissipated: McCarty did play and co-write tracks on a second album, 1972's *Prologue*, but he and the original team – including Paul Samwell-Smith – had otherwise abandoned Renaissance.

"There was a high pressure situation about work," assesses Jim. "I decided to leave, but I wanted to carry on writing for the band. Keith and Louis quit as well. Jane and John kept on for a little while longer and then they went too. The idea was that I was going to keep on writing, and Keith was going to produce, but he wasn't interested." In the light of the last suggestion, Paul Samwell-Smith was not all smiles: "I'd negotiated the deal with Elektra. I got the money for the album, produced the thing, took it to America, sold it, got it sold in Britain, and then Keith and Jim turned around and told me they were going to produce the next one themselves."

One advantage that did accrue to Paul partly through his work with Renaissance was that he was commissioned by Island mogul Chris Blackwell to produce some of the label's other artists, such as Amazing Blondel, Bronco and, most important of all, Jethro Tull – and also Cat Stevens who, on Samwell-Smith's advice, formed a prosperous musical partnership with Alun Davies. Thanks in no small part to his new producer's efforts, Stevens gained world recognition as "a solo singer who could actually sing and play his songs," in Paul's words, "which I could embellish as I wanted". In a *Beat Instrumental* interview, Paul added that Cat's *Mona Bone Jakon* album – arriving several months after Renaissance – was, "the first production of mine to give me real satisfaction".

For McCarty and the Relfs, Renaissance provided less an *entree* to future triumphs than vinyl postscripts that led nowhere important. Decca grabbed Jane for a solo 45, 'Without A Song From You', co-written and co-produced by Jim – who, with Keith, negotiated a one-shot deal with Regal Zonophone to market a composition (published by Renaissance Music) entitled 'Line Of Least Resistance', its text a hybrid of being at one with natural forces and a rejuvenation of the 'Henry's Coming Home' theme. Produced by Amen Corner's Mike Smith, it was attributed to Reign, an act centred on Robin le Mesurier – son of the distinguished actor John – but had no physical state outside the studio.

The quality of 'Line Of Least Resistance' as a song shone through a too-loose arrangement, notable mainly for a guitar solo of clanged chords. It sounded fine to a 'Mr Zero'-'Turn Into Earth' nancy-boy like me when first I listened to it, after Richard MacKay mailed me a tape 15 years after its 1970 release. It took only a few more whirls to take such a vice-like grip on me that I drove everyone in the household nervous for weeks by dirgeing 'Line Of Least Resistance' *sotto voce* like a mantra.

CHAPTER 12

ALL THE
FALLING ANGELS

"I would love to have been a Stone, but they worked at a completely different pace ... They had trouble turning up at the same time."

JEFF BECK

The vast majority of participants in the beat boom had returned to anonymity by the mid-1970s. Getting shot of show-business was like completing National Service, in that your old job was often waiting for you when you got back. Unalluring it might have seemed, but it wasn't too late for some to resume apprenticeships and college courses – or return to the fold as maybe taxi drivers or suburban shopkeepers. If obliged to touch a figurative cap to higher ranking employees years your junior, you'd be ribbed by them for having had ideas above your station, but they'd be less inclined to tease after they'd seen you get up and do a couple of numbers with the band booked for the firm's dinner-and-dance. Then the years would seem to fall away as they glimpsed a profile once defined by a *Ready Steady Go* arc-light.

It hadn't taken long for the old life to seem like a previous existence for Jim McCarty. The most immediate post-Renaissance ripple he made was the penning of 'If You've Got A Little Love To Give' for the only album by Dave Clark & Friends (ie Clark, the Five's singing organist Mike Smith, and assorted session hirelings) in 1972. Nonetheless, each week's new Top 40 hammered home the futility of a 29-year-old wasting time and energy playing pop stars.

McCarty felt sometimes as if he'd never made those hit records, won that acclaim, seen America or done any of the other things spoken of in orgies of maudlin reminiscence about the 'group that had everything it took' back in 1964, when the world was young. He was also dejected by the curtness of old associates who'd say they were "in a meeting", "on another line", "out to lunch" or, damn their impudence, "too busy" to call him back – especially about money he believed he was owed: not that there was a massive amount, since "the record royalties for 'For Your Love', 'Shapes Of Things', all the big stuff, went as part of the settlement with Giorgio. It was half bad luck, half bad advice."

McCarty would be kept waiting for his cash – and for the seasons of pop to rotate. It might have been tempting for him to fling it all back in their faces – if "they" cared at all about a downtrodden drummer from another bunch of poor sods who'd been milked dry and tossed aside when the first serious flop came. To hell with the music industry. Who needed the time-serving incompetence, the fake sincerity, the backstabbing and the contradiction of excessive thrift and heedless expenditure? In what other sphere of the most corrupt business could a dam burst on such a deep river of embezzlement, arm-twisting and concealment of guilty secrets?

Yet for some who'd made their first forays into pop in the 1960s, this was a boom time. Most relevant to this discussion is David Bowie, who was to reach middle age as one of Britain's richest pop stars. He'd been reaping his first million as a prime mover of glam-rock, along with Marc Bolan, Slade – and, in leather jump-suit, chains and hardly any make-up, Suzi Quatro – another Mickie Most production charge – who was seen as an 'answer' to mascara'd men dressed as ladies.

> *"It hadn't taken long for the old life to seem like a previous existence for Jim McCarty"*

Another band to thrive in the glam era were Bryan Ferry's Roxy Music. If I had a tidier mind, I'd argue that Roxy Music were to glam-rock what The Yardbirds had been to 1960s beat. For a start, both contained an entrancing lead singer who was a lover of R&B, a former art student, a maker of solo records, and no Caruso. Each group was patronised by Andy Warhol's arty New York set for their collisions of pop convention and curiously tangential singularities on raw material that didn't take long to 'grow' on you. 'Ladytron', 'In Every Dream Home A Heartache' and other examples of Roxy's music were riddled with abrupt changes of mood and tempo – while 'Sunset' drank from the same pool as 'Farewell' and 'Only The Black Rose' in its gathering of final thoughts as death crept nearer.

Yet before hulking youths became receptive to a wardrobe that was less than brusquely masculine, Roxy Music and like glam-rock icons were conspicuous by their absences on technical college juke boxes, full of album-enhancing 45s by Deep Purple, Man, Black Sabbath and other 'heavy' combos who attracted male consumers recently grown to man's estate.

In their hostel rooms, elongated 'works' (as opposed to three-minute songs) were very much *de rigeur* too. Holland's Focus – featuring Jan Akkerman, 1973's Best Guitarist in a *Melody Maker* poll – offered amplified arrangements of pieces by Bartok and Rodrigo and, as much as Mike Oldfield and his *Tubular Bells*, set the standard for Jethro Tull, Yes, Hawkwind, ELP and many others to make albums as a continuous entity, teeming with interweaving themes, links and *leitmotivs*. Renaissance were to join this list of acts, via 1975's rocked-up crack at Rimsky-Korsakov's 'Scheherazade', at Carnegie Hall with the New York Philharmonic. These – and borderline cases such as The Moody Blues and the post-Syd Barrett Pink Floyd – were to lay the foundations of the new-age meanderings of the 1980s.

> *"BBA was obsolete before it got started ... a nasty horrible noise. When we weren't fighting we were playing trash"*

Though more castigated for preferring technique to instinct, jazz-rock also scored with both musicians and students. If its truer home was the US – which abounded with the ilk of Weather Report, Return To Forever, Jan Hammer Group and The Crusaders – Britain still supplied respectable genre names like East of Eden, Colosseum, former Graham Bond guitarist 'Mahavishnu' John McLaughlin – and Jeff Beck.

Fully recovered from his accident, Beck had issued two albums with his Group, containing drummer Cozy Powell as a foil for his guitar pyrotechnics, prior to the eagerly awaited amalgamation with Tim Bogert and Carmine Appice. This trio, however, "was obsolete before it got started," reckoned Jeff, looking back – principally through lack of new material forcing recreations of past glories as far back as The Yardbirds, and Jeff's dismay at the overall unsubtlety and indiscipline. "I was finished with that style a long time ago, but if you could zero in on the energy, you got the goods – otherwise, it was a cacophonous, nasty, horrible noise. When we weren't fighting, we were playing trash."

Well, you can understand this attitude from one who'd just demonstrated his skills on BBC2's *Guitar Workshop*; as a measure of his standing, other guest tutors included Julian Bream and John Renbourn. Even so, Jan Akkerman had thought highly enough of Appice and Bogert to invite them to play on *Tabernakel*, his 1973 solo album, before he left Focus in 1976 to begin the first of several jazz fusion collections.

Backed by a young outfit called Upp, Jeff previewed a number from the dazzling *Blow By Blow*, an album with session musicians and arrangements by George Martin, The Beatles' former producer. It was also unlike anything Beck had done before, but similar to work by the jazz-rock pioneers he was copying most successfully. Beck's enchantment with the form caused him next to record the instrumental *Wired* album with The Jan Hammer Group, after declining a post in The Rolling Stones when guitarist Mick Taylor resigned in 1974. "I would love to have been a Stone," Jeff said later, "but they worked at a completely different pace. I was used to conceiving a notion, putting it on tape, and having it finished by the evening. They had trouble turning up at the same time."

On a promotional tour with Hammer, Beck emerged as one of the few rock guitarists capable of playing 'fusion' music convincingly, even if, in common with most critics, Jeff himself slagged off a 1977 in-concert album – though his biographer, Annette Carson, felt it was saved by "guitar work of such complexity, it's hard to imagine how he pulled it off live".

At David Bowie's 'retirement' of his Ziggy Stardust alter-ego at London's Hammersmith Odeon in July 1973, the glam-rocker pulled the biggest rabbit from his musical top-hat by bringing on the old Yardbird to slug it out Harrison-Clapton style with Mick Ronson – Ziggy/David's lead guitarist and known Beck admirer – for two encores: Chuck Berry's 'Around And Around', and a revisited 'I'm A Man'. (There was a noticeable similarity between Bowie's 'Jean Genie' and The Yardbirds' arrangement of 'I'm A Man'.)

Later that year Bowie released *Pin-Ups*, a complete LP of cover versions, either to display his talent as an 'interpreter' or simply because he was running out of ideas. Either way, Bowie chose to devote *Pin-Ups* to an affectionate trawl through British beat group classics that included 'I Wish You Would' and 'Shapes Of Things'. Throughout the whole album, Keith Relf seeps insidiously from the speakers as a principal vocal influence – as he was too for Alice Cooper, Iggy Pop and a host of less illustrious singers.

Probably because of his respiratory maladies and general ill-health, Keith lacked the lung power of a Robert Plant or Steve Winwood, but the initial attraction for a Yardbirds fan like Bowie was a voice recognisable instantly for a schneiderian, slightly sinister edge, and a widely expressive if technically limited range stretching from the aching desolation of 'Turn Into Earth' to the contempt of 'Rack My Mind'.

Disenchanted both with being a group's focal point and with the underachievement of the first Renaissance line-up, the monk in Relf had been haunting the back stairs of the record business

> *"Relf functioned too as producer of Medicine Head, a prog-folk duo with an R&B undercurrent"*

as co-writer (with Jim McCarty) of incidental music to a hitherto unissued movie, *Schizom*. He functioned too as publicity-shunning producer of discs by Saturnalia, Hunter Muskett, Kala, Smokestack Crumble, Steamhammer – all either heavy rock, homegrown progressive or both – and, most spectacularly, Medicine Head, a 'prog-folk' duo with an R&B undercurrent, much liked by John Peel, and local to Relf's new Staffordshire home.

It was there that he taped their Top 30 debut, 1971's '(And The) Pictures In The Sky' – in a living room that was an Aladdin's cave of linked-up reel-to-reel tape recorders, editing blocks and jack-to-jack leads. Keith's purchase of increasingly more splendid equipment had freed him from the constraints of a hired studio. This enabled him to potter about with sound, tape the wackiest demos, and begin a day's work with nothing prepared. In theory, every note of his output could be hand-tooled there on equipment that was several technological steps ahead of some professional London equivalents – and a lot more environmentally inviting.

(Some of his recordings from this time were to appear on *Musical Spectrum*, a 1992 cassette tape of a mostly fly-on-the-wall patchwork of sounds not usually thought of as musical, compiled by Richard MacKay from Relf's private, unreleased home recordings. Thanks to Keith's sister Jane, Richard has compiled two cassette albums from about 50 of the singer's personal reel-to-reel tapes – as well as finding sufficient in Jim McCarty's house to create a third LP (*Enchanted Caress*) by Illusion, the band that came after Renaissance.)

Shuttered underground, his headphoned ears like braised chops after thumping out take after rejected take, Jim McCarty could identify only too well with the clinic/doss-house paradox of certain metropolitan studio complexes – where you got to know by sight individual biscuit crumbs, and follow their day-to-day journeyings up and down a ledge, where an empty can of orangeade might also remain for weeks next to a discarded swab-stick made grubby from cleaning tape-heads.

In an unfamiliar role on keyboards and lead vocals – and he was no tyro on either – McCarty demonstrated that, unlike The Beatles, the individual parts of The Yardbirds could sometimes equal the whole, even if his short-lived new outfit, Shoot, fired a commercial blank with 1973's *On The Frontier*.

> *"There was a lively, vivid imagination at work in Shoot, with high standards of performance, production and composition"*

A strip of blue sky as Jim gazed up from the bottom of a psychological ravine during these 'wilderness years', *On The Frontier* was one of those albums that got lost because it came out in a month dominated by the latest from, say, Deep Purple, Rod Stewart and T.Rex. While EMI's distribution network ensured it was filed under 'popular' in the same shops, *On The Frontier*'s front cover – a jungle scene framed in leopard-skin – gave no indication of an ex-Yardbird's presence in the grooves, and was squeezed out of FM radio playlists by guaranteed listener-friendly extracts from *Machine Head*, *Sing It Again Rod* and *Tanx*.

More so than *Yardbirds* in 1966, *On The Frontier*'s artistic worth *per se* was disregarded in accounts ledgers, on computer run-offs and during board meetings. Since then, of course, it has become a prized rarity, however scuffed and scratched. But Shoot's is not one of those vinyl artefacts desired simply for its obscurity or investment potential, becoming just another record when you finally acquire it. There was a lively and vivid imagination at work there, with performance and production matching a high standard of composition. While it made more concessions to prevailing trends than had Renaissance, as epitomised by the obligatory swirls of BJ Cole's pedal steel, *On The Frontier* doesn't sound too dated today. Indeed, if a tape of it was mailed under a pseudonym to certain record company talent scouts, they'd think the group was that longed-for Next Big Thing.

Jokey track 'The Boogie' could have been omitted without any difficulty (and possibly guitarist Dave Green's short and wiry 'Head Under Water' instrumental), but the rest of Jim's "straight songs with no fancy frills" – the antithesis of Renaissance, in fact – shape up to confident and occasionally eccentric arrangements. They also pass the artistic litmus test if stripped down to just voice and solitary keyboard – as they are for half of the confessional 'Old Time Religion', the most immediately memorable piece, along with 'Ships And Sails', the title track (and spin-off A-side, which was recorded later in 1973 as a Renaissance B-side), and 'Sepia Sister', which emits much the same eldritch cry as Robert Plant's 'Big Log' would ten years later.

Supplementary musicians included pianist John Tout from Renaissance – while the libretto of 'On The Frontier' was the work of Betty Thatcher, whose poems were set to music on Renaissance's *Ashes Are Burning* and on later records, which met with greater acclaim in North America than Europe – so much so that the group found it more convenient to take up US residency.

Vague plans to reform the original Renaissance line-up were put on gradually more solid ice when, with an inner ear cocked to the far-off roar of the crowd, Keith Relf stood with Medicine Head either side of him in a press photo prior to a return to stage performance as their bass player. By 1975 he'd stepped further into the limelight as frontman of Armageddon, whose record

> *"The question of whether Armageddon could have reached at least the AOR middle league became academic"*

company (A&M) had intended them to plough a hard rock furrow, capitalising on the same shallow megastardom accrued over 22 US tours by the lately fragmented Humble Pie, formed in 1968 by The Small Faces' Steve Marriott and The Herd's Peter Frampton.

Joined on Armageddon's solitary LP by Louis Cennamo, plus Steamhammer's guitarist and Johnny Winter's drummer, Keith's prospects looked enticing. Without overshadowing companion tracks, 'Silver Tightrope' was worth the whole price of the album – a reconciliation between thunderclap aggression and sedate pulse, in which Keith swerved adeptly from murmured trepidation to strident intensity during the course of a 'power ballad' that was more moving than the more obvious example of Led Zeppelin's famed 'Stairway To Heaven'.

It seemed Armageddon could hardly miss. But although a series of prestigious tour supports in North America were on the calendar, the question of whether Armageddon could have reached at least the middle league of the 'adult-orientated' rock hierarchy became purely academic – partly due to the drummer's drug problems but, more conclusively, because on 14th May 1976 Keith Relf absorbed more than enough high voltage to kill him while using a guitar fed through an unearthed amplifier.

For a while Keith Relf's passing was acknowledged by groups here and there bombarding audiences with a hurriedly-rehearsed Yardbirds number. Among other dedications was singing poet Patti Smith with her inane observation that Keith shared the same initials as Keith Richards, then focus of an unofficial pop press sweepstake with odds-on that his would be the next Big Death. (Around this time I also noticed several instances of urban graffiti reading 'Relf – English Hero', but it turned out this referred to Robert Relf, a recently jailed racist 'martyr'.)

Jim McCarty stared gloomily as handfuls of earth splattered onto his friend's coffin lid, but had decided already to continue as best he could with the Renaissance regrouping project. Prevented from using that name by the 'Northern Lights' hit-makers, he created a unit called Illusion, with himself at the helm of surviving members from the first Renaissance plus guitarist John Knightsbridge, at the time moonlighting in Dana Gillespie's backing band. Illusion, however, proved a disappointing investment for Island, who issued their brace of likeable but unexciting albums, the last produced by Paul Samwell-Smith in 1978.

> "Keith's passing was acknowledged by groups here and there bombarding audiences with a hurriedly-rehearsed Yardbirds number"

Island's marketing division was contending too with the fact that discs featuring former Yardbirds – those who weren't Clapton, Beck or Page – were no longer big events. What Island demanded from Illusion was an injection of up-tempo product, and not just an associated single that might or might not chart, but ideally an unmistakable worldwide smash. When one wasn't forthcoming, McCarty, Cennamo, Jane Relf et al returned briefly to the drawing board, before going separate ways in 1978.

It was rooting through dusty spools in McCarty's attic ten years later that Richard MacKay compiled enough remaindered Illusion tapes for a third collection, 1990's *Enchanted Caress*. Though the prospective buyer should be aware that these are only demos, there is much of the same unvarnished allure about this ragbag as within The Byrds' *Preflyte*, Dylan's *Great White Wonder* – the first pop bootleg – and any number of Yardbirds items not meant originally for public consumption.

MacKay's most fascinating selection for *Enchanted Caress* was 'All The Falling Angels'. For music lovers who collate macabre allusions on disc (whose attention I must also draw to the line "deep within me I die" from 'Only The Black Rose'), there is much enjoyable time-wasting on this, Keith Relf's final recording, taped when he was losing interest in Armageddon. While this opus is bequeathed a perhaps unbearable piquancy for anyone with a glimmer of its creator's personal history, it was as deserved as that for, say, Roy Orbison's 1973 go at 'Danny Boy', or John Lennon's 'Beautiful Boy' after his slaying on a New York sidewalk. There are grounds for criticism of its execution, but 'All The Falling Angels' is a haunting melancholia, strong enough to withstand Keith's tortuous pitching of most of the higher notes.

The companion tracks – mainly the work of McCarty – don't carry the same morbid mystique, but if the arrangements are sketchy at times, some of the songs wouldn't have been out of place on any of

Illusion's – or Renaissance's – Island albums. Examples include Jane Relf's reading of the desolate 'The Man Who Loved The Trees' and her self-penned 'Let's Get Above It All' (an entry in some Irish song contest). But the mood is broken, and evidence presented that Illusion had taken Island's demands to heart, in 'Nights In Paris', an opening salvo that discharges low-life menace and perfumed temptation like that wrought in a Jacques Brel chanson.

Then there's the evocation of bloody reprisal by wide-lapelled hitmen riding on the tail-boards of Buicks in an arrangement of Richard Rodgers' 'Slaughter On Tenth Avenue', demonstrating that John Knightsbridge was as adept a Jeff Beck stylist as Mick Ronson, whose better-known version of the same tune was title track of a 1974 album.

Illusion drowned in the rip-tide of pub-rock and punk as certainly as Van Morrison nearly did, not to mention Led Zeppelin and other hirsute, tight-trousered 'heavy' acts, as well as the wholesomely Americanised likes of Fleetwood Mac, more displaced from the rough-and-ready blues band of yore than the 1968 Yardbirds had been from 'I Ain't Got You'. The 'street level' acclaim granted by publications like the *NME* to pub-rockers such as The Count Bishops, Dr Feelgood, Kilburn & The High Roads and Nine Below Zero was a reaction against the distancing of the humble pop group from the everyday – as in Jimmy Page's rumoured dabbling in the occult in his turreted pile virtually next door to Windsor Castle, and George Harrison's reworking of The Everly Brothers' 'Bye Bye Love' with in-joking lyrical digs at his first wife and "old Clapper" either as a rebuttal to 'Layla' or, to quote from his creamy-velumed autobiography *I Me Mine*, "a piece of self-indulgence, like some other of my songs about things that nobody else knows or cares about."

"For music lovers who collate macabre allusions on disc there is much to enjoy on 'All The Falling Angels' "

Only the craziest Beatle-ologist was interested in this, or in Eric Clapton and the former Mrs Harrison's subsequent wedding during the groom's 47-city tour of the States, and George attending the belated and lavish reception – along with Jeff Beck, Mick Jagger and other famous guests – at the happy pair's Surrey mansion.

By original definition, pub-rock (and, festering beneath it, punk) precluded both air-kissing luvvie affection and paying to see whether this or that dinosaur band was really as terrible as the *NME* made out. How much more pleasurable was a beer-sodden night in the Hope & Anchor in Islington or the Putney Half-Moon, or countless other pubs around the country where acts entertained more thought for the paying customer, and had a sense of humility lacking in the rock prima donna prone to throwing a wobbler at Madison Square Garden because the promoter provided still rather than fizzy mineral water. Even Jimmy Page was keen to show off how hip he was by visiting a London punk club to check out The Damned before it was too late. At one such venue, Bracknell's Bridge House, various bands containing either one or both of Keith Relf's two sons were to alternate with El Seven, The Next – with drummer

Zak Starkey, Ringo Starr's eldest boy – The K9s and other local outfits. In the 1980s, Jason Relf was also to pass through the ranks of east Berkshire's psychedelic Magic Mushroom Band.

With glam and pub-rock as signposts, and punk the final destination, bands like The Count Bishops, Dr Feelgood and Nine Below Zero, instead of exchanging smirks at each other's cleverness, had all latched onto a mean R&B mode a la Animals-Yardbirds-Pretty Things. With committedly backward-looking repertoires also embracing 'Talkin' About You', 'I Ain't Got You', 'I'm A Man' and all manner of Bo Diddley, reformed outfits such as Johnny Kidd's Pirates and even the lowly Rockin' Vickers were on the boards again – and there'd be a place in pub-rock's nicotine-clouded sun for The Downliners Sect too when they reappeared in 1976 like ghosts from the recent past.

Gambling for higher stakes, 1970s rebirths had been attempted already by The Animals, Georgie Fame and *a* Blue Flames, *a* Big Three, Dave Dee, Dozy, Beaky, *a* Mick & Tich, The Temperance Seven, The Walker Brothers, The Small Faces and, for the first of n times, The Pretty Things. Yet hardly any became challengers again, because, as poor sales of doubtful comeback records demonstrated, all that the fans, old and new, wanted were the sounds of yesteryear. As these resounded from Radio One's *All Our Yesterplays*, Mr and Mrs Average became Swinging Sixties teenagers again, lovestruck and irresponsible.

'Art' intruded on guts, however, in over-premeditated 1970s remakes of their old hits by The Hollies, The Troggs, Alan Price, Brian Poole, tell me when to stop... Leaving a comparably peculiar afterglow was David Bowie, making no attempt to hide his cribbing from The Yardbirds in 'TVC15', kicking off with 'Good Morning Little Schoolgirl' oh-oh-oh oh-ohs, and 1977's 'What In The World' where he's in the mood "for your love, for your love, for your love".

Then, as in 1965, and as punk fanzine *Sniffin' Glue* insisted, all you needed was three chords. By winter, not a week was passing without another hot 'New Wave' group ringing some changes. Somehow, most looked and sounded just like The Sex Pistols. Ousted from the Pistols for his advocacy of melody and technical precision, bass guitarist Glen Matlock would be heard years later as a transient member of The Pretty Things who, for originality rather than anything as boring as talent, were among a smattering of Swinging Sixties celebrities to be rated, however begrudgingly, in this punk explosion that had split the decade as the beat boom had the 1960s.

The Yardbirds just about measured up too. Jean-Jacques Burnel of The Stranglers formed a splinter group, The Purple Helmets, playing respective regurgitations of old punk and Sixties stuff – including 'You're A Better Man Than I'.

CHAPTER 13

A BOX OF
FROGS

*"I felt the old energy coming back ...
I liked the recording side, and being friends
once more, but Paul and I didn't want to
become working musicians again."*

CHRIS DREJA

Once, after playing keyboards on-stage (for Screaming Lord Sutch's thunderous Savages), I had ringing in the ears for about three days. I mentioned this to Jim McCarty during the intermission of a far louder extravaganza by Jeff Beck at Hammersmith Odeon, and wasn't surprised to learn that Jeff suffered from tinnitus – as I did myself some years back. Unlike Jeff, I was fortunate and, though it brought me close to suicide when hissing in both ears resolved into a feedback-like squeal, the affliction vanished as suddenly and mysteriously as it had appeared. Hopefully the same will happen to poor Jeff.

Miserable though this legacy of a career in rock is, it doesn't lead directly to death – like a less localised malady did for John Bonham when, to show what a hell of a fellow he was, he held down 16 vodkas during a pub luncheon on 24th September 1980. At a rehearsal-cum-social gathering round at Jimmy Page's that afternoon, he carried on imbibing until he was poured onto a bed to sleep it off. By the next morning, he'd turned blue, and before that creepy day was done, Led Zeppelin had given up the ghost too.

A few months later, Eric Clapton's admission to a hospital in Minnesota necessitated the cancellation of a US tour to promote his latest LP, *Another Ticket*. A combination of first night nerves and a correlated drinking binge had caused an internal haemorrhage requiring several weeks of treatment and convalescence. Boozing seemed to have been his way of dealing with emergence from heroin addiction, but *Another Ticket*, 1982's *Best Of…* and 1983's *Money And Cigarettes* seemed to me to be purchased largely out of habit by the kind of consumer for whom information that a favoured performer's latest disc is "like the one before" is praise indeed. Clapton was also forging an unofficial second career with psychiatrist-couch discourses to his eulogists about his life, his soul, his torment. Eric often bitched about The Yardbirds too. "The guitar players who play with them don't like them," he once assured Jann Wenner of *Rolling Stone* magazine. "I was fooled into joining the group, attracted by the pop thing, the big money and travelling around, and little chicks. You lose a lot of your original values."

> *"Jim approached me about a reformation for the Marquee anniversary, with others including Paul"*

One of Eric's friends, ex-*Melody Maker* writer Chris Welch, would comment disobligingly about Paul Samwell-Smith ("a fat, middle-aged gentleman") when reviewing a group called The Yardbirds who had taken the Marquee stage on 22nd July 1982 as part of the club's celebrations of 20 years in business. There was also a second and final British appearance by this line-up – to raise funds for a children's hospital – at Surbiton's Ritz club on 8th September.

"I was back in London," recalls Chris Dreja of this event, "doing mostly design and advertising, when Jim approached me about a reformation for the Marquee anniversary, with others including Paul." (Dreja had already delved into the past with 1981's *Afternoon Tea*, a spoken-word album of reminiscences with Jim McCarty, with whom Chris was to co-author a 1983 Yardbirds' memoir.) As Keith couldn't make the reunion (for the most absolute reason), and none of Clapton, Beck and Page could be persuaded to pitch in either, Dreja, McCarty and Samwell-Smith went the distance with substitutes: mouth-organist Mark Feltham from Nine Below Zero, John Fiddler, mainstay of Medicine Head, on lead vocals – a poignant touch, bearing in mind Keith's earlier involvement with that band – and John Knightsbridge duplicating Jeff's solos.

If not on the scale of Moses re-appearing before the Israelites from the misted summit of Mount Sinai, the return to the Marquee – bootlegged on a double-album – was at least on the same level as The Animals' reunion bash at Newcastle City Hall. The Yardbirds, just as much as their cramped audience, were ecstatic about being so rabidly remembered. Even the grandchildren of those who'd spent evenings with them in the Craw Daddy knew 'For Your Love', re-released that March: it was an anthem almost as synonymous with Swinging London as 'You'll Never Walk Alone' to Liverpool.

At the Surbiton 'home game', pride in Surrey's cradling of The Yardbirds was rekindled for those who'd stayed in the picture about the group's activities since before 'For Your Love'. For them, Chris, Jim, Paul and the lads' 50-odd minutes on stage were the proverbial 'something to tell your grandchildren about'... Others weren't so sure. Only a miracle could have rescued the show from anti-climax when the buzzing tribes filed out, blood pressure dropping in the early autumn chill. All the same, a spirited 'Heart Full Of Soul' finale had sparked off a delirium of applause. There were also renditions of 'Back In The USA' – 1959 vintage Chuck Berry – Taj Mahal's 'Statesboro' Blues', and self-written 'Back Where I Started', propelled by Canned Heat's patented blues-boogie drone.

'Back Where I Started', in a more melodic and controlled form, was the initial A-side to spring from *A Box Of Frogs*, the first of two albums by the three original Yardbirds plus John Fiddler and studio ancillaries such as Jeff Beck, Rory Gallagher and, from the latter-day Mott The Hoople, Ray Majors – but the live version was more transfixing. You had to have been there.

Much more *Led Zeppelin* than *Yardbirds*, the rest of *A Box Of Frogs* embraced mostly lyrics of un-'Happenings Ten Years Time Ago' clarity on top of other fresh modifications of patterns from the 'contemporary rock' straitjacket the old comrades gladly wore. It was a collection that certain of their more commercially-fêted former associates might have been proud to own among their finest work. Yet repeated spins didn't put more than one or two individual tracks in sharper focus for me, and I started wishing, now and then, for some musical dirt, something a bit coarse, to capsize producer Samwell-Smith's digitised layers of sound.

Somehow it was too pat, too dovetailed, too American... But who the hell was I to criticise *A Box Of Frogs* when it jumped to Number 45 in the *Billboard* list, qualifying Paul's premise that "there's something of the Yardbirds that is of today instead of being history". Chris Dreja was to add: "I felt the old energy coming back, and had written a few bits and pieces. I liked the recording side, and being with friends once more, but Paul and I didn't want to become working musicians again." As it happened, Chris – bearded to the cheek-bones and wearing sunglasses – had stuck it out for a post-Surbiton in-concert TV special in Spain.

Months after its release, I'd bought the 'Back Where I Started' 45 without realising an album came with it. The making of another *Roger The Engineer* album seemed as unlikely as Muhammed Ali regaining his world heavyweight title back in 1975 – though he'd been full of surprises then, hadn't he? Wanting magic, all I got from 'Back Where I Started' was mere music, but I was glad to possess it.

To be brutal, *A Box Of Frogs* was much of a muchness – and its follow-up, 1986's *Strange Land*,

"There is something of The Yardbirds that is of today instead of being history"

even more so. Ian Dury was that album's most negotiable guest, having left Kilburn & The High Roads for solo acclaim, beginning as – so one periodical described him – "a sort of dirty old man of punk". His spitting out of the Chris Dreja-penned 'Average' in characteristic Cockney rather knocked into a cocked hat the contributions of Jimmy Page, Graham Gouldman (on another crack at 'Heart Full Of Soul') and Peter Haycock, guitarist from The Climax Chicago Blues Band, on an album shorn of corporate identity. The critic who imagines himself a wit might have applied the adjective 'average' to the whole of the *Strange Land* effort.

In any case, simply making a record wasn't enough. In the 1980s you had to bawl it from the rooftops. What about the plugger paid to get it on radio playlists? How about the video? Any news on the TV advert to go with it? How about using one of those adenoidal streets-of-Islington voice-overs that people seem to go for nowadays? It could be scheduled before the last part of the *Chart Show* on Friday between 'Britain's noisiest crisps' and the government health warning about AIDS. If all you did was post review copies to the music papers, you might as well have chucked *Strange Land* out of the window.

Where did it fit in anyway? The seasons of pop were continuing on their endless cycle. After punk came a mod revival, a rockabilly craze, and later a resurgence of psychedelia which, when fused with renewed interest in modern jazz, resulted in acid jazz. In among many of the various strands of dance-floor-oriented music that have developed, be it techno, trance, ambient jazz, hardcore, jungle, ragga – many of which display a crossover from reality to a wild dream via LSD and its ecstasy descendant – there's a wealth of instrumental meanderings, perfunctory lyrics, and evidence of painstaking analysis of early Pink Floyd and Jimi Hendrix, as well as The Soft Machine, Hawkwind and Van Der Graaf Generator, and, inevitably, The Yardbirds. Respective lead singers from Echo & The Bunnymen and Bauhaus appropriated aspects of Keith Relf's style, just as Chrissie Hynde of The Pretenders and Adam Ant had with both Relf and Ray Davies. And guitarists everywhere still argued over who was best between Clapton, Page and Beck.

By the early 1980s, after Britain's tax laws had liberated the gypsy in his soul for a year, Jeff Beck had re-ensconced himself in his Sussex manor house, which dated back to the Reformation – as attested by stone-flagged floors and fireplaces with space for half a tree to blaze in them. For a while, the returned owner's life revolved around restoring the building – as far as modern conveniences would permit – to its original state, and tinkering with his collection of hot-rod racing cars. To the consternation of his manager, Jeff was thus inviting injury to digits more precious now that he was inclined not to use plectrums so much (partly, he admits, because he kept dropping them), and was thinking aloud about a fingered acoustic LP: "I'd love to do a way-out album just using classical guitar, probably with an orchestra on a few tracks. Maybe that would be too sweet, so I'd use synthesisers. They don't sound as human, but they're certainly a lot cheaper."

Putting action over debate with another pipe-dream, Beck tried and then scrapped a recording with a big-band: brass, woodwinds, two bass players, two drummers and three additional guitarists. But his 1985 single 'Ambitious' was more in keeping with passing trends, complete with cameos from Donny Osmond and Alice Cooper – both back in Hot 100 favour – on the accompanying video.

In common with Donny, Alice and nearly ever other 1980s pop star, Beck was also doing his bit for charity. The most remarkable instance was him singing a sporting 'Hi Ho Silver Lining' when The Yardbirds' three most illustrious guitarists were persuaded by ex-Small Face Ronnie Lane to appear together on 20th September 1983 at the Royal Albert Hall with other musical paladins in aid of Action for Muscular Sclerosis.

Until then, Jimmy Page had been sighted less often than the Loch Ness Monster. Interest in him had been sustained, however, via the unstoppable Led Zeppelin bootleg industry, his 1982 soundtrack to nasty *Death Wish II*, and reissues of such as *No Introduction Necessary* and further items that had acquired historical importance through his old band's global renown. There was little escape from Led Zeppelin either for John Paul Jones or Robert Plant, who caved in too when pressured to regroup for *Live Aid* and later events, at which John Bonham's son Jason proved very much a chip off the old block. Jimmy Page also formed The Firm with Bad Company's Paul Rodgers, a venture subject to critiques as mixed as those for 1988's solo *Outrider*, and then his teaming-up with David Coverdale from Deep Purple offshoot Whitesnake.

Meanwhile Eric Clapton's extraordinary popularity meant that, from the early 1990s, he could occupy the Royal Albert Hall for a regular few weeks of standing-room-only concerts every winter, with some evenings devoted solely to the blues – as you'd expect from one who'd so furthered the cause.

"The house band at the Station Tavern, led by McCarty, was as near as you'd get to The Yardbirds at the time"

For the price of a pint, you could hear just as much of the stuff at blues sessions held every Wednesday in west London's Station Tavern, just a couple of miles away from the Albert Hall. The house band was led by Jim McCarty, and was as near as you'd get to The Yardbirds at that time, leaning heavily as they did upon that august group's repertoire – just as The Blues Band, formed by Paul Jones and Tom McGuinness in 1979, did on that of Manfred Mann. Finding themselves at the same bookings time and time again, The Blues Band and McCarty's combo had at least the opportunity to form genuine friendships rather than simply play host to starstruck fans. Some fans – especially those still-libidinous matrons, rich enough to follow a favoured act round the country – would feel strangely disappointed that an icon once worshipped from afar was now touchable, offering conversation as a preferred alternative to vanishing into the dark. How ordinary – even boring – he was, noticing whether you'd lost weight or grown a fringe, asking after your family, and bringing you up to date on his own. Yet once he and the others mounted the stage, they could still belt out the old magic, even if no-one was getting any younger.

At 44, Jim McCarty had more than enough hair left to brush forward like a teenager when he was guest of honour with April, Jason and Matthew Relf, Keith's widow and children, holding court to the fewer than 50 devotees who turned out the day Richard MacKay lost his shirt in the cavernous Oxford hall he'd booked for a Yardbirds international convention in September 1987. Chief among its diversions were the playing of a 'modern dance' tape by the Relf brothers, and game Jim rattling the traps and singing 'Train Kept A-Rollin''.

Around this time Jim got together with the original Yardbirds guitarist to form the Top Topham-Jim McCarty Blues Band, a quartet whose 1960s R&B pedigree was enhanced further by bass player Rod Demick, once of The Wheels, who'd tussled with Them for bookings in Belfast's jive hives, and had released 'Gloria' as an EMI A-side a few weeks before Them put it on a Decca B-side. But it was 20-something American guitarist 'Detroit' John Idan who dominated proceedings in the Topham-McCarty band, in the same manner as Steve Winwood had with The Spencer Davis Group. Idan sang all the numbers (bar Demick's 'Gloria' and a McCarty lead vocal) from 'Heart Full Of Soul' and 'For Your Love' to 'Roadrunner', 'Carol' and a 'Smokestack Lightning' that was nowadays more Howlin' Wolf than *Five Live Yardbirds*.

Having elicited a glowing review from a *Guardian* journalist present at the Station Tavern in 1988, the group remained a club attraction until 13th July 1990, when Topham announced his imminent departure after a performance at Reading's *After Dark* – in which, for the last of two encores, 'I Got My Mojo Working', he had abandoned his guitar to shake maracas like a man possessed. Topham was still to be seen guesting on small British stages in the late 1990s.

> *"Jim got together with the original Yardbirds guitarist to form the Topham-McCarty Blues Band"*

The wisdom of the decision to wash his hands of the group might have been confirmed almost two years later had Anthony attended a dismal 12-hour blues festival at Wokingham's Phoenix Plaza leisure centre. It was a bastard of a day. Outside it was not quite a gale, and inside there was so much hanging about that the running-order was well behind schedule by mid-afternoon when the compere did The Downliners Sect no favours by choosing to precede them with a singing spot of his own, which all but emptied the auditorium. It might have defied an Elvis Presley risen from the dead to go down well after that, but the Sect managed it. From tall, gaunt Keith Grant to diminutive Don Craine in his perpetual deerstalker (his "headcoat") they looked a motley crew, but were to be admired for just about winning. Most of the customers had drifted away once more to the bar, the bowling alley and other of the complex's diversions by the time The Jim McCarty Band – with Topham's replacement, Ray Majors – piled into an opening instrumental.

The hall stayed just as empty, and if the ice-breaking 'Heart Full Of Soul' hadn't filled it, nothing else could have – because the only other number directly associated with The Yardbirds was a hard-bought encore that resuscitated 'Jeff's Boogie'. But the self-composed 'Slow Drivers' and the 'Hey Joe' big finish had been strong enough to shine through a sound balance in which words were either incomprehensible or simply inaudible.

The following Wednesday, The Jim McCarty Band were back wowing 'em at the jolly old Station Tavern, where bad experiences like the Phoenix Plaza could sink in backwaters of memory.

Among the difficulties of writing a biography – particularly of a group rather than an individual – is that real life doesn't run as smoothly as fiction. Nevertheless, this seems an appropriate moment to introduce an aspect of The Yardbirds history that hitherto has been discussed in cursory fashion at most. It concerns Jim McCarty's parallel career as a colossus of new-age music.

Association with a non-melodic instrument to the rear of the stage prejudices the acceptance of pop drummers as plausible composers – or plausible anything – by those who imagine that any fool can bash drums. "What I have to combat," Ringo Starr had moaned at the beginning of his life as an ex-Beatle, "is that image of me as the downtrodden drummer. You don't know how hard it is to fight that."

Talents from behind the kit who were also up against such undervaluation included David Essex, comedian Russ Abbott – and Jim McCarty who, despite co-writing The Yardbirds most enduring songs, and his subsequent founding of Renaissance and lesser known but equally scintillating outfits, suffered from years of categorisation as an incorrigible rhythm-and-blues sticksman.

Yet in the same way that George Harrison lent his celebrity to Krishna consciousness, and Reg Presley to research into crop circles, McCarty's name became synonymous with 'new age', the only wave of essentially instrumental music to have reached a mass public since jazz-rock.

Stairway – the UK's most widely acclaimed new-age outfit – was actually Jim and Louis Cennamo (both trained spiritual or 'contact' healers by this time), reactivating in the new idiom the pastoral lyricism, Gregorian chant and other reference points once associated with The Yardbirds and their more subdued artistic descendants.

If you liked 'Still I'm Sad', 'Turn Into Earth' (once part of Stairway's concert repertoire) and, OK, The Herd's 'From The Underworld', then you'd like Stairway, and maybe further acts for whom the abyss between new age and more orthodox pop isn't uncrossable – an off-the-cuff instance from the realms of black R&B is from *Yes We Can*, a 1970 album by Lee Dorsey, in which 'Occapella' switches smoothly from verses jittery with percussion to a choral suspension that might have been lifted by time machine from some mellow new-age compact disc. More germane to this book perhaps is Jeff Beck's funereal-paced 'Final Peace' improvisation from 1980's *There And Back*, derided by one critic as "fuzak" (a cross between muzak and jazz-rock fusion – get it?).

> *"If you liked 'Still I'm Sad', 'Turn Into Earth', and The Herd's 'From The Underworld', then you'd like Stairway"*

Each of these examples would not be regarded as 'pure' new age, far from it. While you might be able to recognise it when it chances upon your ear, pure new age flouts precise definition. Is it music for people who don't like music but think they ought to? Is it merely irritating aural wallpaper? (Even *Sound Waves*, newsletter of the New Age Music Association, is irked by the conveyor-belt creation of "bleeping whale music".) Or is new age rock'n'roll's most exquisite form?

By applying a little mental athleticism, what might be described as rock'n'roll can peep out sometimes from beneath the swirling backwash, but the infrequent vocals on most new-age recordings were – and are – typified by a long (and frequently unhummable) melody line and either wordless singing or a one-line lyric, such as McCarty's 'I Choose Love' from Stairway's *Chakra Dance*.

Jim and Louis, though, usually hedged their bets with two or three tartly-arranged songs per album. Fragrant 'Lavender Down' from *Moonstone* – Stairway's most 'accessible' offering – was to bear re-recording by McCarty in a rock context, and he thought highly enough of the spellbinding 'Bird Of Paradise' from the same album to try it himself later (for a then-unknown purpose), substituting Jane Relf's guest vocal for his own on the same backing track – though he seemed in need of a sharp stick to hit the highest notes when his version was released eventually on a narrowly-circulated compilation cassette, *The Yardbirds Offshoots' Greatest Hits*. Neither 'Bird Of Paradise' nor 'Ship Of Happiness' (from 1987's *Aquamarine*) would have been out of place on *Renaissance*, or even possibly *Yardbirds*.

'Throat Chakra' was one of only two McCarty compositions on *Chakra Dance*, but Jim was the sole writer of the all-instrumental *Medicine Dance*, which featured one-word animal titles – 'Lynx', 'Wolf', 'Horse', 'Deer' and so on – and had him pounding a full drum kit, almost *à la Five Live Yardbirds* on some pieces.

> *"In the ethnic shop, buying joss sticks, you may have been unaware that the music hovering in the background was by a former Yardbird"*

Jim chose, however, to play keyboards when *Medicine Dance* received its concert premiere in 1992, courtesy of the with-it vicar of the capacious St James' Church in London's Piccadilly. In dry-cleaned jumper-and-jeans or 'babytime' garb, a lot of the congregation scorned the pews to either sit preciously cross-legged or, under Stairway's musical sorcery, hurl themselves about in the aisles with beatific self-consciousness like the flower power idiot-dancers they once were. I disliked them intensely.

When stumbling out to the nearest licensed premises, we noticed an array of new-age CDs and cassettes on sale in the church vestibule. During their seven-or-so years of activity, Stairway shifted over 50,000 albums via outlets like this, usually not chart-return shops, otherwise chart placings might well have been found. Instead, in the 'ethnic' shop where he's buying his joss-sticks, the man-in-the-street was unlikely to be aware that the music hovering in the background was by a once and future Yardbird.

Jim's first 'solo' album, *Out Of The Dark* (attributed to James McCarty) was an all-song offering with across-the-board guest musicians such as Jane Relf, Clifford White, Eddie Phillips, Matthew Fisher, Rod Demick and Don Craine. It took several plays for me to get acclimatised to arrangements that adhered to such a just-below-moderato tempo – though as it was issued by a new-age company (with pictures of Stonehenge all over the sleeve) maybe that was almost the point.

Maybe no track was designed to be in higher profile than another – though, strictly speaking, they all kicked against 'low stress' dictates by being about something, albeit via a mix of discursive lyrical abstraction and clear formal definition in the arrangements. Some items stood out eventually – like 'Just Breaking Through', 'Signs From An Age Gone By', 'What If Summer Never Came' (shades of The Mamas & The Papas) and 'Home Is Where The Heart Is', which wouldn't have been out of place on a mid-1980s Eric Clapton album. Ultimately, *Out Of The Dark* was as much a feathery type of soul music as it was new age – it seemed reminiscent at times of a rustic Stylistics or Three Degrees, gorged as it was with the velvet-smooth harmonies and intricate woodwind parts common to both.

It might have been personal bias that caused me to review it as "a strong contender for my favourite album of 1994", but I was able to be more objective about *In Search Of The Dreamchild* and 1996's *Gothic Dream* by Pilgrim. This outfit was the yoking together of McCarty, John Richardson, Carmen Willcox and singer Tania Matchett – all of whom emerged with credit when getting to grips with verses from Keats, Byron, Shelley, Poe (and Willcox) over a production criterion that Jim would call 'organic' – in other words, a superimposition of acoustic instruments that camouflaged the unavoidable electronic programming. And throughout there were melodies that, like 'The Moonlight Skater', may tarry with thee unto death.

CHAPTER 14

SIGNS FROM AN AGE GONE BY

*"We realised there were great audiences
out there, of all ages ... I suddenly thought
there'd be nothing to lose working with Jim
again on a new Yardbirds."*

CHRIS DREJA

In the late 1980s, it was clear that McCarty, Beck, Page *et al* could fan creative fires as vigorously as they liked, but they'd never be as hot as they were in the fabulous 1960s. Like many other Sixties icons they were constantly being told – infuriatingly – that their best work was behind them. Yet there were fiscal advantages in a public of a certain age becoming dazzled by rose-tinted musical memories: at one point in 1987 all but one record in the Top Ten was either a reissue or an arrangement of an old song.

Advertising soundtracks were to prove another lucrative spin-off of the burgeoning nostalgia craze. Them's 'Baby Please Don't Go' leapt out of the small screen with a voice-over extolling the virtues of a new kind of Peugeot. The Kinks, The Dave Clark Five, The Rolling Stones, The Troggs and The Swinging Blue Jeans travelled the same road – and the offices of Miller Lite lager sent The Hollies' 20-year-old 'He Ain't Heavy (He's My Brother)' to the very summit of the Top Ten.

Envious beat group contemporaries watched The Hollies on *Top Of The Pops* and wondered. Some were already regulars at 'Oldies *Nachts*' in Germany, which attracted Cecil B de Mille-sized crowds – of all ages – to be enthralled by hours of performances, one after the other, on stages framed by sky-clawing scaffolding, giant video screens and lighting gantries like oil derricks. When had The Searchers, Freddie & The Dreamers, Dave Dee, Dozy, Beaky, Mick & Tich – or any beat group – ever been as loud and clear or seen so well?

These spectaculars dwarfed any given *Sounds Of The Sixties* evening in Britain, though Dave Dee tried hard with his organisation of a charity extravaganza entitled *Heroes And Villains* at London's Dominion Theatre (a couple of hundred yards from the 100 Club) in October 1985 – perhaps the most pivotal 'live' event to nudge the 1960s revival out of neutral. Current chart status had no meaning on such occasions, but this scene was to become less of an artistic graveyard than it was in the 1970s – though it's open to conjecture whether looking forward to the past is a healthy situation for any musician to be in.

Maybe the Sixties nostalgia trail was the logical conclusion of that bilious music journalism cliché, Growing Old With Your Audience – except that if, like me, you were a child of the 1960s, you were supposed to be settled into a proper job and parenthood, and be saving up for a CD player in order to hear the dandruff falling from the sparse hair of Van Morrison, Phil Collins, Mark Knopfler and other purveyors of cultured contemporary pop. Either that or you disguised your middle-age crisis as a second adolescence – or vice-versa. At any rate, this obsession (far more socially acceptable than, say, collating information about donkeys' false teeth) was pouring huge amounts into the English Tourist Board's coffers for conducted treks around London and Liverpool to such golgothas as the Abbey Road zebra crossing and the dingy terrace where Ringo was born.

Mementos of what your children had missed blared from jukebox, disco turntable and bar-band repertoire; and the original performers of the repromoted old classics would sometimes still be seen setting up their gear at opening time – as was John Mayall, coming up for his 60th birthday, at London's Town And Country Club venue (where his name had been misspelt on the tickets).

> *"It's open to conjecture whether looking forward to the past is a healthy situation for any musician to be in"*

A bygone era was, therefore, faraway no more. For Chris Dreja, there was one evening when it seemed too close for comfort. "Very occasionally, after Box Of Frogs, I sat in with Jim's blues band. One of these was recorded at the 100 Club as a Yardbirds reunion concert. I had a painful cyst on my back, and I didn't enjoy the gig – and more or less decided never to do it again."

In the late 1980s there was little interest in a Yardbirds reassessment among music press hacks. When I rang *Q* magazine ("The modern guide to music and more") to suggest a retrospective, they sniggered – even in the light of exploitation by various corporate and individual entrepreneurs that would place over 30 Yardbirds compilations (including a boxed set of more than 70 tracks) in the shops by 1990.

Some previously unheard items among this lot were intriguing – like the 'real sitar' version of 'Heart Full Of Soul', or a slightly longer 'He's Always There' – but despite selection for grand-sounding umbrella titles like *Classic Cuts* and *Best Of British Rock*, a barrel-scraping majority were documentary rather than recreational: backing tracks, indolent improvisations around 12-bar blues and suchlike digressions. There were enough Yardbirds worshippers still around, though, to push such releases into a profit position after information about them was inserted in retailer catalogues.

There would also be *Top Of The Pops* visitations – either on video or in the chicken-necked flesh – with the latest single releases by such as The Rolling Stones, The Kinks, George Harrison, The Bee Gees, Alice Cooper, Roy Orbison and Cliff Richard – all justifying the words of John McNally of The Searchers: "You don't have to be young to make good records." Even on Sixties nights in the most dismal locations, The Searchers, Dave Dee *et al*, The Troggs and those of corresponding vintage would lure a strikingly young crowd by counterpoising contemporary offerings with the ancient chestnuts.

> *"In the late 1980s there was little interest in a Yardbirds reassessment among music press hacks"*

While there'd be no more 'Hi Ho Silver Lining' after the Albert Hall Multiple Sclerosis benefit, Jeff Beck was to release a self-indulgent revival of The Troggs' 'Wild Thing' in 1986, and trawl through aspects of his own past too – though not quite yet. Demo sessions – some involving Lemmy Kilminster of Motorhead (and former Rockin' Vicker) on bass – were underway for *Guitar Shop*, the next official Beck album, when, at some social gathering in Los Angeles, Jeff had been pleased to meet former Sex Pistols svengali Malcolm McLaren, whose two albums, *Duck Rock* and *Fans*, he owned. In reciprocation, 42-year-old Malcolm gushed that the ex-Yardbird was "the garage mechanic of all time, the rock'n'roll blizzard-maker, the Paganini of the guitar". He was thus delighted – and reckoning up the dollars immediately – when Beck volunteered to play on the follow-up to *Fans*.

There remains bitter division over McLaren. Was he a cynical, manipulative situationist or merely a bourgeois shopkeeper sucked into a vortex of circumstances he was unable to resist? Certainly his management of the Sex Pistols had marked the apogee of punk, and facilitated the promotion of himself as an artist. This had brought forth a body of work that was more fascinating in its blending of often-clashing ideas than anything by his former clients. Fans had put "Un Bel di Vedremo" from Puccini's *Madame Butterfly* into the hit parade – albeit suspended over a disco rhythm and interrupted by a modern interpretation that included McLaren's callous monologue.

But 1989's *Waltz Darling* was to take a flagrant contempt for musical and historical context further via the disparate sounds – and time signatures – of Beck, former James Brown bass guitarist-turned-solo-star Bootsy Collins, and a 60-piece orchestra, to effect a curious but enticing marriage of the Modern Dance and Viennese waltzes. Coinciding with a non-story about Jeff and a model 20 years his junior which dominated *The Sun*'s front page one news-starved morning in August 1989, *Waltz Darling*'s 'House Of the Blue Danube' was the last singles chart entry involving Beck to date – and, bar the recurring reissues of 'Hi Ho Silver Lining', perhaps for all time.

As the 1990s approached there were also Beck guitar cameos (and even bit-parts as an actor) in the British television series *The Comic Strip Presents...* It was on the recommendation of Peter Richardson, one of the Comic Strip stars, that Jeff first checked out 100 Club regulars The Big Town Playboys, who went on to back him on 1993's *Crazy Legs*, a Gene Vincent & The Blue Caps tribute album that recalled his apprenticeship under Cal Danger and Kerry Rapid over a quarter of a century earlier.

He'd reached back over the years more passively by escorting his then-girlfriend along Latimer Road for evenings in the Station Tavern during Jim McCarty's ongoing residency. Jimmy Page, prior to his *UnLedded* reunion with Robert Plant in 1994, was to put his head round the door too, and Eric Clapton had been there late in 1992 when The Jim McCarty Band played the Hard Rock Cafe off Hyde Park.

> *"Jim, Jeff, Jimmy and Chris were there when the Yardbirds were inducted into the Rock & Roll Hall Of Fame"*

After the show, Jim caught Eric's eye and was acknowledged with the merest nod, as if to a common acquaintance. The following January, Clapton wasn't around to join Jim, Jeff, Jimmy and Chris when The Yardbirds were inducted into The Rock & Roll Hall Of Fame at New York's upper-crust Waldorf-Astoria Hotel in front of the cream of the US music industry. The awards were followed by an 'impromptu' jam in which those ex-Yardbirds that took part held their own amid admiring Me-Generation performers, who seemed more than happy to exalt and emulate these middle-aged legends, despite the 'good' foreheads, crow's feet and belts loosened to the last hole.

During the rest of the winter that followed the Hall Of Fame ceremonials, Jim McCarty was in the States again – as a temporary Pretty Thing. "It was the idea of George Paulus, a record archivist," Jim explained, "for Dick Taylor, Phil May and I to record some R&B in Seagrape, a Chicago studio with a library of equipment that the Chess legends might have used, and using US musicians like Richard Hite, bass player from Canned Heat. We taped a lot of Bo Diddley, Chuck Berry – all the usual stuff – and a great version of Aretha Franklin's 'Chain Of Fools'. Phil sang really well – and I've always been surprised at how underrated Dick has been as a guitarist. While we were there, we also managed a few local club gigs, every one of them packed out, despite the freezing cold and constant blizzards."

For me, there's not that much difference between this venture and The Traveling Wilburys, the gathering of George Harrison, Jeff Lynne, Bob Dylan, Roy Orbison and Tom Petty, who began as just five geezers messing about in Dylan's garage over a long afternoon, but became bound in a 'brotherhood'.

Back in England, both Eric Clapton and Steve Winwood had also rolled up with some musical cronies and acoustic guitars to the disbelief of respectful folk club audiences in Surrey and Birmingham (as Steve put it: "You can't really say you have to play 1000 times better in front of 20,000 people than you do in front of 20.") Meanwhile a combine more durable than the reborn (and disappointing) Traffic or The Wilburys had surfaced via the Home Counties R&B old boy network. The British Invasion All-Stars were less noteworthy for their music than how they were turned into a cottage industry by a certain Michael Bernard Ober, a New Yorker who, as an 11-year-old schoolboy, had watched The Beatles' debut on *The Ed Sullivan Show* in 1964, and conceived an unfading passion for British beat groups – as he put it, "sounds that made love to my mind".

> *"Chris Dreja joined the Jim McCarty band for what was billed as* The Yardbirds Reunion Concert*"*

In his own way, Ober did much to keep the flame of 1960s beat groups alive. In 1975, he'd written a most erudite epistle to a UK pop weekly about his own combo, That Hideous Strength, whose EP contained "Vintage English Rock 'N' Roll ... our tribute to the English groups of the 1960s – Downliners Sect, Pretty Things, Who, Creation, Move etc." The Sect's Don Craine remembers keeping a cut-out of that letter, not knowing then that he would meet and work with its writer almost 15 years later. A post as a US government accountant brought Mike Ober to London in 1989 for a stay lasting four years. Like the man who paid to conduct the London Symphony Orchestra at the Albert Hall for just one night, Mike – still crazy about British beat – also had the wherewithal to fulfil a dream.

So began a liaison that was to bring some of Ober's boyhood heroes – including ex-members of The Yardbirds – to a wider public than they might have warranted in the ordinary course of events. With Don Craine appointed general manager of Ober's Brisk Productions company and Promised Land record label, there followed a vast (and not inexpensive) array of vintage and newly-recorded cassettes, CDs and videos, intended to capture "the sound of the future, the beat of the past" – or how some might expect a 1960s beat group to be 30 years of recording technology later.

The enterprise included an (amateurishly made) video called *Guide To Yardbirds Drumming* by Jim McCarty, and a Stairway recital at the Church in Piccadilly. They also branched out into the printed word with *The Downliners Sect* and two softbound volumes of *Yardbirds World* back copies. It was also through Promised Land that Richard MacKay (who'd first introduced McCarty to Ober) was able to get *Musical Spectrum*, *Enchanted Caress* and a Renaissance in-concert album to any interested public.

Ober was on-hand too for a "historic jam", shot one summer's night down Latimer Road, where Craine, Keith Grant and dimmer luminaries of the British blues firmament joined McCarty's band on-stage to run though a ramshackle mixture of 'Roadrunner', 'Hoochie Coochie Man', 'Too Much Monkey Business' and the like, as well as pieces peculiar to both the Sect and The Yardbirds.

From this crowded evening, Brisk/Promised Land's flagship act smouldered into form. The British

Invasion All-Stars started as a tawdry throwing together of Don, Keith, Jim, Ray Phillips from The Nashville Teens – one of the better lead singers of the beat boom – and guitarist Eddie Phillips (no relation), whose 15 minutes with The Creation was long gone. With every fretful quaver costing Mike money, *Regression*, the maiden album of "the ultimate supergroup of the new decade", was a rushed job – brisk, you might say – revealing not the ghost of the 1960s confronting the spirit of the 1990s, but nothing more than merely competent live-in-the-studio stabs at 'House Of The Rising Sun', 'Nadine', 'Train Kept A-Rolling' (with McCarty's lead vocals struggling to be heard from behind the kit), 'Summertime Blues', 'My Generation' and other mutually over-familiar standards. Mike's argument was that "doing obscure material would not generate airplay".

The attendant video went in one eye and out the other. Yet the chaps seemed to have fun in it, notably in a simulated auto-destruction of inflatable toy guitars in 'My Generation'. But rather than this kind of gentle send-up, the video – and more so the record – may have carried more impact if the All-Stars had dug up their own buried gimmicks (Eddie Phillips scraping a violin bow across his guitar strings, for instance). And the pedestrian atmosphere that marred *Regression* may have been lifted had it been an in-concert effort instead. Alternatively, perhaps the All-Stars' time – and Ober's cash – could have been better spent on a fortnight in a proper studio, working on fresh material as Box Of Frogs had. Like The Traveling Wilburys, it wasn't as if the All-Stars were short of songwriters.

That's being wise after the event. At the time, the All-Stars shrugged their shoulders, banked their promptly-paid royalty cheques and returned to everyday activities. They weren't to know then that *Regression*, lost opportunity though it was, represented only the tip of Mike Ober's iceberg. Even the initial batch of Promised Land merchandise proved a worthwhile commercial strategy, particularly in the US and Japan – for whom, as implied by the 'British Invasion' appellation, it was ultimately targeted.

Artistic matters were to improve to varying degrees. *United*, the follow-up to *Regression*, demonstrated there was more to these British Invasion boys than a bunch of has-beens accepting hand-outs from someone with more money than sense. Though retreads of hits from each member's individual catalogue were musical equivalents of genetically-modified food, could any listener not derive vicarious delight from Phil May pitching into 'Shapes Of Things', or Ray Phillips' 'Gimme Some Lovin'? Far healthier was the selection of inventive originals like Grant and Craine's 'Bad Penny' and McCarty's 'Heavy Weather' – which went down nearly as well as his Yardbirds' smashes on the occasion when Chris Dreja joined The Jim McCarty Band for what Mike Ober felt entitled to call *The Yardbirds Reunion Concert* on the subsequent cassette.

As well as planning a Jane Relf solo venture – until she said no – Ober had been agitating for Dreja, McCarty and any other available former Yardbirds to record an interpretation of the first Led Zeppelin album. The closest he came was on 1994's *The Yardbirds Experience* – essentially the All-Stars plus Noel Redding, Jimi Hendrix's bass player – which embraced rehashes of Led Zeppelin's 'Communication Breakdown' and 'Whole Lotta Love' amid copies of previously-released tracks from *United* and further corner-cutting selections such as an ill-advised 'Lavender Down'.

Pukka Stairway items – and Jim McCarty's neo-falsetto 'Bird Of Paradise' – had rounded off *The*

Yardbirds Offshoots Greatest Hits. From the title alone you may imagine wrongly that this cassette album embraced the likes of Beck's 'Hi-Ho Silver Lining' and the Together 45, but what we actually had here were mostly excerpts from Promised Land's output during its first – and most prolific – two years.

Sadly it couldn't last forever. Soon after *The Yardbirds Experience* was mastered (at Abbey Road, no less), Mike Ober's day job took him back to New York (and thence to Virginia) where he conducted fruitless negotiations for an All-Stars tour of the States while overseeing Brisk Productions – in the same fashion as George III tried to fight the American War of Independence from Whitehall. Over his ledgers and computer run-offs, Mike continues to daydream about a wondrous parallel dimension in which Westlife, Robbie Williams and Busta Rhymes mean nothing, and The Yardbirds, The Sect, The Pretty Things and their ilk reign supreme.

In the early 1990s you could still hear Yardbirds numbers whenever The Jim McCarty Band trod the boards, and on disc in the Brisk reprises and, more authentically, on ever more specialist repackagings. The Sonny Boy Williamson tracks were to appear on CD for the first time, and yet another pressing of the *Blowup* soundtrack was on the way too, along with a further CD boxed-set (*Train Kept A-Rollin: The Complete Giorgio Gomelsky Productions)*, bloated with unforgiving hours of everything – and I mean everything – that the band ever commited to tape with Gomelsky.

> "In 1994 Jim McCarty anchored himself to the notion that he was going to be a Yardbird again"

Who bought this stuff? Who had the patience to sit through four takes of the same backing track, a fractionally shorter edit of some rotten Italian B-side, a false start of 'Got To Hurry', one more fantastic version of 'I'm A Man' – and then spend infinitely less time actually listening to the recordings than discussing how 'interesting' its contents were? Yet to The Yardbirds' most painfully committed fans, its intrinsic worth and high retail price hardly mattered. And displayed between, say, *The Koto Music Of Japan* and *Aznavour Sings Aznavour Volume Three*, it served as a fine detail of interior decor and a handy conversational ice-breaker.

Yardbirds talk became more animated among the faithful in 1994. That's when Jim McCarty experienced a revelation. It told him there was to be no more circling around the issue with blues bands and All-Stars. He anchored himself to the notion that he was going to be a Yardbird again. Almost as if sensing what was on his mind, Peter Barton, a northern agent (and "mad bundle of energy"), approached McCarty that summer with a mighty powerful financial incentive to find a new edition of the group for an exploratory tour of Germany which might lead to more grandiose developments.

From his management offices in Lancashire, Barton also represented Animals II – a unit formed by Hilton Valentine and John Steel, the guitarist and drummer from the Eric Burdon days; then there was John Coghlan's Status Quo, Trevor Burton's Next Move and similarly cobbled-together acts. It seemed you just required the rights to an old name, no matter how obscure, to find work. You didn't even necessarily have to adapt the name and call yourselves something like The Walker Cousins, Baltej Patel's Searchers or Teddie & The Dreamers; roaming Britain in 1994, for instance, was a Hedgehoppers Anonymous with no connection whatsoever with either the 1965 one-hit-wonders (who sang 'It's Good News Week'), or with Wittering, the town from whence they came.

This kind of touring was quite different from these groups' early experiences. All an ersatz or genuine Hedgehoppers Anonymous – or an ersatz or genuine anyone – needed to take with them for these shows were instruments, a pair of drumsticks and the computer-printed folder of details about venues, where they'd find that a 'backline' of instrument amps, a megawatt PA and any keyboards needed would be ready and waiting on-stage.

You might have become too civilised to sleep in the van any more, but you didn't always have to. You could choose to fly, and be picked up at the terminal by minibus. The accommodation – Holiday Inns mostly – and meals were laid on too. There were other perks too – some of them providing solid heads of families with excuses to behave like teenagers again... but the less said about that the better.

Technical innovations like programmable desks and graphic equalisers (to help do battle against adverse venue acoustics) were among the factors that made the idea of doing it all again as attractive to Jim McCarty as it would seem to Chris Dreja in 1995 when Peter Barton rang. "I suddenly thought there'd be nothing to lose in working with Jim again on a new Yardbirds," says Chris. "We realised there were great audiences of all ages out there – even in Eastern Europe."

OUT OF
THE DARK

Y ou could argue that the future is the past all over again for The Yardbirds, as much as it was for any other entertainer stuck, however unwillingly, in a 1960s repetend. Exacerbating the situation were repackaging factories in full production, churning out merchandise like an *Ultimate Yardbirds* collection of old tracks on two CDs for Rhino Records. In 2000, however, it was gratifying to find a Yardbirds retrospective – *Cumular Limit*, another double CD – which didn't plough the same tired furrow as the others. While the outer artwork was almost unreadable (blue text on turquoise background) you couldn't wish for a more comprehensive booklet – by compiler Greg Russo – on an audio (and, if you have the technology, visual) documentary of The Yardbirds' final flight, circa 1967-1968.

As well as rediscovered media interviews and live approximations of some old smashes, there were nascent or dismantled versions of desperate studio efforts – including previously unheard compositions, along with glimpses of the future. While Led Zeppelin were telegraphed most conspicuously in a version of 'Dazed And Confused' for French TV, 'Spanish Blood', an instrumental prefacing a hilariously bungled recitation by McCarty, anticipates Jim's ventures into new age.

"The problem we face with any new record," sighs Chris Dreja, " is that, although we'd sell a lot on the strength of the name, people, especially Americans, don't like you messing with their memories. But The Yardbirds aren't a nostalgia band. The excitement, the energy still winds me up, and I'll always be a fan of The Yardbirds as much as I am a player. It's a band I'd be proud to take anywhere."

And Chris was to do so more and more as the tempo of work quickened. Whatever they may have anticipated – perhaps that an end-of-century Yardbirds comeback would be typified by less-than-half-capacity turn-outs – here they were, wowing 15,000 ticket-holders at one of many annual fixtures across Europe, featuring nigh-on 12 hours-worth of hoary old groups. Such jubilees also provided opportunities to renew forgotten friendships and rivalries with those performers either on the bill or showing up simply to watch, and regale each other with endless anecdotes about what Brian Poole said to Phil May at the Basildon Locarno in 1965.

For Chris Dreja and Jim McCarty, their ancient smashes were both milestones and millstones – The Yardbirds were far less likely to be lynched for quitting the stage without giving 'em, say, 'Back Where I Started' or 'Heavy Weather' than they would be for missing out the triumvirate of 'For Your Love', 'Heart Full Of Soul' and 'Shapes Of Things'.

Time and time again they'd find themselves at the same high-paying venues, where incorrigible old mods, rockers and hippies and their offspring didn't mind squeezing into the prescribed 'smart casuals'. As overseas representatives of Britain's performing arts, The Yardbirds had graduated from fly-in-fly-out dates in the US to coast-to-coast tours. There was a trip to Australasia in 1997, and, thanks to the opening of the eastern bloc eight years earlier, they'd been seen in territories once *verboten* to all decadent beat groups from the West.

More swiftly, they'd slipped into a domestic routine of one-nighters and further wallows in nostalgia, like the one in Minehead, and a round-Britain trek in 2002 with The Troggs and a Spencer Davis Group. Coming to terms with both their past and present situation, The Yardbirds had long understood that, whether it's Rod Demick with his Wheels in a North London pub, or The Rolling Stones at Madison Square Garden satellite-linked to unseen millions, all an intact 1960s act had to do was to be an archetypal, self-contained and comprehensive unit, spanning every familiar avenue of its professional life – all the timeless chartbusters, every change of image, every bandwagon jumped or anticipated. This included, in the Yardbirds' case, the well-received inclusion in recent concerts of 'Dream Within A Dream' from Pilgrim's *Gothic Dream*, and the title track of McCarty's *Out Of The Dark*.

While The Yardbirds could be proud, even boastful, about how well they still went down after all these years, there were no rock star-ish 'dark nights of the ego' about obesity, wrinkles and galloping alopecia – or rock star-ish anything else. Mingling with the customers in the foyer after a standing-room-only show in 1997 at Guildford Civic Hall (by tradition the final date of every Eric Clapton UK tour), they were chatting easily and offending no one queueing to be photographed with them by refusing to autograph a *Best Of The Legendary Yardbirds* straight from the merchandising stall, or someone's dog-eared *Five Live Yardbirds* sleeve, depicting Chris Dreja with most of his hair still on his head.

Mother Nature seemed to have been a little less kind to Chris than to Jim when their faces had filled the screen during a half-hour devoted to The Yardbirds in an edition of Channel Four's interrogatory *Without Walls* series in 1995. But they looked no worse than anyone else of their age, these two Yardbird survivors, as they stood joking and swapping banter between songs in the Civic Hall, while peals of laughter set the whole house off.

Musically, The Yardbirds didn't renege on their distinguished past; digging down to 'Smokestack Lightning' and working through as many later items as could be crammed into a trim 45 minutes. Spoilt for choice, there was no satisfying some people. Personally, I missed 'Still I'm Sad' (though they did perform a shortened version on a later tour), and even 'Five Long Years' would have been a more appropriate downbeat number than 'Sitting On Top Of The World'.

Perhaps the Yardbirds story could have ended there with a settling down to a prosperous artistic lassitude as British show-business treasures, guaranteed work for as long as they can stand. Like the happy ending in a Victorian novel – all the villains bested and the inheritance claimed.

Instead, a new chapter began. The group embarked on their first non-compilation LP since *Little Games*. Sessions were booked in a west London studio with olde-tyme valve equipment – albeit under conditions unthinkable in the beat boom, when (it's not much of an exaggeration to say) the order of the day had been little more than sticking a microphone in front of a band and hoping for the best. However, in 2002 The Yardbirds flew to Los Angeles to try again in more high-tech surroundings. The resulting new album is scheduled for release in March 2003 on Steve Vai's Favored Nations label.

Whatever their quality, new Yardbirds songs are free-flowing again. "Jim and I have been composing together," elucidates Chris Dreja. "It's a good partnership. I can come from an emotive riff, a progression, a sound point of view – and I enjoy writing lyrics – and Jim can come from a melodic, more musical structure."

One of their late-1990s collaborations was the song 'Original Man': "It's about Keith," explains Chris. "He was a total one-off with no role model. His look alone remains as contemporary as Oasis and The Verve." It's undeniable that the 1990s Britpop brigade – Oasis, The Verve, Kula Shaker, Pulp, Blur and the rest – relied on musical ideas from the monochrome 1960s as well as image and photographic poses. These plagiarisms, bowdlerisations, whatever, could also be heard in totally undisguised form via the spreading epidemic of 'tribute bands' – like The Bootleg Beatles, The Counterfeit Stones and The Artificial Animals. Unusually, no-one has yet had the nerve to put together a fake Yardbirds – perhaps because they caked their pop with a substance so singularly penetrating it would have been indelible even if the group retired after 'Shapes Of Things', an accomplishment that still blinds the common critic to the quality of most former members' output.

Yet for the disciples – whether there from the beginning or Box Of Frogs latecomers – everything concerning The Yardbirds will always be special – as exemplified by a homecoming charity concert for Twickenham Museum at the town's York House auditorium in October 1998. On the same Thursday evening, one of their former colleagues was appearing before a considerably larger gathering at Earl's Court. But for fate, Eric Clapton might have been brought on to duel with Gypie Mayo on the 'Smokestack Lightning' encore. Instead, Anthony 'Top' Topham was drawn from rural Wiltshire to endure the sweet torment of acclaim by association on one of these proverbial "greatest nights anyone could ever remember".

Paul Samwell-Smith was present, but not participating. Giorgio Gomelsky and Jane Relf were there too. The fire-regulation-breaking crowd contained not only elderly individuals who might once have been part of a screaming mass as amorphous as frogspawn when The Yardbirds supported The Beatles at Hammersmith Odeon, but also a younger contingent which showed they could mouth the words of 'Back Where I Started' just as accurately as 'Heart Full Of Soul'.

You name it, The Yardbirds probably delivered it: all the hits, even if 'Still I'm Sad' was but a flash of past glory; a full-blown version of 1967's last-gasp 'Little Games'; highlights from *Five Live Yardbirds*, *Roger The Engineer*, and the Box Of Frogs episode; Eric's blues pretensions in 'Sitting On Top Of The World', and nearer to the present with 'Out Of The Dark' – one of two solo vocals by Jim McCarty, as much the drummer-leader of the present group as Dave Clark had been of his Five. The lion's share of the lead singing, though, was still by Detroit John Idan, while the spirit of Keith Relf effused as abundantly from the harmonica (and 'For Your Love' bongos) of blueswailing Alan Glen – a visual hybrid of Eric Burdon and Just William but with 100 per cent proof stage presence behind mysterious sunglasses, and the latest addition to a stunning new edition of The Yardbirds, whose spell on the boards that night flew by as quickly as reading the most page-turning thriller.

THE YARDBIRDS
DIARY 1963-1968

BY DOUG HINMAN & JOE McMICHAEL

The Yardbirds have always been the stuff of rock'n'roll legend – and as is so often the case the facts behind that legend are long lost to time or at the very least shrouded in myth. The diary that follows of The Yardbirds' gigs, recordings and broadcasts began its life back in 1996 when the two compilers joined forces, hoping to answer a nagging question: "Where the hell else did these guys play besides the Craw Daddy and the Fillmore?" Pooling their research skills, already sharpened on projects concerning The Kinks and The Who, they set to their task, methodically piecing the puzzle together from scratch. Some of their results turned up in Christopher Hjort's acclaimed *Jeff's Book* (2000), while the material on the Clapton and Page years was intended for a similar book presenting a Yardbirds chronology. Now their entire work appears in distilled form here, the first detailed study based largely on original research. They are justifiably proud of the result – and hope that it finally reveals the answer to that worrying question from '96.

Jimmy Page scribbles, 1966: "Dear diary, another day on bass, but I'll be on guitar soon..."

THE YARDBIRDS
DIARY 1963-1968

The layout of this diary of The Yardbirds' live, studio and broadcasting activities is intended to be straightforward. Material has had to be condensed, but about the only abbreviation you'll see is for broadcast, as 'b/c' or 'b/cast'. Note also that geographic descriptions are present-day. Otherwise, prepare to marvel at the working life of a very, very busy band.

JUNE 1963

RELF+TOPHAM+DREJA+S-SMITH+McCARTY

sat	1	
sun	2	
mon	3	
tue	4	
wed	5	
thu	6	
fri	7	
sat	8	
sun	9	
mon	10	
tue	11	
wed	12	
thur	13	
fri	14	SOME TIME THIS MONTH THE GROUP WHICH WOULD BECOME KNOWN AS THE YARDBIRDS BEGIN REHEARSALS. THE AS-YET UNNAMED BAND WAS A MERGER OF MEMBERS OF TWO GROUPS,
sat	15	THE METROPOLIS BLUES QUARTET (KEITH RELF & PAUL SAMWELL-SMITH) AND THE COUNTRY GENTLEMAN (ANTHONY "TOP" TOPHAM, CHRIS
sun	16	DREJA & JIM McCARTY).

mon	17
tue	18
wed	19
thu	20
fri	21
sat	22
sun	23
mon	24
tue	25
wed	26
thu	27
fri	28
sat	29
sun	30

JULY 1963

mon	1	wed	17	
tue	2	thu	18	
wed	3	fri	19	
thu	4	sat	20	
fri	5	sun	21	
sat	6	mon	22	
sun	7	tue	23	
mon	8	wed	24	
tue	9	thu	25	
wed	10	fri	26	
thu	11	sat	27	
fri	12	sun	28	
sat	13	mon	29	
sun	14	**EEL PIE ISLAND HOTEL BALLROOM** TWICKENHAM, LONDON. SUPPORT CYRIL DAVIES ALLSTARS, BAND'S 1st GIG (DATE UNCONFIRMED)	tue	30
mon	15	wed	31	
tue	16			

AUGUST 1963

thu	1	sat	17	
fri	2	sun	18	
sat	3	mon	19	
sun	4	tue	20	
mon	5	wed	21	
tue	6	**RAILWAY HOTEL** HARROW, LONDON. YARDBIRDS DEP FOR CYRIL DAVIES ON ONE OF HIS REGULAR TUE GIGS AROUND THIS TIME	thu	22
wed	7	fri	23	
thu	8	sat	24	
fri	9	sun	25	
sat	10	mon	26	
sun	11	tue	27	
mon	12	wed	28	
tue	13	thu	29	
wed	14	fri	30	
thu	15	sat	31	
fri	16			

SEPTEMBER 1963

sun	1	
mon	2	
tue	3	
wed	4	
thu	5	
fri	6	**STUDIO 51** LONDON, ENGLAND. *BILLED AS THE BLUE-SOUNDS. EARLIEST DOCUMENTED DATE FOR THIS REGULAR FRIDAY RESIDENCY.*
sat	7	
sun	8	
mon	9	
tue	10	
wed	11	
thu	12	
fri	13	**STUDIO 51** LONDON, ENGLAND. *BILLED AS THE BLUE SOUNDS.*
sat	14	
sun	15	
mon	16	
tue	17	
wed	18	
thu	19	
fri	20	**STUDIO 51** LONDON, ENGLAND. *BILLED AS YARD-BIRDS.*
sat	21	
sun	22	ROLLING STONES' RESIDENCY AT CRAW DADDY, RICHMOND, LONDON, ENDS TODAY.
mon	23	
tue	24	
wed	25	
thu	26	
fri	27	**STUDIO 51** LONDON, ENGLAND. *BILLED AS YARD-BIRDS.*
sat	28	
sun	29	**STUDIO 51** LONDON, ENGLAND (4pm). **CRAW DADDY** RICHMOND, LONDON (7.45pm). *TAKE OVER FROM ROLLING STONES*
mon	30	**STUDIO 51** LONDON, ENGLAND. *BILLED AS YARD-BIRDS (AS WAS YESTERDAY'S APPEARANCE).*

OCTOBER 1963

tue	1	
wed	2	
thu	3	
fri	4	**CRAW DADDY** RICHMOND (7.45pm). **STUDIO 51** LONDON (MIDNIGHT-6am) "YARD-BIRDS", PLUS JIMMY POWELL, & GUESTS.
sat	5	
sun	6	**STUDIO 51** LONDON, ENGLAND (4pm). BILLED AS "YARD-BIRDS".
mon	7	
tue	8	
wed	9	
thu	10	
fri	11	
sat	12	
sun	13	**STUDIO 51** LONDON (4pm) "YARD-BIRDS". **CRAW DADDY** RICHMOND (7.45pm). *LIKELY ERIC CLAPTON SITS IN AROUND NOW*
mon	14	
tue	15	
wed	16	
thu	17	
fri	18	
sat	19	
sun	20	**STUDIO 51** LONDON, (4pm). **CRAW DADDY** RICHMOND (7.45pm). *POSSIBLY CLAPTON'S FIRST GIGS AS MEMBER, REPLACING TOPHAM.*
mon	21	
tue	22	
wed	23	
thu	24	
fri	25	
sat	26	
sun	27	**CRAW DADDY** RICHMOND, LONDON, ENGLAND.
mon	28	
tue	29	
wed	30	
thu	31	

NOVEMBER 1963

fri	1	
sat	2	**CRAW DADDY** STAR HOTEL, CROYDON, LONDON, ENGLAND.
sun	3	**CRAW DADDY** RICHMOND, LONDON, ENGLAND.
mon	4	
tue	5	
wed	6	
thu	7	
fri	8	**EDWINA'S** FINSBURY PARK, LONDON, ENGLAND. *GRAND OPENING OF THIS NEW CLUB.*
sat	9	**CRAW DADDY** STAR HOTEL, CROYDON, LONDON, ENGLAND.
sun	10	**CRAW DADDY** RICHMOND, LONDON. BILLED AS "THE GROUP THAT GOT SONNY BOY WILLIAMSON REAL SATISFIED".
mon	11	
tue	12	
wed	13	
thu	14	
fri	15	**EDWINA'S** FINSBURY PARK, LONDON, ENGLAND.
sat	16	**CRAW DADDY** STAR HOTEL, CROYDON, LONDON, ENGLAND.
sun	17	**CRAW DADDY** RICHMOND, LONDON, ENGLAND.
mon	18	
tue	19	
wed	20	**RICKY TICK** STAR & GARTER HOTEL, WINDSOR, ENGLAND. *UNCONFIRMED.*
thu	21	
fri	22	**EDWINA'S** FINSBURY PARK, LONDON, ENGLAND.
sat	23	**CRAW DADDY** STAR HOTEL, CROYDON, LONDON, ENGLAND.
sun	24	**CRAW DADDY** RICHMOND, LONDON, ENGLAND.
mon	25	
tue	26	
wed	27	
thu	28	
fri	29	**EDWINA'S** FINSBURY PARK, LONDON, ENGLAND.
sat	30	**CRAW DADDY** STAR HOTEL, CROYDON, LONDON, ENGLAND.

DECEMBER 1963

sun	1	**CRAW DADDY** RICHMOND, LONDON, ENGLAND.
mon	2	
tue	3	
wed	4	
thu	5	
fri	6	**EDWINA'S** FINSBURY PARK, LONDON, ENGLAND.
sat	7	**CRAW DADDY** STAR HOTEL, CROYDON, LONDON, ENGLAND.
sun	8	**CRAW DADDY** RICHMOND, RECORDING WITH SONNY BOY WILLIAMSON; ENGINEER: KEITH GRANT, OLYMPIC STUDIOS' GEAR.
mon	9	
tue	10	**R.G.JONES STUDIO** MORDEN, LONDON, RECORDING DEMOS 'BOOM BOOM', 'HONEY IN YOUR HIPS', 'TALKIN 'BOUT YOU'.
wed	11	
thu	12	
fri	13	**CLUB A GO GO** NEWCASTLE UPON TYNE, ENGLAND. *ALSO ALL-NIGHTER SESSION AT DOWNBEAT, NEWCASTLE, AT THIS TIME.*
sat	14	**CRAW DADDY** STAR HOTEL, CROYDON, LONDON, ENGLAND.
sun	15	**CIVIC HALL** GUILDFORD, SURREY, ENGLAND. SUPPORTING ROLLING STONES, PLUS GEORGIE FAME, GRAHAM BOND ETC.
mon	16	**R.G.JONES STUDIO** MORDEN, LONDON (LIKELY DATE) RECORDING 'BABY WHAT'S WRONG'; PRODUCER: MIKE VERNON.
tue	17	**RICKY TICK** STAR & GARTER HOTEL, WINDSOR, ENGLAND. WITH SONNY BOY WILLIAMSON.
wed	18	
thu	19	
fri	20	**PLAZA BALLROOM** GUILDFORD, SURREY, ENGLAND.
sat	21	**CRAW DADDY** STAR HOTEL, CROYDON, LONDON, ENGLAND.
sun	22	**OLYMPIA BALLROOM** READING, ENGLAND, "READING R&B" (pm). **CRAW DADDY** RICHMOND (evening) + SONNY BOY WILLIAMSON.
mon	23	ERIC CLAPTON LEAVES FOR HOLIDAY; ROGER PEARCE TAKES OVER ON GUITAR FOR REMAINING DECEMBER DATES.
tue	24	**RICKY TICK** STAR & GARTER HOTEL, WINDSOR, ENGLAND.
wed	25	
thu	26	
fri	27	
sat	28	**CRAW DADDY** STAR HOTEL, CROYDON, LONDON, ENGLAND.
sun	29	**CRAW DADDY** RICHMOND, LONDON, ENGLAND. BILLED AS "BACK FROM THEIR CONQUEST OF THE NORTH".
mon	30	
tue	31	

JANUARY 1964

wed 1

thu 2

fri 3

sat 4 **CRAW DADDY** STAR HOTEL, CROYDON, LONDON, ENGLAND.

sun 5 **CRAW DADDY** RICHMOND, LONDON, ENGLAND.

mon 6

tue 7 **RICKY TICK** STAR & GARTER HOTEL, WINDSOR, ENGLAND.

wed 8

thu 9

fri 10

sat 11 **CRAW DADDY** STAR HOTEL, CROYDON, LONDON, ENGLAND.

sun 12 **CRAW DADDY** RICHMOND, LONDON, ENGLAND.

mon 13

tue 14 **RICKY TICK** STAR & GARTER HOTEL, WINDSOR, ENGLAND.

wed 15

thu 16

fri 17 **RICKY TICK** PLAZA BALLROOM, GUILDFORD, SURREY, ENGLAND. WITH SONNY BOY WILLIAMSON.

sat 18 **CRAW DADDY** STAR HOTEL, CROYDON, LONDON, ENGLAND.

sun 19 **CRAW DADDY** RICHMOND, LONDON, ENGLAND.

mon 20 **TOBY JUG HOTEL** TOLWORTH, LONDON, ENGLAND.

tue 21 **RICKY TICK** STAR & GARTER HOTEL, WINDSOR, ENGLAND.

wed 22 **CAVERN** LIVERPOOL, ENGLAND. WITH SONNY BOY WILLIAMSON. PLUS THE MASTER SOUNDS, THE PAWNS, THE CHAMPIONS.

thu 23 **MARQUEE** LONDON, ENGLAND. SUPPORTING THE ALL-STARS (LONG JOHN BALDRY).

fri 24 **RICKY TICK** ST JOHN'S AMBULANCE HALL, READING, BERKS, ENGLAND.

sat 25 **CRAW DADDY** STAR HOTEL, CROYDON, LONDON, ENGLAND.

sun 26 **CRAW DADDY** RICHMOND, LONDON, ENGLAND.

mon 27 **TOBY JUG HOTEL** TOLWORTH, LONDON, ENGLAND. *PRESS RELEASE ANNOUNCES DECCA TO SIGN YARDBIRDS (THEY DON'T).*

tue 28 **RICKY TICK** STAR & GARTER HOTEL, WINDSOR, ENGLAND. **FLAMINGO** LONDON, "CYRIL DAVIES BENEFIT CONCERT".

wed 29

thur 30 **MARQUEE** LONDON. SUPPORTING THE ALL-STARS (LONG JOHN BALDRY).

fri 31 **RICKY TICK** ST JOHN'S AMBULANCE HALL, READING, BERKS, ENGLAND.

FEBRUARY 1964

sat 1 **RICKY TICK** PEARCE HALL, MAIDENHEAD, ENGLAND. WITH SONNY BOY WILLIAMSON.

sun 2 **CRAW DADDY** RICHMOND, LONDON, ENGLAND.

mon 3 PRESS RELEASE (LIKELY TODAY) ANNOUNCES CBS MAY ISSUE 'BOOM BOOM' SINGLE.

tue 4 **PLAZA BALLROOM** GUILDFORD, SURREY, ENGLAND.

wed 5 DECCA RECORD COMPANY DECIDES NOT TO SIGN YARDBIRDS TO A RECORDING CONTRACT.

thu 6 **MARQUEE** LONDON. SUPPORTING LONG JOHN BALDRY & HIS HOOCHIE COOCHIE MEN.

fri 7 **RICKY TICK** ST JOHN'S AMBULANCE HALL, READING, BERKS, ENGLAND.

sat 8 **RICKY TICK** PEARCE HALL, MAIDENHEAD, ENGLAND. **GALAXY** TOWN HALL, BASINGSTOKE, HANTS, ENGLAND. PLUS THE EVIL EYES.

sun 9 **CRAW DADDY** RICHMOND, LONDON, ENGLAND.

mon 10

tue 11 **CORONATION HALL** KINGSTON UPON THAMES, LONDON, ENGLAND.

wed 12

thu 13 **MARQUEE** LONDON, ENGLAND. SUPPORTING LONG JOHN BALDRY & HIS HOOCHIE COOCHIE MEN.

fri 14 **CRAW DADDY** STAR HOTEL, CROYDON, LONDON, ENGLAND.

sat 15 **CRAW DADDY** RICHMOND, LONDON, ENGLAND.

sun 16 **RICKY TICK** PEARCE HALL, MAIDENHEAD, ENGLAND. **OLYMPIA BALLROOM** READING, BERKS, ENGLAND.

mon 17

tue 18

wed 19

thu 20 **MARQUEE** LONDON. SUPPORTING LONG JOHN BALDRY & HIS HOOCHIE COOCHIE MEN.

fri 21 **FAIRFIELD HALLS** CROYDON, LONDON, ENGLAND. "CYRIL DAVIES BENEFIT CONCERT".

sat 22 **RICKY TICK** PEARCE HALL, MAIDENHEAD, ENGLAND.

sun 23 **CRAW DADDY** RICHMOND, LONDON, ENGLAND.

mon 24

tue 25

wed 26 **CAVERN** LIVERPOOL. PLUS THE UNDERTAKERS (LUNCH); WITH SONNY BOY WILLIAMSON, PLUS ROADRUNNERS ETC (EVENING).

thu 27 **MARQUEE** LONDON, ENGLAND. SUPPORTING LONG JOHN BALDRY & HIS HOOCHIE COOCHIE MEN.

fri 28 **TOWN HALL** BIRMINGHAM. "1st RHYTHM & BLUES FESTIVAL", WITH SONNY BOY WILLIAMSON, RECORDED AND LATER ISSUED.

sat 29 **RICKY TICK** PEARCE HALL, MAIDENHEAD, ENGLAND.

UNKNOWN STUDIO *LIKELY AROUND FEB/MAR RECORDING MORE DEMOS, INCLUDING: 'I WISH YOU WOULD', 'A CERTAIN GIRL', 'YOU CAN'T JUDGE A BOOK'.*

MARCH 1964

sun 1 **CRAW DADDY** RICHMOND, LONDON, ENGLAND.

mon 2

tue 3 **CORONATION HALL** KINGSTON UPON THAMES, LONDON. **TOWN HALL** FARNBOROUGH, LONDON, WITH SONNY BOY WILLIAMSON.

wed 4

thu 5 **MARQUEE** LONDON. SUPPORTING LONG JOHN BALDRY & HOOCHIE COOCHIE MEN. *CLUB'S LAST NIGHT AT ITS OXFORD STREET LOCATION.*

fri 6 **TELEPHONE HOUSE** WIMBLEDON, LONDON, ENGLAND

sat 7 **RICKY TICK** PEARCE HALL, MAIDENHEAD, ENGLAND.

sun 8 **REFECTORY** GOLDERS GREEN, LONDON, ENGLAND. **CRAW DADDY** RICHMOND, LONDON, ENGLAND.

mon 9

tue 10

wed 11 **CRAW DADDY** STAR HOTEL, CROYDON, LONDON, ENGLAND.

thu 12

fri 13 **MARQUEE** LONDON. WITH LONG JOHN BALDRY, SONNY BOY WILLIAMSON. *OPENING OF NEW WARDOUR STREET LOCATION.*

sat 14 **CRAW DADDY** STAR HOTEL, CROYDON, LONDON, ENGLAND.

sun 15 **CRAW DADDY** RICHMOND, LONDON, ENGLAND.

mon 16

tue 17

wed 18

thu 19

fri 20 **MARQUEE** LONDON, ENGLAND. *FIRST NIGHT OF RESIDENCY AS HEADLINERS. POSSIBLE DATE OF RECORDING FIVE LIVE YARDBIRDS LP.*

sat 21 **CRAW DADDY** STAR HOTEL, CROYDON, LONDON, ENGLAND.

sun 22 **CRAW DADDY** RICHMOND, LONDON, ENGLAND.

mon 23

tue 24

wed 25

thu 26

fri 27 **MARQUEE** LONDON, ENGLAND.

sat 28 **STAR HOTEL** CROYDON, LONDON, ENGLAND.

sun 29 **CRAW DADDY** RICHMOND, LONDON, ENGLAND. *KEITH RELF ILL, BRIAN JONES SUBSTITUTES.*

mon 30

tue 31

OLYMPIC STUDIOS LONDON, PROBABLY LATE MAR/EARLY APR, RECORDING 'I WISH YOU WOULD', 'A CERTAIN GIRL' (1st SINGLE).

APRIL 1964

wed 1

thu 2

fri 3 **MARQUEE** LONDON, ENGLAND. PLUS THE IMPULSIONS

sat 4 **CRAW DADDY** ST PETER'S HALL, KINGSTON UPON THAMES, LONDON, ENGLAND.

sun 5 **CRAW DADDY** RICHMOND, LONDON, ENGLAND.

mon 6 **REFECTORY** GOLDERS GREEN, LONDON, ENGLAND. **TOWN HALL** HIGH WYCOMBE, BUCKS, ENGLAND.

tue 7

wed 8

thu 9

fri 10 **MARQUEE** LONDON, ENGLAND. PLUS THE IMPULSIONS.

sat 11 **STAR HOTEL** CROYDON, LONDON, ENGLAND.

sun 12 **CRAW DADDY** RICHMOND, LONDON, ENGLAND.

mon 13

tue 14

wed 15

thu 16

fri 17 **MARQUEE** LONDON, ENGLAND. PLUS THE IMPULSIONS.

sat 18 **STAR HOTEL** CROYDON, LONDON, ENGLAND.

sun 19 **CRAW DADDY** RICHMOND, LONDON, ENGLAND.

mon 20 **CELLAR CLUB** KINGSTON UPON THAMES, LONDON, ENGLAND.

tue 21

wed 22

thu 23 **TOWN HALL** HIGH WYCOMBE, BUCKS, ENGLAND.

fri 24 **UNKNOWN VENUE** WALES. *A NIGHT OFF FROM THEIR MARQUEE RESIDENCY TO PLAY OUT OF TOWN.*

sat 25 **TOWN HALL** ABERGAVENNY, MONMOUTH, WALES.

sun 26 **CRAW DADDY** RICHMOND, LONDON, ENGLAND. PLUS THE GREBBELS.

mon 27

tue 28

wed 29

thu 30 **OLYMPIA BALLROOM** READING, BERKS, ENGLAND.

MAY 1964

fri 1 **MARQUEE** LONDON, ENGLAND. PLUS THE AUTHENTICS. **UK RELEASE** 'I WISH YOU WOULD' 45.

sat 2 **STAR HOTEL** CROYDON, LONDON, ENGLAND.

sun 3 **CRAW DADDY** RICHMOND, LONDON, ENGLAND. PLUS THE GREBBELS.

mon 4 **BROMEL CLUB** BROMLEY COURT HOTEL, BROMLEY, LONDON, ENGLAND. **DECCA STUDIOS** CLAPTON AT OTIS SPANN SESSION.

tue 5

wed 6 **REFECTORY** GOLDERS GREEN, LONDON, ENGLAND.

thu 7

fri 8 **MARQUEE** LONDON, ENGLAND. PLUS THE AUTHENTICS.

sat 9 **STAR HOTEL** CROYDON, LONDON, ENGLAND.

sun 10 **CRAW DADDY** RICHMOND, LONDON, ENGLAND. PLUS THE GREBBELS.

mon 11 **CELLAR CLUB** KINGSTON UPON THAMES, LONDON, ENGLAND. UNCONFIRMED.

tue 12

wed 13 **BROMEL CLUB** BROMLEY COURT HOTEL, BROMLEY, LONDON. **PRIVATE PERFORMANCE** LORD TED WILLIS'S HOUSE, CHISLEHURST, KENT.

thu 14

fri 15 **MARQUEE** LONDON, ENGLAND. PLUS THE AUTHENTICS.

sat 16 **STAR HOTEL** CROYDON, LONDON, ENGLAND.

sun 17 **CRAW DADDY** RICHMOND, LONDON, ENGLAND. PLUS THE GREBBELS.

mon 18

tue 19

wed 20

thu 21 **TOWN HALL** HIGH WYCOMBE, BUCKS, ENGLAND.

fri 22 **MARQUEE** LONDON. PLUS THE AUTHENTICS. **REDIFFUSION TV** LONDON, PERFORM 'I WISH YOU WOULD' ON READY STEADY GO.

sat 23

sun 24 **CRAW DADDY** RICHMOND, LONDON, ENGLAND. PLUS THE GREBBELS.

mon 25 **CELLAR CLUB** KINGSTON UPON THAMES, LONDON, ENGLAND. PLUS THE GREBBELS.

tue 26

wed 27 **BECKENHAM BALLROOM** LONDON. **TV WEST & WALES** BRISTOL, ENGLAND. (LIKELY) TAPING FOR DISCS A GO GO BROADCAST JUN 1st.

thu 28

fri 29 **MARQUEE** LONDON, ENGLAND. PLUS THE AUTHENTICS.

sat 30

sun 31 **CRAW DADDY** RICHMOND, LONDON, ENGLAND. PLUS THE GREBBELS.

JUNE 1964

mon 1

tue 2

wed 3 **TWISTED WHEEL** MANCHESTER, ENGLAND.

thu 4

fri 5 **MARQUEE** LONDON, ENGLAND. PLUS THE AUTHENTICS.

sat 6 **TRADE UNION HALL** WATFORD, HERTS, ENGLAND.

sun 7 **CRAW DADDY** RICHMOND, LONDON, ENGLAND.

mon 8 **CELLAR CLUB** KINGSTON UPON THAMES, LONDON, ENGLAND.

tue 9 **TOWN HALL** HIGH WYCOMBE, BUCKS, ENGLAND.

wed 10 **BLUE MOON** HAYES, LONDON, ENGLAND.

thu 11 **THE DOME** BRIGHTON, ENGLAND.

fri 12 **MARQUEE** LONDON, ENGLAND. PLUS THE AUTHENTICS.

sat 13 **CLUB NOREIK** TOTTENHAM, LONDON, ENGLAND. **FLEUR DE LYS** HAYES, LONDON, ENGLAND.

sun 14 **WIMBLEDON PALAIS** WIMBLEDON, LONDON, PLUS GREBBELS. REGULAR CRAW DADDY RICHMOND DATE LIKELY CANCELLED.

mon 15 **BBC TV** NOTTINGHAM ICE STADIUM, AROUND THIS TIME, TAPING 'I WISH YOU WOULD', 'A CERTAIN GIRL' FOR COOL SPOT b/c JUL 7th.

tue 16 **UNIVERSITY HALL** CAMBRIDGE UNIVERSITY, CAMBRIDGE, ENGLAND.

wed 17

thu 18 **TWISTED WHEEL** MANCHESTER, ENGLAND.

fri 19 **MARQUEE** LONDON, ENGLAND. PLUS THE AUTHENTICS.

sat 20 **SHOWGROUND** UXBRIDGE, LONDON, ENGLAND. **OSTERLEY RUGBY GROUND** NORWOOD GREEN, LONDON.

sun 21 **CRAW DADDY** RICHMOND, LONDON, ENGLAND.

mon 22 **CELLAR CLUB** KINGSTON UPON THAMES, LONDON, ENGLAND.

tue 23 **ASSEMBLY HALL** AYLESBURY, BUCKS, ENGLAND.

wed 24 **TV WEST & WALES** BRISTOL, ENGLAND, TAPING FOR DISCS A GO GO BROADCAST JUN 29th.

thu 25 **ATTIC CLUB** HOUNSLOW, LONDON, ENGLAND. PLUS THE SNOWBALLS.

fri 26 **RACECOURSE** REDCAR, ENGLAND. "NORTHERN JAZZ FESTIVAL" PLUS MANFRED MANN, LONG JOHN BALDRY, THE CRAWDADDIES ETC.

sat 27

sun 28 **CRAW DADDY** RICHMOND, LONDON, ENGLAND.

mon 29 **CELLAR CLUB** KINGSTON UPON THAMES, LONDON, ENGLAND. PLUS THE GREBBELS.

tue 30 **CASINO HOTEL** TAGS ISLAND, TWICKENHAM, LONDON, ENGLAND. PLUS THE GREBBLES, THE T.BONES.

JULY 1964

wed	1	**BLU-BEAT CLUB** LORD WAKEFIELD HALL, HAYES, LONDON, ENGLAND.
thu	2	
fri	3	**MARQUEE** LONDON, ENGLAND. PLUS THE AUTHENTICS.
sat	4	
sun	5	**CAVERN** LIVERPOOL, ENGLAND. PLUS THE GREBBELS AND LOCAL ACTS.
mon	6	
tue	7	**TUESDAY BLUES CLUB** CHURCHILL HALL, HARROW, LONDON, ENGLAND.
wed	8	**BLU-BEAT CLUB** LORD WAKEFIELD HALL, HAYES, LONDON, ENGLAND.
thu	9	**OLYMPIA BALLROOM** READING, BERKS, ENGLAND. PLUS THE BLUES COMMITTEE.
fri	10	**MARQUEE** LONDON, ENGLAND. PLUS THE AUTHENTICS.
sat	11	**RHODES CENTRE** BISHOP'S STORTFORD, HERTS, ENGLAND. PLUS SHANE & THE SHANE GANG.
sun	12	**SCALA BALLROOM** DARTFORD, KENT, ENGLAND.
mon	13	**THE SPARROWHAWK** EDGWARE, LONDON, ENGLAND.
tue	14	**TUESDAY BLUES CLUB** CHURCHILL HALL, HARROW, LONDON, ENGLAND.
wed	15	**IL RONDO** LEICESTER, ENGLAND.
thu	16	**OLYMPIA BALLROOM** READING, BERKS, ENGLAND.
fri	17	**MARQUEE** LONDON, ENGLAND. PLUS THE AUTHENTICS.
sat	18	**DAM PARK** AYR, SCOTLAND. "2nd SCOTTISH JAZZ & BLUES FESTIVAL".
sun	19	**COMMODORE BALLROOM** RYDE, ISLE OF WIGHT, ENGLAND.
mon	20	**CELLAR CLUB** KINGSTON UPON THAMES, LONDON, ENGLAND.
tue	21	**TUESDAY BLUES CLUB** CHURCHILL HALL, HARROW, LONDON, ENGLAND.
wed	22	**TWISTED WHEEL** MANCHESTER; **GRANADA TV** MANCHESTER, 2 SONGS B/CAST ON *GO TELL IT TO THE MOUNTAINS*.
thu	23	**TWISTED WHEEL** MANCHESTER; **QUEEN'S BALLROOM** CLEVELEYS, LANCS, PLUS JIMMY POWELL & THE FIVE DIMENSIONS.
fri	24	**MARQUEE** LONDON, ENGLAND. PLUS THE AUTHENTICS.
sat	25	**KING GEORGE'S HALL** ESHER, SURREY, ENGLAND.
sun	26	**CRAW DADDY** RICHMOND, LONDON, ENGLAND.
mon	27	**TOWN HALL** CLACTON-ON-SEA, ESSEX, ENGLAND. PLUS BERN ELLIOT & THE KLAN, THE FABULOUS McCOYS.
tue	28	**TUESDAY BLUES CLUB** CHURCHILL HALL, HARROW, LONDON, ENGLAND.
wed	29	**BROMEL CLUB** BROMLEY COURT HOTEL, BROMLEY, LONDON, ENGLAND.
thu	30	**LOCARNO BALLROOM** SWINDON, ENGLAND.
fri	31	**MARQUEE** LONDON, ENGLAND. PLUS THE AUTHENTICS.

AUGUST 1964

sat	1	**TOWN HALL** TORQUAY, TORBAY, ENGLAND.
sun	2	**CRAW DADDY** RICHMOND, LONDON, ENGLAND. PLUS THE GREBBELS.
mon	3	
tue	4	**FENDER CLUB** KENTON CONSERVATIVE HALL, KENTON, LONDON, ENGLAND. PLUS THE GREBBELS
wed	5	
thu	6	**FLAMINGO** REDRUTH, CORNWALL, ENGLAND. PLUS THE GOPHERS. **QUEENS BALLROOM** BARNSTAPLE, DEVON (POSSIBLY RESCHEDULED).
fri	7	**MARQUEE** LONDON, ENGLAND. PLUS THE BRAKEMEN. *RELF ILL; MICK O'NEILL STANDS IN ON VOCALS.*
sat	8	**UNKNOWN VENUE** & LOCATION. *RELF'S LUNG CONDITION WORSENS AND HE IS HOSPITALISED, SPENDS 6 WEEKS RECOVERING.*
sun	9	**4th NATIONAL JAZZ/BLUES FESTIVAL** RICHMOND, LONDON. *FROM NOW MICK O'NEILL TAKES OVER FROM RELF ON VOCALS.*
mon	10	**OLYMPIC STUDIOS** LONDON, RECORDING 'GOOD MORNING LITTLE SCHOOLGIRL' (BACKING TRACK); POSSIBLY ALSO NOW 'GOT TO HURRY'. *DATE OF THESE RECORDINGS UNCERTAIN, BUT LIKELY A FEW DAYS EITHER SIDE OF AUG 9th.*
tue	11	
wed	12	
thu	13	
fri	14	**INTERNATIONAL JAZZ DAYS FESTIVAL** ASCONA, SWITZERLAND. PLUS MOSE ALLISON ETC. *EXACT DAY(S) PERFORMING UNCERTAIN.*
sat	15	**INTERNATIONAL JAZZ DAYS FESTIVAL** ASCONA, SWITZERLAND. PLUS MOSE ALLISON ETC. *EXACT DAY(S) PERFORMING UNCERTAIN.*
sun	16	**INTERNATIONAL JAZZ DAYS FESTIVAL** ASCONA, SWITZERLAND. PLUS MOSE ALLISON ETC. *EXACT DAY(S) PERFORMING UNCERTAIN.*
mon	17	**LUGANO HOTEL** LUGANO, SWITZERLAND. BEGIN NIGHTLY PERFORMANCES ON HOTEL TERRACE AROUND THIS TIME. REPORTS SUGGEST FOR 5 OR 7 NIGHTS; BAND ON HOLIDAY THEREAFTER. **US RELEASE** 'I WISH YOU WOULD' 45.
tue	18	
wed	19	
thu	20	
fri	21	
sat	22	
sun	23	
mon	24	
tue	25	
wed	26	
thu	27	
fri	28	
sat	29	**TOWN HALL** ABERGAVENNY, WALES. *UNCONFIRMED. MICK O'NEILL STILL VOCALS (MIKE VERNON ALSO STOOD IN AT SOME POINT).*
sun	30	
mon	31	

SEPTEMBER 1964

tue	1	
wed	2	**TV WEST/WALES** BRISTOL, (LIKELY) TAPING '...LITTLE SCHOOLGIRL' FOR DISCS A GO GO BROADCAST SEP 7th. *CLAPTON SINGS.*
thu	3	
fri	4	**MARQUEE** LONDON, ENGLAND. PLUS THE DISSATISFIEDS. *MICK O'NEILL CONTINUES TO DEP ON VOCALS; RELF STILL ILL.*
sat	5	
sun	6	**CRAW DADDY** RICHMOND, LONDON, ENGLAND. PLUS GREBBELS. *RELF LEAVES HOSPITAL, ORDERED NOT TO SING YET, CONVALESCES.*
mon	7	
tue	8	**TUESDAY BLUES CLUB** CHURCHILL HALL, HARROW, LONDON, ENGLAND. *MICK O'NEILL CONTINUES ON VOCALS.*
wed	9	**IL RONDO HALL** LEICESTER, ENGLAND.
thu	10	
fri	11	**MARQUEE** LONDON, ENGLAND. PLUS THE MOODY BLUES.
sat	12	**PAVILION BALLROOM** BUXTON, DERBYS, ENGLAND. PLUS THE PATHFINDERS.
sun	13	**CRAW DADDY** RICHMOND, LONDON, ENGLAND. PLUS THE GREBBELS.
mon	14	
tue	15	**TOWN HALL** HIGH WYCOMBE, BUCKS, ENGLAND.
wed	16	**CORN EXCHANGE** BRISTOL, ENGLAND. PLUS MARK ROMAIN & THE JAVELINS.
thu	17	
fri	18	TOUR WITH BILLY J KRAMER & DAKOTAS DUE TO START; TONIGHT'S OPENING GIG CANCELLED AS TWO OTHER ARTISTS NO-SHOW.
sat	19	**OLYMPIC STUDIOS** LONDON, RELF DUBS VOCALS/HARP TO 'SCHOOLGIRL', + LIKELY RECORDING 'I AIN'T GOT YOU'.
sun	20	**ODEON CINEMA** LEWISHAM, LONDON. *YARDBIRDS CANCEL TONIGHT (AND (LAST NIGHT IN BRISTOL).*
mon	21	**GRANADA CINEMA** MAIDSTONE, KENT. *THE RETURN OF RELF; THE SINGER REJOINS THE BAND AFTER HIS 6-WEEK ILLNESS.*
tue	22	**GRANADA CINEMA** GREENFORD, LONDON, ENGLAND. *OTHER ARTISTS ON KRAMER TOUR: CLIFF BENNETT & THE REBEL ROUSERS...*
wed	23	**GAUMONT CINEMA** IPSWICH, SUFFOLK, ENGLAND. *...ALSO BILL BLACK COMBO, THE RONETTES, THE NASHVILLE TEENS.*
thu	24	**ODEON CINEMA** SOUTHEND-ON-SEA, ENGLAND.
fri	25	**ABC CINEMA** NORTHAMPTON, ENGLAND.
sat	26	**GRANADA CINEMA** MANSFIELD, NOTTS, ENGLAND.
sun	27	**EMPIRE THEATRE** LIVERPOOL, ENGLAND.
mon	28	**CAIRD HALL** DUNDEE, SCOTLAND.
tue	29	**ABC CINEMA** EDINBURGH, SCOTLAND.
wed	30	**ODEON THEATRE** GLASGOW, SCOTLAND.

OCTOBER 1964

thu	1	**ADELPHI THEATRE** DUBLIN, IRELAND. *BILLY J KRAMER TOUR CONTINUES.*
fri	2	**ABC CINEMA** BELFAST, NORTHERN IRELAND.
sat	3	**SAVOY THEATRE** CORK, IRELAND. *ORIGINALLY SCHEDULED FOR CITY HALL, SHEFFIELD.*
sun	4	**ABC CINEMA** STOCKTON-ON-TEES, ENGLAND.
mon	5	
tue	6	
wed	7	**ABC CINEMA** CARLISLE, CUMBRIA, ENGLAND. *THE KINKS REPLACE THE RONETTES ON THIS 2nd LEG OF THE KRAMER TOUR.*
thu	8	**ODEON CINEMA** BOLTON, MANCHESTER, ENGLAND.
fri	9	**GRANADA CINEMA** GRANTHAM, LINCS, ENGLAND.
sat	10	**ABC CINEMA** (KINGSTON UPON) HULL, ENGLAND.
sun	11	**GRANADA CINEMA** EAST HAM, LONDON, ENGLAND.
mon	12	**CRAW DADDY** HANWORTH, LONDON, ENGLAND. *INDEPENDENT BOOKING, NOT PART OF TOUR.*
tue	13	**GRANADA CINEMA** BEDFORD, ENGLAND.
wed	14	**GRANADA CINEMA** BRIXTON, LONDON, ENGLAND.
thu	15	**ODEON CINEMA** GUILDFORD, SURREY, ENGLAND.
fri	16	**ABC CINEMA** SOUTHAMPTON, ENGLAND.
sat	17	**ABC CINEMA** GLOUCESTER, ENGLAND.
sun	18	**GRANADA CINEMA** TOOTING, LONDON, ENGLAND. *BILLY J KRAMER TOUR ENDS.*
mon	19	
tue	20	
wed	21	**TWISTED WHEEL** MANCHESTER, ENGLAND.
thu	22	
fri	23	**MARQUEE** LONDON, ENGLAND. PLUS THE DISSATISFIEDS.
sat	24	**GOLDHAWK SOCIAL CLUB** SHEPHERD'S BUSH, LONDON, ENGLAND.
sun	25	**CRAW DADDY** RICHMOND, LONDON, ENGLAND. PLUS THE GREBBELS.
mon	26	**GLENLYN BALLROOM** FOREST HILL, LONDON, ENGLAND.
tue	27	
wed	28	**BBC TV** (REGIONAL) B/CAST ON TOWN AND AROUND (POSSIBLY TAPED PREVIOUS DAY, 27th).
thu	29	**LAKESIDE R&B** HENDON, LONDON. **BBC RADIO** LONDON, TAPING 4 SONGS FOR RHYTHM & BLUES BROADCAST NOV 21st.
fri	30	**MARQUEE** LONDON, ENGLAND. **REDIFFUSION TV** LONDON, PERFORM '...MORNING LITTLE SCHOOLGIRL' ON READY STEADY GO.
sat	31	**UK RELEASE** 'GOOD MORNING LITTLE SCHOOLGIRL' 45.

NOVEMBER 1964

sun	1	**CRAW DADDY** RICHMOND, LONDON, ENGLAND. PLUS THE GREBBELS
mon	2	
tue	3	**TOWN HALL** HIGH WYCOMBE, BUCKS, ENGLAND.
wed	4	**TV WEST & WALES** BRISTOL, ENGLAND. TAPING ' ', 'LITTLE SCHOOLGIRL' FOR DISCS A GO GO BROADCAST NOV 9th.
thu	5	
fri	6	**UK RELEASE** ON THE SCENE MULTI-ACT LP WITH 'A CERTAIN GIRL', 'I WISH YOU WOULD'. THE YARDBIRDS' 1st OUTING ON ALBUM.
sat	7	**MEMORIAL HALL** NORTHWICH, CHES, ENGLAND.
sun	8	**CRAW DADDY** RICHMOND, LONDON, ENGLAND. PLUS THE GREBBELS.
mon	9	**IBC STUDIOS** LONDON (AROUND THIS TIME) RECORDING 'SWEET MUSIC'. PRODUCER: MANFRED MANN.
tue	10	**TUESDAY BLUES CLUB** CHURCHILL HALL, HARROW, LONDON, ENGLAND.
wed	11	**CORN EXCHANGE** BRISTOL, ENGLAND. PLUS THE PENTAGONS.
thu	12	
fri	13	
sat	14	**TWISTED WHEEL** MANCHESTER, ENGLAND.
sun	15	
mon	16	
tue	17	
wed	18	
thu	19	**PIER PAVILION** WORTHING, WEST SUSSEX, ENGLAND. PLUS THE OTIS BAND.
fri	20	
sat	21	**RICKY TICK** PLAZA BALLROOM, GUILDFORD, SURREY, ENGLAND.
sun	22	**HIPPODROME** BRIGHTON. PLUS JERRY LEE LEWIS, TWINKLE, QUIET FIVE. SAMWELL-SMITH PLAYS BASS FOR LEWIS WITH NASHVILLE TEENS.
mon	23	
tue	24	**REDIFFUSION TV** LONDON, PERFORMING ON FIVE O'CLOCK CLUB.
wed	25	
thu	26	
fri	27	**TOWN HALL** LEAMINGTON SPA, WARKS, ENGLAND.
sat	28	
sun	29	**CRAW DADDY** RICHMOND, LONDON, ENGLAND.
mon	30	

OLYMPIC STUDIOS LONDON (LATE NOV/EARLY DEC) RECORDING 'PUTTY (IN YOUR HANDS)'; ALSO POSSIBLY 'GOT TO HURRY'.

DECEMBER 1964

tue	1	
wed	2	
thu	3	
fri	4	**RICKY TICK** WINDSOR, ENGLAND.
sat	5	**ST GEORGE'S BALLROOM** HINCKLEY, LEICS, ENGLAND.
sun	6	
mon	7	**ROYAL ALBERT HALL** LONDON, ENGLAND. 'TOP BEAT SHOW'. BROADCAST ON BBC-2 TV, DEC 9th.
tue	8	**ASSEMBLY HALLS** TUNBRIDGE WELLS, KENT, ENGLAND.
wed	9	
thu	10	**OLYMPIA BALLROOM** READING, ENGLAND.
fri	11	
sat	12	**PALAIS** PETERBOROUGH, CAMBS, ENGLAND.
sun	13	**MOJO** SHEFFIELD, SOUTH YORKS, ENGLAND.
mon	14	**GRAND PAVILION** PORTHCAWL, BRIDGEND, WALES.
tue	15	
wed	16	
thu	17	**LAKESIDE BALLROOM** HENDON, LONDON, ENGLAND.
fri	18	**CO-OP HALL** GRAVESEND, KENT, ENGLAND.
sat	19	
sun	20	**CRAW DADDY** RICHMOND, LONDON, ENGLAND.
mon	21	
tue	22	
wed	23	
thu	24	**ODEON CINEMA** HAMMERSMITH, LONDON, ENGLAND. 20-DATE SEASON AS SUPPORT IN 'THE BEATLES SHOW'.
fri	25	
sat	26	**ODEON CINEMA** HAMMERSMITH, LONDON, ENGLAND. 'THE BEATLES SHOW'.
sun	27	**CRAW DADDY** RICHMOND, LONDON, ENGLAND. PLUS THE GREBBELS. RESIDENCY GIG ON DAY-OFF FROM 'BEATLES SHOW'.
mon	28	**ODEON CINEMA** HAMMERSMITH, LONDON, ENGLAND. 'THE BEATLES SHOW'.
tue	29	**ODEON CINEMA** HAMMERSMITH, LONDON, ENGLAND. 'THE BEATLES SHOW'.
wed	30	**ODEON CINEMA** HAMMERSMITH, LONDON, ENGLAND. 'THE BEATLES SHOW'.
thu	31	**ODEON CINEMA** HAMMERSMITH, LONDON, ENGLAND. 'THE BEATLES SHOW'. **UK RELEASE** FIVE LIVE YARDBIRDS LP.

JANUARY 1965

fri 1 **ODEON CINEMA** HAMMERSMITH, LONDON, ENGLAND. *"THE BEATLES SHOW".*

sat 2 **ODEON CINEMA** HAMMERSMITH, LONDON, ENGLAND. *"THE BEATLES SHOW".*

sun 3 **CRAW DADDY** RICHMOND, LONDON, ENGLAND. PLUS THE GREBBELS. *RESIDENCY GIG ON DAY-OFF FROM "BEATLES SHOW".*

mon 4 **ODEON CINEMA** HAMMERSMITH, LONDON, ENGLAND. *"THE BEATLES SHOW".*

tue 5 **ODEON CINEMA** HAMMERSMITH, LONDON, ENGLAND. *"THE BEATLES SHOW".*

wed 6 **ODEON CINEMA** HAMMERSMITH, LONDON, ENGLAND. *"THE BEATLES SHOW".*

thu 7 **ODEON CINEMA** HAMMERSMITH, LONDON, ENGLAND. *"THE BEATLES SHOW".*

fri 8 **ODEON CINEMA** HAMMERSMITH, LONDON, ENGLAND. *"THE BEATLES SHOW".*

sat 9 **ODEON CINEMA** HAMMERSMITH, LONDON, ENGLAND. *"THE BEATLES SHOW".*

sun 10 **CRAW DADDY** RICHMOND, LONDON, ENGLAND. PLUS THE GREBBELS. *RESIDENCY GIG ON DAY-OFF FROM "BEATLES SHOW".*

mon 11 **ODEON CINEMA** HAMMERSMITH, LONDON, ENGLAND. *"THE BEATLES SHOW".*

tue 12 **ODEON CINEMA** HAMMERSMITH, LONDON, ENGLAND. *"THE BEATLES SHOW".*

wed 13 **ODEON CINEMA** HAMMERSMITH, LONDON, ENGLAND. *"THE BEATLES SHOW".*

thu 14 **ODEON CINEMA** HAMMERSMITH, LONDON, ENGLAND. *"THE BEATLES SHOW".*

fri 15 **ODEON CINEMA** HAMMERSMITH, LONDON, ENGLAND. *"THE BEATLES SHOW".*

sat 16 **ODEON CINEMA** HAMMERSMITH, LONDON, ENGLAND. *FINAL SHOW IN 20-DATE "BEATLES SHOW" SEASON.*

sun 17 **CRAW DADDY** RICHMOND, LONDON, ENGLAND. PLUS THE GREBBELS

mon 18 **PAVILION** BATH, ENGLAND.

tue 19

wed 20 **BROMEL CLUB** BROMLEY COURT HOTEL, BROMLEY, LONDON, ENGLAND.

thu 21

fri 22 **MARQUEE** LONDON, ENGLAND.

sat 23 **ASTORIA BALLROOM** RAWTENSTALL, LANCS, ENGLAND. PLUS THE BRYSTALS, THE THUNDERBIRDS.

sun 24

mon 25 **MAJESTIC BALLROOM** READING, ENGLAND.

tue 26

wed 27

thu 28

fri 29 **TRENTHAM GARDENS** TRENTHAM, STOKE, ENGLAND.

sat 30 **FLORAL HALL** MORECAMBE, LANCS, ENGLAND

sun 31

FEBRUARY 1965

mon 1 **MARQUEE** LONDON. PLUS MARK LEEMAN FIVE. **IBC STUDIOS** LONDON, RECORDING 'FOR YOUR LOVE'. **REDIFFUSION TV** LONDON, PERFORMING 'FOR YOUR LOVE' ON *THAT'S FOR ME*

tue 2

wed 3 **IBC STUDIOS** LONDON, ENGLAND (AROUND THIS TIME) RECORDING 'SOMEONE TO LOVE ME'.

thu 4

fri 5 **DUNGEON** NOTTINGHAM, ENGLAND.

sat 6 **WHISKY A GO GO** BIRMINGHAM, ENGLAND.

sun 7 **CAVERN** MANCHESTER, ENGLAND.

mon 8 **TOWN HALL** BASINGSTOKE, HANTS, ENGLAND.

tue 9 **TOWN HALL** HIGH WYCOMBE, BUCKS, ENGLAND.

wed 10 **TOWN HALL** FARNBOROUGH, HANTS, ENGLAND.

thu 11

fri 12 *ERIC CLAPTON AROUND THIS TIME ANNOUNCES INTENTION TO LEAVE BECAUSE 'FOR YOUR LOVE' CHOSEN AS NEW SINGLE A-SIDE*

sat 13 *MANAGER GOMELSKY AROUND THIS TIME CALLS JIMMY PAGE WHO DECLINES OFFER TO JOIN BUT RECOMMENDS HIS FRIEND JEFF BECK.*

sun 14 **COMMUNITY CENTRE** SOUTHALL, LONDON, ENGLAND.

mon 15 **MARQUEE** LONDON. *GOMELSKY APPROACHES BECK AT TRIDENTS GIG AT NEARBY 100 CLUB & OFFERS JOB TO REPLACE CLAPTON.*

tue 16

wed 17 **MARQUEE** LONDON. *PROBABLY THIS DAY AT A PRIVATE CLUB SESSION BECK AUDITIONS TO REPLACE CLAPTON*

thu 18

fri 19

sat 20

sun 21 **R&B RENDEZVOUS** KIMBELLS, SOUTHSEA, PORTSMOUTH, ENGLAND. PLUS THE J CROW COMBO.

mon 22

tue 23

wed 24

thu 25

fri 26 **BATHS** LEYTON, LONDON, ENGLAND.

sat 27

sun 28 **CRAW DADDY** RICHMOND, LONDON, ENGLAND. *CLAPTON COUNTING DOWN HIS REMAINING DAYS AS A YARDBIRD*

mon	1	
tue	2	**TOWN HALL** LYDNEY, GLOS, ENGLAND.
wed	3	**BRISTOL CORN EXCHANGE** BRISTOL. *CLAPTON'S LAST SHOW WITH THE BAND; HE DOES PLAY THE OFFENDING 'FOR YOUR LOVE'.*
thu	4	
fri	5	**FAIRFIELD HALL** CROYDON, LONDON. PLUS MOODY BLUES. *JEFF BECK'S 1ST GIG AS A YARDBIRD.* **UK RELEASE** *'FOR YOUR LOVE' 45.*
sat	6	**UNIVERSITY OF MANCHESTER** MANCHESTER, ENGLAND. *UNCONFIRMED.*
sun	7	
mon	8	**MARQUEE** LONDON, ENGLAND. **RADIO LUXEMBOURG** EMI, LONDON, TAPING *FRIDAY SPECTACULAR* FOR BROADCAST 12th.
tue	9	**GROSVENOR BALLROOM** BOROUGH ASSEMBLY HALL, AYLESBURY, BUCKS, ENGLAND.
wed	10	**WOLSEY HALL** CHESHUNT, HERTS, ENGLAND.
thu	11	**THORNGATE BALLROOM** GOSPORT, HANTS, ENGLAND. PLUS THE ROADRUNNERS.
fri	12	**HILLSIDE BALLROOM** HEREFORD, ENGLAND. PLUS THE SOULENTS.
sat	13	**LOUGHBOROUGH COLLEGE** LOUGHBOROUGH, LEICS, ENGLAND. **TWISTED WHEEL** MANCHESTER, ENGLAND.
sun	14	**CRAW DADDY** RICHMOND, LONDON, ENGLAND. *UNCONFIRMED.*
mon	15	**ADVISION STUDIOS** LONDON, ENGLAND. (LIKELY) RECORDING 'STEELED BLUES', 'I AIN'T DONE WRONG'. *FIRST SESSION WITH BECK.*
tue	16	**BBC RADIO** LONDON, ENGLAND. TAPING 5 SONGS INC 'FOR YOUR LOVE' FOR *SATURDAY CLUB* BROADCAST MAR 20th.
wed	17	
thu	18	**GRANADA TV** *SCENE AT 6.30.* **BBC TV** *TOP OF THE POPS.* TWO MANCHESTER TV BROADCASTS MIMING 'FOR YOUR LOVE'.
fri	19	**WIMBLEDON PALAIS** LONDON. **REDIFFUSION TV** LONDON, PLAY 'FOR YOUR LOVE' ON TONIGHT'S *READY STEADY GO.*
sat	20	**ASSEMBLY HALL** FARNBOROUGH TECHNICAL COLLEGE, FARNBOROUGH, HANTS, ENGLAND.
sun	21	
mon	22	**BBC RADIO** LONDON, ENGLAND. TAPING 5 SONGS INC 'FOR YOUR LOVE' FOR *TOP GEAR* BROADCAST APRIL 10th.
tue	23	**BURTON'S BALLROOM** UXBRIDGE, LONDON, ENGLAND.
wed	24	**TV WEST & WALES** BRISTOL, ENGLAND. TAPING 'FOR YOUR LOVE' FOR *DISCS A GO GO* BROADCAST MAR 29th/APR 3rd.
thu	25	**ASTORIA BALLROOM** OLDHAM, LANCS, ENGLAND. **BBC TV** MANCHESTER MIMING 'FOR YOUR LOVE' ON *TOP OF THE POPS.*
fri	26	**LYNX CLUB** BOREHAMWOOD, HERTS, ENGLAND.
sat	27	**ROYAL HOTEL** LOWESTOFT, SUFFOLK, ENGLAND. PLUS THE STATESMEN.
sun	28	**CRAW DADDY** RICHMOND, LONDON, ENGLAND.
mon	29	**MARQUEE** LONDON, ENGLAND. PLUS THE MARK LEEMAN FIVE.
tue	30	**CAPITOL THEATRE** ABERDEEN, SCOTLAND. *REPLACING THE KINKS AT SHORT NOTICE.*
wed	31	

thu	1	**BBC TV** MANCHESTER, ENGLAND. MIMING 'FOR YOUR LOVE' ON TODAY'S *TOP OF THE POPS* BROADCAST.
fri	2	**DUNGEON CLUB** NOTTINGHAM. **REDIFFUSION TV** LONDON PERFORM 'FOR YOUR LOVE' ON TODAY'S *READY STEADY GOES LIVE.*
sat	3	**ST GEORGE'S BALLROOM** HINCKLEY, LEICS, ENGLAND. PLUS THE STAGERLEES.
sun	4	**ULTRA CLUB** DOWNS HOTEL, HASSOCKS, WEST SUSSEX, ENGLAND. PLUS THE SHADES.
mon	5	**GUILDHALL** SOUTHAMPTON, ENGLAND.
tue	6	**RADIO LUXEMBOURG** LONDON, TAPING SONG(S) FOR *READY STEADY RADIO* BROADCAST APRIL 11th.
wed	7	**BBC TV** MANCHESTER, ENGLAND, TAPING 'FOR YOUR LOVE' FOR *TOP OF THE POPS;* NOT BROADCAST.
thu	8	**McILROYS BALLROOM** SWINDON, ENGLAND.
fri	9	**LONDON ARCHITECTURAL ASSOC** DANCE. **BBC RADIO** TAPING *SATURDAY SWINGS.* **REDIFFUSION TV** *READY STEADY GOES LIVE.*
sat	10	**CORN EXCHANGE** BRISTOL, ENGLAND.
sun	11	**ROYAL STAR** MAIDSTONE, KENT, ENGLAND.
mon	12	**US RELEASE** 'FOR YOUR LOVE' 45.
tue	13	**ADVISION STUDIOS** LONDON, RECORDING 'I'M NOT TALKING', '...SLOOPY', 'HEART FULL OF SOUL'. **TOWN HALL** HIGH WYCOMBE.
wed	14	
thu	15	**COOKS FERRY INN** EDMONTON, LONDON
fri	16	**RICKY TICK** THAMES HOTEL, WINDSOR, ENGLAND. **REDIFFUSION TV** LONDON, APPEAR ON TONIGHT'S *READY STEADY GOES LIVE.*
sat	17	**PLAZA BALLROOM** OSWESTRY, SHROPSHIRE, ENGLAND.
sun	18	**COMMUNITY CENTRE** SOUTHALL, LONDON, ENGLAND.
mon	19	**MARQUEE DANCE CLUB** BIRMINGHAM, ENGLAND. (LIKELY) PLUS THE CRAWDADDIES.
tue	20	**ADVISION STUDIOS** LONDON, PROBABLE DATE OF RE-RECORDING 'HEART FULL OF SOUL' (RELEASED VERSION).
wed	21	**BROMEL CLUB** BROMLEY COURT HOTEL, BROMLEY, KENT, ENGLAND.
thu	22	**LAKESIDE BALLROOM** HENDON, LONDON, ENGLAND.
fri	23	**KING'S COURT HOTEL** LONDON, ENGLAND.
sat	24	**CORN EXCHANGE** CHELMSFORD, ESSEX, ENGLAND.
sun	25	**WINTER GARDENS** DROITWICH SPA, WORCS, ENGLAND.
mon	26	**MARQUEE** LONDON, ENGLAND. PLUS THE MARK LEEMAN FIVE.
tue	27	**ASSEMBLY HALL** TUNBRIDGE WELLS, KENT, ENGLAND.
wed	28	
thu	29	
fri	30	**ADELPHI CINEMA** SLOUGH. *FIRST GIG 21-DATE TOUR SUPPORTING KINKS.* **BBC RADIO** LIVE BROADCAST ON *JOE LOSS POP SHOW.*

MAY 1965

sat	1	**GRANADA CINEMA** WALTHAMSTOW, LONDON, ENGLAND. *SUPPORT SLOT ON 21-DATE KINKS TOUR CONTINUES.*
sun	2	**ODEON CINEMA** LEWISHAM, LONDON, ENGLAND.
mon	3	**MARQUEE** LONDON, ENGLAND. PLUS THE MARK LEEMAN FIVE. *RESIDENCY COMMITMENT ON DAY-OFF FROM KINKS TOUR.*
tue	4	**GUILDHALL** PORTSMOUTH, ENGLAND. *KINKS TOUR CONTINUES.*
wed	5	
thu	6	**GRANADA CINEMA** KINGSTON UPON THAMES, LONDON, ENGLAND.
fri	7	**GRANADA CINEMA** EAST HAM, LONDON, ENGLAND.
sat	8	**GAUMONT CINEMA** HANLEY, STOKE, ENGLAND.
sun	9	**COVENTRY THEATRE** COVENTRY, WEST MIDLANDS, ENGLAND.
mon	10	
tue	11	**ODEON CINEMA** SWINDON, ENGLAND.
wed	12	**ODEON CINEMA** SOUTHEND-ON-SEA, ESSEX, ENGLAND.
thu	13	**GRANADA CINEMA** BEDFORD, BEDS, ENGLAND.
fri	14	**GRANADA CINEMA** TOOTING, LONDON, ENGLAND.
sat	15	**WINTER GARDENS** BOURNEMOUTH, ENGLAND.
sun	16	**GAUMONT CINEMA** IPSWICH, SUFFOLK, ENGLAND.
mon	17	**MARQUEE** LONDON, ENGLAND. *RESIDENCY COMMITMENT ON DAY-OFF FROM KINKS TOUR.*
tue	18	**GAUMONT CINEMA** TAUNTON, SOMERSET, ENGLAND. *KINKS TOUR CONTINUES.*
wed	19	**CAPITOL CINEMA** CARDIFF, WALES. *KINKS REPLACED BY WALKER BROTHERS AFTER ON-STAGE BRAWL AT THIS TOUR DATE.*
thu	20	**GAUMONT CINEMA** WOLVERHAMPTON, WEST MIDLANDS, ENGLAND. *YARDBIRDS REPLACED BY HOLLIES AFTER THIS DATE.*
fri	21	**RAITH BALLROOM** KIRKCALDY, FIFE, SCOTLAND. PLUS ANDY ROSS ORCHESTRA. *FIRST GIG ON 9-DATE YARDBIRDS SCOTTISH TOUR.*
sat	22	**CITY HALL** PERTH, SCOTLAND. PLUS THE COURIERS.
sun	23	**TOP 10 CLUB** PALAIS, DUNDEE, SCOTLAND. PLUS THE POUR SOULS, THE EXECUTIVES, AND "MISS HOLIDAY TOP TEN FINAL".
mon	24	**ASSEMBLY ROOMS** WICK, HIGHLAND, SCOTLAND. PLUS THE ACTUAL FACTS.
tue	25	**LOCARNO BALLROOM** MONTROSE, ANGUS, SCOTLAND. PLUS GARY SUMMERS & THE HIGHLANDERS.
wed	26	
thu	27	**PAISLEY ICE RINK** GLASGOW, SCOTLAND. PLUS ROB & THE CLANSMEN, THE POETS, THE BEATSTALKERS, THE BOOTS.
fri	28	**DRILL HALL** DUMFRIES, SCOTLAND.
sat	29	**UNKNOWN VENUE** SCOTLAND.
sun	30	**NEW HALL** NEWTONGRANGE, MIDLOTHIAN, SCOTLAND. *YARDBIRDS SCOTTISH TOUR ENDS.*
mon	31	

JUNE 1965

tue	1	**BBC RADIO** LONDON, ENGLAND. TAPING 3 SONGS INC 'HEART FULL OF SOUL' FOR *SATURDAY CLUB* BROADCAST JUNE 5th.
wed	2	**COUNTRY CLUB** MUDEFORD, DORSET. **BBC RADIO** LONDON, TAPING 3 SONGS FOR *JOE LOSS POP SHOW* BROADCAST JULY 2nd.
thu	3	
fri	4	**FENDER CLUB** HARROW. **BBC RADIO** *SATURDAY SWINGS* b/c JUN 12th. **TV** *READY STEADY GO*. **UK RELEASE** 'HEART FULL OF SOUL' 45.
sat	5	**PETERBOROUGH PALAIS** PETERBOROUGH, CAMBS, ENGLAND.
sun	6	**ELM PARK** ROMFORD, LONDON, ENGLAND.
mon	7	**COUNTRY CLUB** BORLEY, ESSEX, ENGLAND.
tue	8	**MARQUEE** LONDON, ENGLAND. PLUS THE MARK LEEMAN FIVE.
wed	9	**BBC RADIO** LONDON, ENGLAND. TAPING 'HEART FULL OF SOUL' FOR *KEN DODD SHOW* BROADCAST JUNE 20th & 23rd.
thur	10	**MARQUEE** LONDON, ENGLAND. *AFTERNOON REHEARSAL.*
fri	11	**WINTER GARDENS** BLACKPOOL. **REDIFFUSION TV** LONDON, PLAYING 'HEART FULL OF SOUL' ON TONIGHT'S *READY STEADY GO*.
sat	12	**STAFFORD RUGBY CLUB** STAFFORD, ENGLAND.
sun	13	**ABC TV** ASTON, BIRMINGHAM, MIMING 'HEART FULL OF SOUL' FOR *THANK YOUR LUCKY STARS* BROADCAST JUNE 19th.
mon	14	**PARR HALL** WARRINGTON, ENGLAND. **GRANADA TV** MANCHESTER, PERFORMING ON *SCENE AT 6.30*.
tue	15	**STAMFORD HALL** ALTRINCHAM, MANCHESTER, ENGLAND. PLUS THE BUMBLIES.
wed	16	**RICKY TICK** WINDSOR, ENGLAND (& OUTSIDE). PROMO FILM SHOT (LIKELY TODAY) FOR US TV OF 'FOR YOUR LOVE' IN MEDIEVAL COSTUME.
thu	17	**PIER PAVILLION** WORTHING, WEST SUSSEX, ENGLAND.
fri	18	**UNIVERSITY OF BIRMINGHAM** BIRMINGHAM, ENGLAND.
sat	19	**STARLIGHT ROOM** GLIDERDROME, BOSTON, LINCS, ENGLAND. PLUS THE YES'N'NO, THE ESSEX.
sun	20	**PALAIS DES SPORTS** PARIS, FRANCE. *ONE-OFF SUPPORT SLOT ON OPENING DATE OF THE BEATLES' SHORT EUROPEAN TOUR.*
mon	21	**BBC RADIO** LONDON, ENGLAND. TAPING 3 SONGS INC 'HEART FULL OF SOUL' FOR *TOP GEAR* BROADCAST JUNE 26th.
tue	22	**TOWN HALL** HIGH WYCOMBE, BUCKS, ENGLAND.
wed	23	**CITY HALL** SALISBURY, WILTS, ENGLAND. PLUS THE TROGGS.
thu	24	**KAVE DWELLERS CLUB** BILLINGHAM, STOCKTON-ON-TEES, ENGLAND. *CANCELLED AS BECK AND SAMWELL-SMITH ILL.*
fri	25	**OASIS CLUB** MANCHESTER, ENGLAND. *CANCELLED AS BECK AND SAMWELL-SMITH ILL.*
sat	26	**DRILL HALL** SCUNTHORPE, NORTH LINCS, ENGLAND. *CANCELLED AS BECK AND SAMWELL-SMITH ILL.*
sun	27	**CRAW DADDY** RICHMOND, LONDON, ENGLAND.
mon	28	
tue	29	
wed	30	**CORN EXCHANGE** BRISTOL, ENGLAND. **TV WEST & WALES** BRISTOL, ENGLAND, PERFORMING ON *DISCS A GO GO*.

JULY 1965

thu	1	**DREAMLAND BALLROOM** WINTER GARDENS, MARGATE, KENT, ENGLAND.
fri	2	**PALAIS** WIMBLEDON, LONDON, ENGLAND. **REDIFFUSION TV** LONDON, TAPING FOR *READY STEADY GO* BROADCAST JULY 9th.
sat	3	**WHITEHALL** EAST GRINSTEAD. **BBC RADIO** LONDON, TAPING 2 SONGS INC 'HEART FULL OF SOUL' FOR *EASY BEAT* BROADCAST 4th.
sun	4	**STARLITE BALLROOM** GREENFORD, LONDON, ENGLAND. PLUS LULU, GOLDIE & THE GINGERBREADS.
mon	5	**BATH PAVILLION** BATH, ENGLAND. **US RELEASE** *FOR YOUR LOVE* LP.
tue	6	**MARQUEE** LONDON, ENGLAND.
wed	7	
thu	8	**BBC TV** LONDON, ENGLAND, MIMING 'HEART FULL OF SOUL' ON TODAY'S *TOP OF THE POPS* BROADCAST.
fri	9	**ASSEMBLY HALL** FARNBOROUGH TECHNICAL COLLEGE, FARNBOROUGH, HANTS, ENGLAND. PLUS THE SOLE-TONES.
sat	10	**CORN EXCHANGE** CAMBRIDGE, ENGLAND.
sun	11	
mon	12	
tue	13	
wed	14	
thu	15	**WINTER GARDENS** GREAT YARMOUTH, NORFOLK, ENGLAND.
fri	16	**WHADDON FOOTBALL GROUND** CHELTENHAM, GLOS, ENGLAND. PLUS THE WHO.
sat	17	**BIRDCAGE CLUB** KIMBEL'S BALLROOM, SOUTHSEA, PORTSMOUTH, ENGLAND. *YARDBIRDS FAIL TO PLAY THIS BOOKING.*
sun	18	**ABC TV** ASTON, BIRMINGHAM, SESSION PLANNED FOR *LUCKY STARS SUMMER SPIN*, BUT YARDBIRDS ARRIVE TOO LATE TO APPEAR.
mon	19	**MAJESTIC BALLROOM** NEWCASTLE UPON TYNE, ENGLAND. **US RELEASE** 'HEART FULL OF SOUL' 45.
tue	20	**QUEEN'S BALLROOM** CLEVELEYS, LANCS, ENGLAND.
wed	21	START OF SHORT SCOTTISH TOUR IN DUNFERMLINE DELAYED: SHOW RESCHEDULED FOR JUL 26th.
thu	22	
fri	23	**CITY HALL** PERTH, SCOTLAND.
sat	24	**TOWN HALL** INVERURIE, ABERDEEN, SCOTLAND.
sun	25	**TOWN HALL** BRODICK, ISLE OF ARRAN, SCOTLAND.
mon	26	**KINEMA BALLROOM** DUNFERMLINE, FIFE, SCOTLAND. *SCOTTISH TOUR ENDS.*
tue	27	**OLYMPIC** LONDON. (LIKELY) RECORDING BACKING TRACK TO 'STILL I'M SAD'. ENGINEER: KEITH GRANT.
wed	28	**FLORAL HALL** MORECAMBE, LANCS, ENGLAND. PLUS THE PEEPS.
thu	29	
fri	30	**RICKY TICK** WINDSOR. *CANCELLED, BECK ILL, BUT HE DID MAKE…* **REDIFFUSION TV** LONDON, PERFORMING ON *READY STEADY GO*.
sat	31	**BOATING LAKE GROUNDS** CLEETHORPES, LINCS, ENGLAND. 'EAST COAST JAZZ/MODERN MUSIC FESTIVAL', MANY OTHER ACTS.

AUGUST 1965

sun	1	
mon	2	**SAVOY BALLROOM** SOUTHSEA, PORTSMOUTH, ENGLAND. PLUS THE KLIMAKS. *MAKE-UP DATE FOR NO-SHOW ON JULY 17th.*
tue	3	
wed	4	
thu	5	**ASSEMBLY HALL** WORTHING, SUSSEX. **BBC RADIO** LONDON, TAPING 5 SONGS FOR *SATURDAY SWINGS* BROADCAST AUG 14th.
fri	6	**5th NATIONAL JAZZ/BLUES FESTIVAL** RICHMOND. FILMED FOR US *SHINDIG* TV. **BBC RADIO** FOR *YOU REALLY GOT* b/c AUG 30th.
sat	7	**OASIS CLUB** MANCHESTER, ENGLAND. *MAKE-UP DATE FOR NO-SHOW ON JUNE 25th.* **UK RELEASE** (YESTERDAY, 6th) *5 YARDBIRDS* EP.
sun	8	**NORTH PIER PAVILLION** BLACKPOOL, ENGLAND. PLUS DAVE BERRY & THE CRUISERS, BILLY BURDEN, THE HOBOS.
mon	9	**BBC RADIO** MANCHESTER, ENGLAND, TAPING 3 SONGS INC 'HEART FULL OF SOUL' FOR *THE BEAT SHOW* BROADCAST AUG 13th.
tue	10	**TWICKENHAM STUDIOS** LONDON (THIS DAY AND/OR 11th) FILMING 4 SONGS FOR US TV *SHINDIG* BROADCAST SEP & DEC.
wed	11	
thu	12	
fri	13	
sat	14	
sun	15	**THE PIER** LLANDUDNO, CONWY, WALES. *CANCELLED.*
mon	16	
tue	17	**ADVISION STUDIOS** LONDON. (LIKELY) RECORDING 'EVIL HEARTED YOU', 'STILL I'M SAD', 'HEART FULL OF SOUL' (ITALIAN VOCAL).
wed	18	
thu	19	**US TOUR** DUE TO START TODAY. *BUT POSTPONED DUE TO MUDDLE OVER US UNION AND LABOR RULES. EVENTUALLY RESET FOR SEP 2nd.*
fri	20	
sat	21	
sun	22	
mon	23	**ADVISION STUDIOS** LONDON, RE-RECORDING 'EVIL HEARTED YOU' (AND MASTERED AUG 26th).
tue	24	
wed	25	
thu	26	
fri	27	**REDIFFUSION TV** LONDON, APPEARING ON TONIGHT'S *READY STEADY GO* BROADCAST.
sat	28	
sun	29	
mon	30	
tue	31	

SEPTEMBER 1965

wed **1**

thu **2**

fri **3** **OKLAHOMA STATE FAIRGROUNDS GRANDSTAND** OKLAHOMA CITY, OK, US. *START OF RESCHEDULED 1st NORTH AMERICAN TOUR.*

sat **4** **VIP CLUB** JAYCEES HALL, PHOENIX, AZ, US. PLUS THE SPIDERS *(A BAND THAT INCLUDES RELF-INSPIRED SOON-NAMED ALICE COOPER).*

sun **5** BAND AND MANAGER GIORGIO GOMELSKY CONTINUE THEIR DRIVE ACROSS ROUTE 66 IN HIRED CAR.

mon **6**

tue **7** **RCA STUDIO** HOLLYWOOD, CA, US. RECORDING OF 'I'M A MAN' (UNISSUED VERSION). *TODAY OR AROUND THIS TIME.*

wed **8** **PRIVATE PARTY** MARKLEY FAMILY HOUSE, HOLLYWOOD, CA, US. *TODAY OR AROUND THIS TIME; ARRANGED BY KIM FOWLEY.*

thu **9** **TV STUDIO** LOS ANGELES, CA, US (LIKELY) MIMING 'FOR YOUR LOVE' FOR DICK CLARK'S *WHERE THE ACTION IS.* NOT BROADCAST.

fri **10** **THE CLEARPOOL** MEMPHIS, TN, US (LIKELY). **SKATELAND FRAYSER** MEMPHIS, TN, US. *TWO SHOWS TODAY.*

sat **11** **ROBINSON AUDITORIUM** LITTLE ROCK, AR, US. PLUS THE GIANTS, THE COMMOTIONS, THE GROUPE.

sun **12** **SUN STUDIOS** MEMPHIS, TN, US. RECORDING INC 'TRAIN KEPT A ROLLIN' & 'YOU'RE A BETTER MAN THAN I'. ENGINEER: SAM PHILLIPS.

mon **13** **NBC TV STUDIOS** NEW YORK, NY, US. PLANNED TAPING FOR *HULLABALOO* HALTED BY US DEPT OF LABOR.

tue **14**

wed **15** **NBC TV STUDIOS** NEW YORK, NY, US. *DEPT OF LABOR OBJECTIONS CLEARED UP; YARDBIRDS REHEARSE FOR HULLABALOO.*

thu **16** **NBC TV STUDIOS** NEW YORK, NY, US. *TODAY'S PLANNED TAPING FOR HULLABALOO AGAIN HALTED.*

fri **17** **ROLLING STONE DISCOTHEQUE** NEW YORK, NY, US. PLUS THE MERSEY LADS. *US RECORD COMPANY EPIC'S RECEPTION.*

sat **18** **ARIE CROWN THEATER** CHICAGO, IL, US. PLUS THE HOLLIES.

sun **19** **CHESS STUDIOS** CHICAGO, IL, US. RECORDING 'I'M A MAN'. ENGINEER: RON MALO.

mon **20** **NBC TV STUDIOS** NEW YORK, NY, US. REHEARSALS FOR *HULLABALOO.*

tue **21** **NBC** 'I'M A MAN' FOR *HULLABALOO* DEC 6th. **COLUMBIA STUDIOS** NY. ADDING TO BACKING TRACKS AND RECORDING.

wed **22** FIRST US TOUR ENDS. *BAND TRAVELS TO NETHERLANDS.*

thu **23** **NRCV TV STUDIOS** BUSSUM, NETHERLANDS. TAPING 'FOR YOUR LOVE' FOR *TIENER MAGAZINE* BROADCAST DEC 3rd.

fri **24**

sat **25** BAND RETURNS TO ENGLAND.

sun **26** **ABC TV** ASTON, BIRMINGHAM. TAPING 'EVIL HEARTED YOU' FOR *THANK YOUR LUCKY STARS* BROADCAST OCT 2nd.

mon **27** **BBC RADIO** LONDON, ENGLAND. TAPING 5 SONGS INC 'EVIL HEARTED YOU' FOR *SATURDAY CLUB* BROADCAST OCT 2nd.

tue **28** **GRANADA TV** MANCHESTER, PERFORMING 'EVIL HEARTED YOU' ON *SCENE AT 6.30.*

wed **29** **TV WEST & WALES** BRISTOL, ENGLAND, PERFORMING 'EVIL HEARTED YOU' ON *DISCS A GO GO.*

thu **30** **LOCARNO BALLROOM** SWINDON, ENGLAND.

OCTOBER 1965

fri **1** **REDIFFUSION TV** LONDON, PLAYING 'EVIL HEARTED YOU' ON *READY STEADY GO.* **UK RELEASE** 'EVIL HEARTED YOU' 45.

sat **2** **DRILL HALL** GRANTHAM, LINCS, ENGLAND. PLUS THE MANIAX, THE OMRUDS.

sun **3**

mon **4** **BBC RADIO** LONDON, TAPING 3 SONGS INC 'EVIL HEARTED YOU' AND 'STILL I'M SAD' FOR *BEAT SHOW* BROADCAST OCT 7th.

tue **5**

wed **6** **THE WITCH DOCTOR** HASTINGS, EAST SUSSEX, ENGLAND.

thu **7** **RICKY TICK** THAMES HOTEL, WINDSOR, ENGLAND.

fri **8** **TOWN HALL** STAINES, SURREY. **BBC RADIO** LONDON, TAPING 4 SONGS FOR *THIS MUST BE THE PLACE* BROADCAST OCT 18th.

sat **9** **CALIFORNIA BALLROOM** DUNSTABLE, BEDS. **BBC RADIO** LONDON, TAPING 2 SONGS FOR *EASY BEAT* BROADCAST OCT 10th.

sun **10**

mon **11** **MAJESTIC BALLROOM** RHYL, DENBIGH, WALES. **US RELEASE** 'I'M A MAN' 45.

tue **12** **MARQUEE** LONDON, ENGLAND. PLUS THE MARK LEEMAN FIVE.

wed **13** **TV WEST & WALES** BRISTOL, ENGLAND, LIKELY DATE FOR TAPING FOR *DISCS A GO GO* BROADCAST OCT 20th.

thu **14** **QUEENS HALL** BARNSTAPLE, DEVON, ENGLAND.

fri **15** **GUILDHALL** AXMINSTER, DEVON, ENGLAND.

sat **16** **TRADE UNION HALL** WATFORD, HERTS, ENGLAND.

sun **17**

mon **18**

tue **19** **TOWN HALL** HIGH WYCOMBE, BUCKS, ENGLAND.

wed **20** **TOWN HALL** STOURBRIDGE, WEST MIDLANDS, ENGLAND.

thu **21** **WINTER GARDENS** CLEETHORPES. **BBC TV** MANCHESTER, MIMING 'EVIL HEARTED YOU' ON TONIGHT'S *TOP OF THE POPS.*

fri **22** **MARINE BALLROOM** CENTRAL PIER, MORECAMBE, LANCS, ENGLAND. PLUS THE EXECUTIVES, HAROLD GRAHAM (ORGANIST!).

sat **23** **STUDENT UNION** UNIVERSITY OF LEEDS, LEEDS, ENGLAND. PLUS THE DETROITS, AL CROSSLAND, THE UNWANTED PREGNANCIES.

sun **24** **OASIS CLUB** MANCHESTER, ENGLAND.

mon **25** **QUEENS BALLROOM** WOLVERHAMPTON, WEST MIDLANDS, ENGLAND.

tue **26** **SHERWOOD ROOMS** NOTTINGHAM, ENGLAND.

wed **27**

thu **28**

fri **29** **REDIFFUSION TV** LONDON, PLAYING 'EVIL HEARTED YOU' ETC ON TONIGHT'S *READY STEADY GO.*

sat **30** **BATHS** LEYTON, LONDON, ENGLAND.

sun **31**

NOVEMBER 1965

mon	1	**PAVILLION** BATH, ENGLAND.
tue	2	**FLORAL HALL** GORLESTON, NORFOLK.
wed	3	**ORCHID BALLROOM** PURLEY, LONDON, ENGLAND.
thu	4	
fri	5	**ABC THEATRE** CLEETHORPES, LINCS, ENGLAND. *REPLACEMENT FOR BILLY FURY ON HERMAN'S HERMITS/WAYNE FONTANA TOUR.*
sat	6	**MARCAM HALL** MARCH, CAMBS, ENGLAND.
sun	7	
mon	8	**BATHS** ELTHAM, LONDON, ENGLAND.
tue	9	**K-52** FRANKFURT, GERMANY. *OPENING DATE OF SHORT EUROPEAN TOUR.*
wed	10	TRAVEL DAY TO MUNICH.
thu	11	
fri	12	**BIG APPLE** MUNICH, GERMANY.
sat	13	**TV STUDIO** BRUSSELS, BELGIUM. TAPING 'STILL I'M SAD' & 'FOR YOUR LOVE' FOR *ADAMOROSO (THE ADAMO SHOW)* BROADCAST NOV 21st.
sun	14	
mon	15	**COLSTON HALL** BRISTOL, ENGLAND. *CANCELLED.*
tue	16	**BBC RADIO** LONDON. TAPING 4 SONGS INC 'STILL I'M SAD' FOR *THE SOUND OF BOXING DAY* BROADCAST DEC 27th.
wed	17	**LOCARNO BALLROOM** STEVENAGE, HERTS, ENGLAND.
thu	18	**ABC CINEMA** STOCKTON-ON-TEES, ENGLAND. *FIRST DATE OF "MARQUEE SHOW" UK TOUR WITH MANFRED MANN AND …*
fri	19	**ABC CINEMA** CHESTERFIELD, DERBYS, ENGLAND. *TOUR ALSO FEATURES … THE SCAFFOLD, THE RYAN TWINS, MARK LEEMAN FIVE*
sat	20	**GAUMONT CINEMA** DERBY, ENGLAND. *TOUR ALSO FEATURES … GARY FARR & THE T-BONES, GOLDIE & THE GINGERBREADS.*
sun	21	
mon	22	**GAUMONT CINEMA** BRADFORD, WEST YORKS, ENGLAND. *YARDBIRDS MISS FIRST OF TWO SHOWS HERE AFTER VAN TROUBLE.*
tue	23	**RITZ CINEMA** LUTON, BEDS, ENGLAND.
wed	24	**RITZ CINEMA** CHATHAM, KENT, ENGLAND.
thu	25	**RITZ CINEMA** CAMBRIDGE, ENGLAND.
fri	26	**ABC CINEMA** SOUTHAMPTON, ENGLAND.
sat	27	**GRANADA CINEMA** EAST HAM, LONDON, ENGLAND.
sun	28	**COVENTRY THEATRE** COVENTRY, WEST MIDLANDS, ENGLAND.
mon	29	**ABC CINEMA** NORTHAMPTON, ENGLAND.
tue	30	**GUILDHALL** PORTSMOUTH, ENGLAND. *US RELEASE HAVING A RAVE UP WITH THE YARDBIRDS LP.*

DECEMBER 1965

wed	1	**ADVISION STUDIOS** LONDON. RELF DUBS ITALIAN-LANGUAGE VOCAL ON TO 'STILL I'M SAD'. *UNRELEASED.*
thu	2	**GRANADA CINEMA** BEDFORD, ENGLAND. *"MARQUEE SHOW" TOUR CONTINUES.*
fri	3	**COLSTON HALL** BRISTOL, ENGLAND. PLUS JIMMY JAMES & THE VAGABONDS.
sat	4	**ABC CINEMA** PLYMOUTH, ENGLAND.
sun	5	**ABC CINEMA** EXETER, DEVON, ENGLAND.
mon	6	**ADELPHI CINEMA** SLOUGH, ENGLAND. *LAST DATE OF "MARQUEE SHOW" TOUR.*
tue	7	
wed	8	**TOWER HALL** NEW BRIGHTON, MERSEYSIDE, ENGLAND. *"ZOWIE 1" BALL FOR PIRATE STATION RADIO CAROLINE, PLUS BRIAN POOLE ETC.*
thu	9	
fri	10	
sat	11	**ARIE CROWN THEATER** CHICAGO, IL, US. **ROCK RIVER ROLLER PALACE** ROCKFORD, IL, US. *START OF 2nd NORTH AMERICAN TOUR.*
sun	12	**IMA AUDITORIUM** FLINT, MI, US. PLUS THE BEAU BRUMMELS, THE STRANGELOVES, TERRY & THE PACK.
mon	13	
tue	14	LIKELY THIS DAY AT HOWLIN' WOLF'S BIG SQUEEZE CLUB, CHICAGO, THAT BECK JAMS WITH WOLF'S BAND INC GUITARIST HUBERT SUMLIN.
wed	15	**RENFRO'S** EMPORIA, KS, US.
thu	16	
fri	17	**UNKNOWN VENUE** MID-WESTERN HIGH SCHOOL END-OF-SEMESTER CONCERT.
sat	18	**DANCELAND BALLROOM** CEDAR RAPIDS, IA, US. PLUS THE R-TISTICS.
sun	19	**SURF OF THE FOUR SEASONS BALLROOM** CLEAR LAKE, IA, US. *VENUE THAT BUDDY HOLLY PLAYED BEFORE FATAL AIR CRASH 1959.*
mon	20	REHEARSALS AT THUMBS UP CLUB, CHICAGO, IL, FOR TOMORROW'S RECORDING SESSION.
tue	21	**CHESS STUDIOS** CHICAGO, IL, US. RECORDING BACKING TRACK FOR 'SHAPES OF THINGS'.
wed	22	**CHESS STUDIOS** CHICAGO, IL, US. VOCAL DUBS AND INITIAL MIXING 'SHAPES OF THINGS'.
thu	23	**ALEXANDRIA ROLLER RINK** ALEXANDRIA, VA, US. *YARDBIRDS SUPPORT HEADLINING SHANGRI-LAS AS 2ND US TOUR CONTINUES.*
fri	24	
sat	25	**PEPPERMINT STICK** WHEATFIELD, NY, US. *THRU SNOWSTORMS, BAND REPORTEDLY PLAYS TO 10 PEOPLE ON RE-JIGGED XMAS DATE.*
sun	26	**DANIEL'S DEN** SAGINAW, NI, US. PLUS THE JAY HAWKERS.
mon	27	**WILL ROGERS MEMORIAL COLISEUM** FORT WORTH, TX, US. PLUS MOUSE & THE TRAPS, LARRY & THE BLUE NOTES, THE BAD SEEDS.
tue	28	**CIVIC ARENA** PITTSBURGH, PA, US. *"CHRISTMAS SHOWER OF STARS" INC FOUR SEASONS, CHUCK BERRY, SIMON & GARFUNKEL.*
wed	29	TRAVEL DAY TO SAN FRANCISCO.
thu	30	**TEEN CENTER** SILVER $ FAIRGROUND, CHICO, CA, US. **SKATELAND** MARYSVILLE, CA, US.
fri	31	**UNIVERSITY OF PUGET** TACOMA, WA. PLUS BEACH BOYS. POSSIBLE AD-LIB PERFORMANCE LATER @ **EVERGREEN BALLROOM** OLYMPIA, WA.

JANUARY 1966

sat	1	**SEATTLE CENTER COLISEUM** SEATTLE, WA, US, "1966 NEW YEAR SPECTACULAR" PLUS BEACH BOYS. *2nd US TOUR CONTINUES.*
sun	2	
mon	3	**KABC TV STUDIO** HOLLYWOOD, CA, US, TAPING 'I'M A MAN', 'HEART FULL OF SOUL' FOR *SHIVAREE* BROADCAST JAN 8th.
tue	4	**PRIVATE PARTY** KIM FOWLEY'S HOUSE, HOLLYWOOD, CA, US. **KHJ-TV** LOS ANGELES, PROBABLE BROADCAST ON *9th STREET WEST.*
wed	5	**HULLABALOO CLUB** HOLLYWOOD, CA, US. *START OF 4-DATE RESIDENCY.*
thu	6	**HULLABALOO CLUB** HOLLYWOOD, CA, US. PLUS THE PALACE GUARD. *SAME VENUE & ACTS TOMORROW NIGHT TOO.*
fri	7	**COLUMBIA STUDIO** HOLLYWOOD, +VOCALS 'SHAPES ...'. **UK RELEASE** *SONNY BOY WILLIAMSON &... LP.* **HULLABALOO** HOLLYWOOD.
sat	8	**MEMORIAL AUDITORIUM** SACRAMENTO, CA, US. PLUS THE BEAU BRUMMELS, THE LOVIN' SPOONFUL, JOHN ROSASCO QUARTET.
sun	9	**HULLABALOO CLUB** HOLLYWOOD, CA, US. PLUS THE PALACE GUARD. *END OF 4-DATE RESIDENCY.*
mon	10	**RCA STUDIOS** HOLLYWOOD, CA, US. *POSSIBLY RECORDING, OR REHEARSING SONGS FOR UPCOMING SAN REMO FESTIVAL, ITALY.*
tue	11	**KCOP-TV** HOLLYWOOD, CA, US (LIKELY) PERFORMING 'FOR YOUR LOVE', 'SHAPES...' FOR *LLOYD THAXTON SHOW* BROADCAST FEB 1st.
wed	12	BAND TRAVELS TO NEW YORK CITY.
thu	13	
fri	14	
sat	15	**EUDOWOOD GARDENS** BALTIMORE, MD, US. **ANNAPOLIS NATIONAL GUARD ARMORY** ANNAPOLIS, MD, US.
sun	16	BAND RETURNS TO NEW YORK CITY.
mon	17	**COLUMBIA STUDIOS** NEW YORK. RECORDING 'QUESTA VOLTA' & 'PAFFF...BUM' FOR RICORDI RECORDS, ITALY. *LIKELY TODAY OR 18th.*
tue	18	
wed	19	
thu	20	
fri	21	**VALPARAISO ARMORY** VALPARAISO, IN, US.
sat	22	**ARAGON BALLROOM** CHICAGO, IL, US. *BAND'S 2ND NORTH AMERICAN TOUR ENDS.*
sun	23	BAND RETURNS TO LONDON.
mon	24	
tue	25	BAND TRAVELS TO ITALY.
wed	26	
thu	27	**CASINO MUNICIPALE** SAN REMO, ITALY. *REHEARSALS FOR SONG FESTIVAL.*
fri	28	**CASINO MUNICIPALE** SAN REMO, ITALY. "16TH FESTIVAL ITALIAN SONGS", BROADCAST ITALIAN TV, YARDBIRDS PLAY 'QUESTA VOLTA'.
sat	29	**CASINO MUNICIPALE** SAN REMO, ITALY. FESTIVAL CONTINUES, YARDBIRDS PLAY 'PAFFF...BUM'. *NEITHER SONG MAKES FINAL.*
sun	30	BAND MEMBERS DEPART FROM ITALY.
mon	31	

FEBRUARY 1966

tue	1	
wed	2	
thu	3	**ORTF TV** PARIS, FRANCE, TAPING (PROBABLY) FOR *MUSIC HALL DE FRANCE* BROADCAST FEB 12th.
fri	4	**GOLF DRUOT** PARIS, FRANCE. *ORGANISED BY LOCAL FAN CLUB.* **ITALIAN RELEASE** 'QUESTA VOLTA' 45 & SAN REMO 66 LP.
sat	5	**PLACE DE LA MUTUALITÉ** PARIS, FRANCE. PLUS THE MOODY BLUES, RONNIE BIRD, ANTOINE & VIGON.
sun	6	BAND TAKES A SHORT BREAK.
mon	7	**US RELEASE** SONNY BOY WILLIAMSON & THE YARDBIRDS LP.
tue	8	
wed	9	
thu	10	
fri	11	
sat	12	
sun	13	
mon	14	
tue	15	
wed	16	
thu	17	REHEARSAL DAY IN LONDON.
fri	18	**REDIFFUSION TV** LONDON, PLAYING 'SHAPES OF THINGS' ON TONIGHT'S *READY STEADY GO!*
sat	19	**BATHS HALL** SCUNTHORPE, NORTH LINCS, ENGLAND.
sun	20	**ABC TV** ASTON, BIRMINGHAM, MIMING 'SHAPES OF THINGS' FOR *THANK YOUR LUCKY STARS* BROADCAST FEB 26th.
mon	21	
tue	22	
wed	23	
thu	24	
fri	25	**IRON CURTAIN CLUB** ST MARY CRAY, LONDON, ENGLAND. **UK RELEASE** 'SHAPES OF THINGS' 45.
sat	26	
sun	27	**MARQUEE** LONDON, ENGLAND. *BROADCAST ON PIRATE RADIO LONDON FROM THIS CLUB, SPONSORED BY INECTO.*
mon	28	**BBC RADIO** LONDON, TAPING 5 SONGS FOR *SATURDAY CLUB* BROADCAST MAR 5th. **US RELEASE** 'SHAPES OF THINGS' 45.

MARCH 1966

tue	1	**REDIFFUSION TV** LONDON, PERFORMING 'SHAPES OF THINGS' ON *FIVE O'CLOCK CLUB*.
wed	2	**TV WEST & WALES** BRISTOL, ENGLAND, PERFORMING ON *NOW!*.
thu	3	
fri	4	**REDIFFUSION TV** LONDON, PLAYING 'SHAPES OF THINGS' ON TONIGHT'S *READY STEADY GO!*.
sat	5	**CORN EXCHANGE** CAMBRIDGE, ENGLAND.
sun	6	
mon	7	**TOWN HALL** CHATHAM, KENT, ENGLAND.
tue	8	REHEARSAL DAY IN LONDON.
wed	9	**CORN EXCHANGE** BRISTOL, ENGLAND. PLUS THE FANATICS.
thu	10	**BBC TV** LONDON, ENGLAND, MIMING 'SHAPES OF THINGS' ON TONIGHT'S *TOP OF THE POPS* BROADCAST.
fri	11	**RICKY TICK** STAINES, SURREY, ENGLAND.
sat	12	**ST GEORGE'S BALLROOM** HINCKLEY, LEICS, ENGLAND. **BBC RADIO** LONDON, TAPING 2 SONGS FOR *EASY BEAT* b/c MAR 13th.
sun	13	
mon	14	**PAVILION** BATH, ENGLAND.
tue	15	**MARQUEE** LONDON, ENGLAND. PLUS THE CLAYTON SQUARES. *LIKELY DATE THAT ERIC CLAPTON JAMS WITH THE YARDBIRDS.*
wed	16	**GRANADA TV** MANCHESTER, PERFORMING 'SHAPES OF THINGS' ON *SCENE* AT 6.30.
thu	17	**ROYAL ALBERT HALL** (EXTERIOR) LONDON, MIMING 4 SONGS FOR US TV SHOW *WHERE THE ACTION IS* B/CAST APR 15th & MAY 11th.
fri	18	
sat	19	**JIGSAW CLUB** MANCHESTER, ENGLAND. PLUS THE POWERHOUSE SIX.
sun	20	
mon	21	**QUEEN'S BALLROOM** WOLVERHAMPTON, WEST MIDLANDS, ENGLAND.
tue	22	**WINTER GARDENS** GREAT MALVERN, WORCS, ENGLAND.
wed	23	**MAJESTIC BALLROOM** LEEDS, WEST YORKS, ENGLAND.
thu	24	**VIRGINIA BALLROOM** CHESTERFIELD, DERBYS, ENGLAND.
fri	25	
sat	26	**IMPERIAL BALLROOM** NELSON, LANCS, ENGLAND. PLUS THE MUTINEERS, GIDION'S WAYS.
sun	27	
mon	28	**ADVISION STUDIOS** LONDON, RECORDING (LIKELY NOW) BACK-TRACKS FOR NEW ALBUM, INCLUDING 'JEFF'S BLUES', 'WHAT DO YOU WANT', 'POUNDS & STOMPS', 'SOMEONE TO LOVE ME', 'HERE 'TIS', 'CHRIS'S NUMBER', 'CRIMSON CURTAIN', 'LIKE JIMMY REED'.
tue	29	
wed	30	
thu	31	**BBC TV** LONDON, ENGLAND, MIMING 'SHAPES OF THINGS' ON TONIGHT'S *TOP OF THE POPS* BROADCAST.

APRIL 1966

fri	1	**LA LOCOMOTIVE CLUB** PARIS, FRANCE, PERFORMING FOR TONIGHT'S *READY STEADY ALLEZ* BROADCAST ON BRITISH TV.
sat	2	**UNKNOWN VENUE** SOUTH OF FRANCE. *SHORT EUROPEAN TOUR UNDERWAY.*
sun	3	**L'OMNIBUS** MARSEILLES, FRANCE. PLUS LES MESSENGERS. *BECK COLLAPSES ON-STAGE, FOOD POISONING, RETURNS LONDON.*
mon	4	**TV STUDIO** SWITZERLAND. *YARDBIRDS CONTINUE AS QUARTET WITHOUT BECK. TODAY'S TV DATE NOT CONFIRMED.*
tue	5	**TV STUDIO** BREMEN, GERMANY, TAPING FOR *BEAT CLUB*. *PROBABLY NOT BROADCAST (STILL NO BECK).*
wed	6	
thu	7	**KB HALLEN** COPENHAGEN, DENMARK. 'YOUNG PEOPLE'S BALL'. **FYNS FORUM** ODENSE, FYN, DENMARK. *BOTH MINUS BECK.*
fri	8	BAND RETURNS HOME. *IN DAYS FOLLOWING GIORGIO GOMELSKY DROPPED AS MANAGER AND SIMON NAPIER-BELL TAKES OVER.*
sat	9	**RHODES CENTRE** BISHOP'S STORTFORD, HERTS, ENGLAND. *PROBABLY CANCELLED.*
sun	10	**AGINCOURT BALLROOM** CAMBERLEY, SURREY, ENGLAND. *PROBABLY CANCELLED.*
mon	11	**CONCERTGEBOUW** HAARLEM, NETHERLANDS, MINUS BECK. 'HET HARTEWENS FESTIVAL'. + TAPING HERE *TEEN SCENE* TV b/c APR 13th.
tue	12	**TOWN HALL** HIGH WYCOMBE, BUCKS, ENGLAND. *POSTPONED. CHANGEOVER IN MANAGEMENT ANNOUNCED TO PRESS.*
wed	13	**BBC RADIO** *PARADE OF THE POPS* APPEARANCE POSTPONED TO MAY 4th.
thu	14	**DE LANE LEA STUDIOS** LONDON, APPROXIMATE TIMING OF RELF SOLO SESSION, RECORDING 'MR ZERO', 'KNOWING'.
fri	15	
sat	16	**FLORAL HALL** SOUTHPORT, MERSEYSIDE, ENGLAND. *BECK REJOINS YARDBIRDS, BUT FROM THIS POINT SEEMS UNHAPPY WITHIN BAND.*
sun	17	**COSMOPOLITAN CLUB** CARLISLE, CUMBRIA, ENGLAND.
mon	18	
tue	19	**ADVISION STUDIOS** LONDON, RECORDING 'OVER UNDER SIDEWAYS DOWN', 'JEFF'S BOOGIE'.
wed	20	**ADVISION STUDIOS** LONDON, RECORDING 'OVER UNDER SIDEWAYS DOWN', 'JEFF'S BOOGIE'.
thu	21	**PIER PAVILION** WORTHING, WEST SUSSEX, ENGLAND.
fri	22	**PALAIS** WIMBLEDON, LONDON, ENGLAND.
sat	23	**STUDENT UNION** UNIVERSITY OF BRISTOL, BRISTOL, ENGLAND.
sun	24	
mon	25	**SILVER BLADES ICE RINK** BIRMINGHAM, ENGLAND.
tue	26	**TOWN HALL** CRAYFORD, LONDON, ENGLAND.
wed	27	**LOCARNO BALLROOM** STEVENAGE, HERTS, ENGLAND.
thu	28	
fri	29	**MANCHESTER TECHNICAL COLLEGE** MANCHESTER. **REDIFFUSION TV** LONDON, PERFORMING 'JEFF'S BOOGIE' ON *READY STEADY GO*.
sat	30	**CALIFORNIA BALLROOM** DUNSTABLE, BEDS, ENGLAND.

MAY 1966

sun **1** EMPIRE POOL WEMBLEY. "NME 66 POLLWINNERS CONCERT", PLUS BEATLES, STONES, WHO ETC. FILMED FOR ABC TV B/CAST MAY 15th.

mon **2**

tue **3** MARQUEE LONDON, ENGLAND. PLUS THE CLAYTON SQUARES.

wed **4** TOP RANK SUITE SOUTHAMPTON, ENGLAND. **BBC RADIO** LONDON, 2 SONGS LIVE BROADCAST FOR *PARADE OF THE POPS*.

thu **5**

fri **6** BBC RADIO LONDON, TAPING 6 SONGS INC 'OVER UNDER...', 'JEFF'S BOOGIE' FOR *SATURDAY SWINGS* BROADCAST MAY 21st.

sat **7** NETHERLANDS VISIT ARRANGED FOR THIS WEEKEND IS CANCELLED.

sun **8**

mon **9**

tue **10** TOWN HALL HIGH WYCOMBE, BUCKS, ENGLAND. *MUCH RESCHEDULED DATE.*

wed **11**

thu **12** RITZ ENTERTAINMENT CLUB SKEWEN, NEATH PORT TALBOT, WALES. PLUS THE EYES OF BLUE, THE IVEYS, MISS SKEWEN CONTEST.

fri **13** REGAL BALLROOM AMMANFORD, CARMAR, WALES. PLUS THE KINGBEES, ETC. **UK RELEASE** 'MR ZERO' 45 BY KEITH RELF.

sat **14** PAVILION GARDENS BALLROOM BUXTON, DERBYS, ENGLAND.

sun **15** BIRMINGHAM THEATRE BIRMINGHAM, ENGLAND. *THERE NOW FOLLOWS AN OFFICIAL WEEK-OFF FOR THE BAND.*

mon **16** IBC STUDIOS LONDON. BECK RECORDS 'BECK'S BOLERO' WITH JIMMY PAGE, JOHN PAUL JONES, NICKY HOPKINS, KEITH MOON.

tue **17** IBC STUDIOS LONDON. BECK CONTINUES SOLO RECORDING OF 'BECK'S BOLERO', PERSONNEL AS 16th.

wed **18**

thu **19**

fri **20**

sat **21**

sun **22** SCHEDULED TV/RADIO WORK IN BELGIUM ON 23rd/24th IS CANCELLED.

mon **23**

tue **24**

wed **25** TOP RANK SUITE DONCASTER, SOUTH YORKS, ENGLAND.

thu **26** LOCARNO BALLROOM BRISTOL, ENGLAND.

fri **27** BLUESVILLE CLUB MANOR HOUSE, LONDON. **REDIFFUSION TV** PLAYING ON *READY STEADY GO*. **UK RELEASE** 'OVER UNDER...' 45.

sat **28** DREAMLAND BALLROOM MARGATE, KENT, ENGLAND.

sun **29** KENTUCKY PALACE WOLUWE-ST-LAMBERT, BRUSSELS, BELGIUM PLUS THE SETTLERS, FERRE GRIGNARD.

mon **30** LINCOLN CITY FOOTBALL CLUB LINCOLN, ENGLAND. PLUS THE KINKS, WHO, CREATION, SMALL FACES, LORD SUTCH, ETC.

tue **31** ADVISION STUDIOS LONDON. RECORDING SESSION STARTS; FOR DETAILS SEE JUN 1st.

JUNE 1966

wed **1**

thu **2** ADVISION STUDIOS LONDON. RECORDING FOR ALBUM, INCLUDING: 'LOST WOMAN', 'THE NAZZ ARE BLUE', 'RACK MY MIND', 'FAREWELL', 'HOT HOUSE OF OMAGARARSHID', 'HE'S ALWAYS THERE', 'TURN INTO EARTH', 'WHAT DO YOU WANT?', 'EVER SINCE THE WORLD BEGAN'. ENGINEER: ROGER CAMERON ('ROGER THE ENGINEER'). PRODUCER: SIMON NAPIER-BELL.

fri **3**

sat **4** MIDDLESEX BOROUGH COLLEGE ISLEWORTH, LONDON. **ADVISION STUDIOS** LONDON. COMPLETE RECORDING SESSION.

sun **5**

mon **6**

tue **7**

wed **8** BBC TV LONDON, ENGLAND. MIMING 'OVER UNDER SIDEWAYS DOWN' ON TODAY'S *A WHOLE SCENE GOING* BROADCAST.

thu **9** BBC TV LONDON, MIMING 'OVER UNDER...' ON *TOP OF THE POPS*. **BBC RADIO** TAPING 3 SONGS FOR *JOE LOSS* B/CAST JUL 1st.

fri **10** RICKY TICK THAMES HOTEL, WINDSOR, ENGLAND. *RELF BETTER AFTER ASTHMA ATTACK MEANT NO-SHOW FOR LONDON GIG ON 9th.*

sat **11** ZAMBESI CLUB HOUNSLOW, LONDON, ENGLAND. "BLUES FESTIVAL". **BBC RADIO** TAPING 2 SONGS FOR *EASY BEAT* B/CAST JUL 12th.

sun **12** STARLITE BALLROOM GREENFORD, LONDON, ENGLAND.

mon **13** GAY TOWER BALLROOM BIRMINGHAM, ENGLAND. **US RELEASE** 'OVER UNDER SIDEWAYS DOWN' 45.

tue **14** IBC STUDIOS LONDON. APPROX TIMING OF RECORDING ONE MORE SONG, 'I CAN'T MAKE YOUR WAY' FOR NEW LP.

wed **15** LONDON (LIKELY DATE) MIMING 'OVER UNDER...', 'TURN INTO EARTH' FOR US WABC-TV *IT'S A MOD MOD WORLD*, BROADCAST AUG 13th.

thu **16** CITY HALL SALISBURY, WILTS, ENGLAND.

fri **17** CORN EXCHANGE NEWBURY, WEST BERKS, ENGLAND.

sat **18** QUEEN'S COLLEGE OXFORD UNIVERSITY. "MAY BALL". *SAMWELL-SMITH LEAVES YARDBIRDS; JIMMY PAGE OFFERS TO TAKE OVER ON BASS.*

sun **19** ULTRA CLUB DOWNS HOTEL, HASSOCKS, WEST SUSSEX. *CANCELLED.*

mon **20**

tue **21** MARQUEE LONDON, ENGLAND. *DEBUT OF PAGE-ON-BASS LINE-UP. FROM START, ULTIMATE AIM IS FOR DREJA TO PLAY BASS, PAGE GUITAR.*

wed **22**

thu **23** MECCA PALAIS ASHTON-UNDER-LYNE, MANCHESTER, ENGLAND.

fri **24** UNIVERSITY OF DURHAM DURHAM, ENGLAND. "JUNE BALL 66", PLUS THE ROULETTES, THE ACTION, GRAHAM BOND ETC.

sat **25** PALAIS DE DANSE BURY, MANCHESTER, ENGLAND. PLUS FRANKENSTEIN & HIS MONSTERS, THE SHEFFIELDS.

sun **26** LE WEEKEND CLUB PARIS, FRANCE.

mon **27** PROVINS, FRANCE. "PROVINS ROCK FESTIVAL" ON CASTLE SITE. FILMED FOR FRENCH TV SHOW *MUSIC HALL DE FRANCE* BROADCAST JUL 2nd.

tue **28** UNKNOWN STUDIO *UNCONFIRMED RECORDING SESSION PROBABLY AROUND THIS TIME.*

wed **29** BROMEL CLUB BROMLEY COURT HOTEL, BROMLEY, LONDON.

thu **30**

fri	1	**CHISLEHURST CAVES** CHISLEHURST, LONDON, ENGLAND.
sat	2	**RAM JAM CLUB** BRIXTON, LONDON, ENGLAND.
sun	3	**NORTH PIER PAVILION** BLACKPOOL, ENGLAND. PLUS THE TROGGS.
mon	4	**US RELEASE** 'MR ZERO' 45 BY KEITH RELF.
tue	5	**WINTER GARDENS** GREAT MALVERN, WORCS, ENGLAND.
wed	6	
thu	7	**TOWN HALL** ELGIN, MORAY, SCOTLAND.
fri	8	**RAITH BALLROOM** KIRKCALDY, FIFE, SCOTLAND.
sat	9	**BASS RECREATION GROUNDS** DERBY, ENGLAND.
sun	10	**PIER PAVILION** HASTINGS, EAST SUSSEX, ENGLAND.
mon	11	
tue	12	**MARQUEE STUDIOS** LONDON, LIKELY TIMING OF BECK-LESS RECORDING GREAT SHAKES AD, LOOSELY BASED ON 'OVER UNDER'.
wed	13	**UNKNOWN VENUE** PARIS, FRANCE. PROBABLY CANCELLED.
thu	14	**TOWN HALL** KIDDERMINSTER, WORCS, ENGLAND.
fri	15	**PALAIS DE DANSE** COWDENBEATH, SCOTLAND. **CITY HALL** PERTH, SCOTLAND. **UK RELEASE** THE YARDBIRDS ('ROGER THE ENGINEER') LP.
sat	16	**ICE RINK** AYR, SCOTLAND. PLUS MAUREEN & THE THUNDERBIRDS.

sun	17	**VICTORIA BALLROOM** DUNBAR, EAST LOTHIAN, SCOTLAND.
mon	18	
tue	19	
wed	20	**TOWN HALL** STOURBRIDGE, WEST MIDLANDS, ENGLAND
thu	21	**ASSEMBLY ROOMS** WORTHING, WEST SUSSEX, ENGLAND.
fri	22	**CO-OP HALL** GRAVESEND, KENT, ENGLAND. **REDIFFUSION TV** LONDON, PERFORMING 2 SONGS ON READY STEADY GO.
sat	23	**PAVILION GARDENS BALLROOM** BUXTON, DERBYS, ENGLAND.
sun	24	
mon	25	**PAVILION** BATH, ENGLAND.
tue	26	**IBC STUDIOS** LONDON, SCHEDULED RECORDING OF NEW SINGLE, LIKELY CANCELLED
wed	27	**BBC TV** LONDON, ENGLAND, TAPING 'RACK MY MIND' FOR HEY PRESTO – IT'S ROLF BROADCAST JUL 29th.
thu	28	**PALACE THEATRE** DOUGLAS, ISLE OF MAN. CANCELLED DUE TO ILL BECK.
fri	29	
sat	30	**6th NATIONAL JAZZ/BLUES FESTIVAL** WINDSOR, ENGLAND. YARDBIRDS APPEARANCE CANCELLED DUE TO STILL-ILL BECK.
sun	31	

mon	1	**US RELEASE** OVER UNDER SIDEWAYS DOWN LP.
tue	2	**US TOUR** TRAVEL SHOULD HAVE STARTED TODAY, BUT POSTPONED BECAUSE OF BECK'S ILL-HEALTH.
wed	3	
thu	4	BAND FLIES OUT FROM LONDON TO START 3rd NORTH AMERICAN TOUR, DESPITE BECK "NOT 100 PER CENT".
fri	5	**DAYTON'S AUDITORIUM** MINNEAPOLIS, MN, US, PLUS THE ESCAPADES. **COL BALLROOM** DAVENPORT, IA, US, PLUS THE XLs.
sat	6	**CIVIC OPERA HOUSE** CHICAGO, IL, US. THE AMERICAN TOUR CONTINUES; PAGE PLAYS BASS AND DREJA RHYTHM GUITAR.
sun	7	**MAPLE LAKE PAVILION** MENTOR, MN, US. ONE OF SEVERAL ODD BOOKINGS ON THIS TOUR AT REMOTE VENUES.
mon	8	**DETROIT LAKES PAVILION** DETROIT LAKES, MN, US. PLUS UNBELIEVABLE UGLIES.
tue	9	**ROOF GARDEN BALLROOM** ARNOLDS PARK, IA, US. PLUS THE DARK KNIGHTS.
wed	10	**GREEN'S PAVILION** LAKEVIEW PARK, MANITOU BEACH, MI, US. NAPIER-BELL HAS HIRED PRIVATE PLANE FOR BAND DUE TO US AIR STRIKE
thu	11	
fri	12	**INDIANA BEACH BALLROOM** MONTICELLO, IN, US. **COLD SPRING RESORT** HAMILTON, IN, US.
sat	13	**CHECKMATE YOUNG ADULT CLUB** AMARILLO, TX, US. PLUS THE PAGE BOYS.
sun	14	**4-H BUILDING** STATE FAIRGROUNDS, GREAT FALLS, MT, US.
mon	15	**COTILLION BALLROOM** WICHITA, KS, US. PLUS THE FRANTICS.
tue	16	

wed	17	**JP'S PALACE** SANTA FE, NM, US. PROBABLE DATE.
thu	18	**TULSA ASSEMBLY CENTER EXHIBIT HALL** OK, US. BAND ONLY OCCASIONALLY USING OWN AMPS, SO SOUND OFTEN POOR.
fri	19	**WEDGEWOOD AMUSEMENT PARK** OKLAHOMA CITY, OK, US.
sat	20	**WEDGEWOOD AMUSEMENT PARK** OKLAHOMA CITY, OK, US
sun	21	**THRIFT CITY ON SPEEDWAY** TUCSON, AZ, US. PLUS LEWALLEN BROS, THE FIVE OF US, SHOWMEN, THE BOW STREET RUNNERS.
mon	22	**SUNSET SOUND STUDIOS** LA, (LIKELY DATE) NAPIER-BELL CUTS BACKING TRACK FOR 'SHAPES IN MY MIND' WITH SESSION PLAYERS.
tue	23	**CASINO BALLROOM** AVALON, CATALINA ISLAND, CA, US. "MOONLIGHT CRUISE TO CATALINA". PLUS THE DANES ETC.
wed	24	**UNKNOWN VENUE** MONTEREY, CA, US. CANCELLED.
thu	25	**CAROUSEL BALLROOM** SAN FRANCISCO, BECK ILL WITH TONSILLITIS; PAGE TAKES OVER ON GUITAR, DREJA SHIFTS TO BASS.
fri	26	**ROLLARENA** SAN LEANDRO, CA, US. PLUS HARBINGER COMPLEX ETC. REMAINING US DATES MINUS BECK, PAGE GUITAR, DREJA BASS.
sat	27	**EARL WARREN SHOWGROUNDS** SANTA BARBARA, CA, US. **VENTURA HIGH SCHOOL AUDITORIUM** VENTURA, CA, US.
sun	28	**CONVENTION HALL** SAN DIEGO, CA, US. CANCELLED DAY OF SHOW.
mon	29	
tue	30	**SAN JOSE CIVIC AUDITORIUM** SAN JOSE, CA, US.
wed	31	**ROSE GARDEN BALLROOM** PISMO BEACH, CA, US. PROBABLE DATE.

SEPTEMBER 1966

thu	1	**CIVIC AUDITORIUM** STOCKTON, CA, US. *TOUR CONTINUES MINUS "ILL" BECK, WITH PAGE ON GUITAR AND DREJA ON BASS.*
fri	2	
sat	3	**SALEM ARMORY AUDITORIUM** SALEM, OR, US. "OREGON STATE FAIR, TEEN FESTIVAL".
sun	4	**HIC EXHIBITON HALL** HONOLULU, HI, US. "BACK TO SCHOOL FALL IN DANCE".
mon	5	
tue	6	
wed	7	**CIVIC AUDITORIUM** SANTA MONICA, CA, US. "SUMMER AT THE CIVIC".
thu	8	**COLUMBIA STUDIOS** NEW YORK, RELF ADDS VOCAL TO 'SHAPES IN MY MIND'. *ALSO EPIC RECORDS PRESS PARTY IN NEW YORK.*
fri	9	**ALEXANDRIA ROLLER RINK** ALEXANDRIA, VA, US. "TEEN FAIR", PLUS ASSORTED LOCAL BANDS.
sat	10	**BALTIMORE CIVIC CENTER** BALTIMORE, MD, US. PLUS THE SYNDICATE OF SOUND, THE CYRKLE.
sun	11	RELF FLIES HOME; REST OF THE BAND, INCLUDING "BETTER" BECK, FOLLOW LATER; CANCEL 2nd DAY OF BALTIMORE BOOKING.
mon	12	
tue	13	
wed	14	
thu	15	REMAINING BAND MEMBERS FLY HOME FROM NYC.
fri	16	
sat	17	
sun	18	
mon	19	
tue	20	**DE LANE LEA STUDIOS** LONDON. RECORDING BASIC TRACK FOR 'HAPPENINGS TEN YEARS TIME AGO'. DUBS OVER NEXT 2 WEEKS. ALSO AROUND THIS TIME RECORD 'PSYCHO DAISIES' – BECK GUITAR, PAGE BASS, McCARTY DRUMS ONLY.
wed	21	
thu	22	
fri	23	**ROYAL ALBERT HALL** LONDON, ENGLAND. *START OF 2-WEEK UK TOUR SUPPORTING ROLLING STONES, PLUS OTHERS... (SEE 24th).*
sat	24	**ODEON CINEMA** LEEDS, ENGLAND. *ALSO IKE & TINA TURNER, PETER JAY & THE JAYWALKERS. YARDBIRDS ARE THIRD ON THE BILL.*
sun	25	**EMPIRE THEATRE** LIVERPOOL, ENGLAND. *FROM START OF TOUR YARDBIRDS LINE-UP SETTLED AT BECK & PAGE GUITARS, DREJA BASS.*
mon	26	
tue	27	
wed	28	**ABC CINEMA** ARDWICK, MANCHESTER, ENGLAND.
thu	29	**ABC CINEMA** STOCKTON-ON-TEES, ENGLAND.
fri	30	**ODEON CINEMA** GLASGOW, SCOTLAND.

OCTOBER 1966

sat	1	**CITY HALL** NEWCASTLE UPON TYNE, ENGLAND. *ROLLING STONES TOUR CONTINUES.*
sun	2	**GAUMONT CINEMA** IPSWICH, SUFFOLK, ENGLAND. *ALSO, BECK ADDS GUITAR OVERDUBS TO 'HAPPENINGS TEN YEARS TIME AGO'.*
mon	3	**SOUND TECHNIQUES** LONDON. (LIKELY DATE) RECORDING 'STROLL ON', A SLIGHTLY RE-ARRANGED VERSION OF 'THE TRAIN KEPT A-ROLLIN', FOR SOUNDTRACK AND BAND'S FORTHCOMING APPEARANCE IN *BLOWUP* MOVIE. DIRECTOR MICHELANGELO ANTONIONI DECIDED ON YARDBIRDS OVER ORIGINAL CHOICE, TOMORROW, AFTER SEEING THEM LIVE AT ALBERT HALL SEP 23rd.
tue	4	
wed	5	
thu	6	**ODEON CINEMA** BIRMINGHAM, ENGLAND. *ROLLING STONES TOUR CONTINUES.*
fri	7	**COLSTON HALL** BRISTOL, ENGLAND.
sat	8	**CAPITOL THEATRE** CARDIFF, WALES.
sun	9	**GAUMONT CINEMA** SOUTHAMPTON, ENGLAND. *LAST DATE OF STONES TOUR. YARDBIRDS EARNED ABOUT £40 PER NIGHT EACH.*
mon	10	
tue	11	
wed	12	**ELSTREE FILM STUDIOS** BOREHAMWOOD, HERTS, ENGLAND. FILMED MIMING 'STROLL ON' FOR MOVIE *BLOWUP* ON THE SET'S RECONSTRUCTION OF WINDSOR'S RICKY TICK CLUB. BECK SMASHES PROP HOLLOWBODY GUITAR MADE FOR STEVE HOWE OF ORIGINAL MOVIE-CHOICE GROUP, TOMORROW.
thu	13	
fri	14	
sat	15	
sun	16	
mon	17	PRESS REPORTS OF IMMINENT YARDBIRDS SPLIT ARE CONSISTENTLY DENIED AROUND THIS TIME.
tue	18	
wed	19	**BBC TV** LONDON, ENGLAND. TAPING 'HAPPENINGS TEN YEARS TIME AGO' FOR *TOP OF THE POPS* BROADCAST NOV 17th.
thu	20	
fri	21	**COMIC STRIP** WORCESTER, MA, US. *1ST DATE OF 4th AMERICAN TOUR.* **UK RELEASE** 'HAPPENINGS TEN YEARS TIME AGO' 45.
sat	22	**STAPLES HIGH SCHOOL AUDITORIUM** WESTPORT, CT, US. *THIS & 21ST/23RD ONLY STRETCHING-OUT DATES FOR 2-GUITAR LINE-UP.*
sun	23	**FILLMORE AUDITORIUM** SAN FRANCISCO, CA, US. PLUS COUNTRY JOE & THE FISH. *BY ALL ACCOUNTS A GREAT SHOW.*
mon	24	
tue	25	**ABC TV CENTER** LOS ANGELES, CA, US. TAPING 'HAPPENINGS...' FOR *THE MILTON BERLE SHOW* BROADCAST DEC 2nd.
wed	26	
thu	27	
fri	28	
sat	29	**DALLAS MEMORIAL AUDITORIUM** DALLAS, TX, US. *FIRST DATE OF DICK CLARK'S "CARAVAN OF STARS" PACKAGE TOUR WITH 7 OTHERS.*
sun	30	**HARLINGEN CIVIC AUDITORIUM** HARLINGEN, TX, US. **MEMORIAL COLISEUM** CORPUS CHRISTI, TX. *BECK DECIDES TO LEAVE FOR LA.*
mon	31	**MUNICIPAL AUDITORIUM** BEAUMONT, TX, US. *CONTINUE MINUS BECK.* **US RELEASE** 'HAPPENINGS TEN YEARS TIME AGO' 45.

NOVEMBER 1966

tue 1 **PARRISH COLISEUM** LOUISIANA STATE UNIVERSITY, ALEXANDRIA, LA, US. *BAND CONTINUES MINUS BECK; PAGE NOW SOLE GUITARIST.*

wed 2 **SOUTHERN STATE COLLEGE FIELD HOUSE** MAGNOLIA, AR, US. *REVIEW OF SHOW CONFIRMS BECK NOT PRESENT.*

thu 3 **DECATUR HIGH SCHOOL AUDITORIUM** DECATUR, AL, US.

fri 4 **BARTON COLISEUM** LITTLE ROCK, AR, US. *SCHEDULED BUT APPARENTLY CANCELLED.*

sat 5 **MEMORIAL BUILDING AUDITORIUM** KANSAS CITY, KS, US.

sun 6 **BARTLESVILLE CIVIC CENTER** BARTLESVILLE, OK, US. **TULSA ASSEMBLY CENTER** TULSA, OK, US.

mon 7 **CHANUTE AUDITORIUM** CHANUTE, KS, US.

tue 8 **RKO ORPHEUM THEATER** DAVENPORT, IA, US.

wed 9 **MEMORIAL FIELD HOUSE** INDIANA STATE UNIVERSITY, TERRE HAUTE, IN, US.

thu 10 **KIEL AUDITORIUM** ST LOUIS, MO, US.

fri 11 **INDIANA FAIRGROUNDS COLISEUM** INDIANAPOLIS, IN, US.

sat 12 **AKRON CIVIC THEATER** AKRON, OH, US. **GROVER CENTER** OHIO UNIVERSITY, ATHENS, OH, US.

sun 13 **BALTIMORE CIVIC CENTER ARENA** BALTIMORE, MD, US.

mon 14 **PAINTSVILLE HIGH SCHOOL GYMNASIUM** PAINTSVILLE, KY, US.

tue 15 **DIDDLE ARENA** UNIVERSITY OF WESTERN KENTUCKY, BOWLING GREEN, KY, US.

wed 16 **MEMORIAL GYMNASIUM** TENNESSEE TECHNOLOGICAL UNIVERSITY, COOKEVILLE, TN, US.

thu 17 **FIELD HOUSE** UNIVERSITY OF TENNESSEE, MARTIN ,TN, US. *CLARK TOUR GRINDS ON WITH YARDBIRDS AS QUARTET, PAGE SOLE GUITARIST.*

fri 18 **MICHIGAN STATE FAIR COLISEUM** DETROIT, MI, US. PLUS THE VELVET UNDERGROUND & NICO.

sat 19 **MICHIGAN STATE FAIR COLISEUM** DETROIT, MI, US. PLUS THE VELVET UNDERGROUND & NICO.

sun 20 **MICHIGAN STATE FAIR COLISEUM** DETROIT, MI, US. PLUS THE VELVET UNDERGROUND & NICO.

mon 21 **RICHMOND CIVIC HALL** RICHMOND, IN, US.

tue 22

wed 23 **PITTSBURGH CIVIC ARENA** PITTSBURGH, PA, US. PLUS SONNY & CHER, TONIGHT ONLY. DINO DESI & BILLY REPLACE LEWIS HEREAFTER.

thu 24 **RALEIGH COUNTY ARMORY** BECKLEY, WV, US. **CHARLESTON CIVIC CENTER** CHARLESTON, WV. *NO-SHOW BY YARDBIRDS .*

fri 25 **MEMORIAL COLISEUM** WINSTON-SALEM, NC, US. *NO-SHOW BY YARDBIRDS.* **UK RELEASE** 'SHAPES IN MY MIND' 45 BY KEITH RELF.

sat 26 **WASHINGTON COLISEUM** WASHINGTON DC, US. PLUS LITTLE ANTHONY & THE IMPERIALS, THIS DATE ONLY.

sun 27 **CABELL COUNTY MEMORIAL FIELD HOUSE** HUNTINGTON, WV, US. *LAST DATE OF GRUELLING DICK CLARK "CARAVAN OF STARS" TOUR.*

mon 28

tue 29

wed 30 MANAGER SIMON NAPIER-BELL IN LONDON INFORMS PRESS THAT BECK IS LEAVING YARDBIRDS DUE TO "PERSISTENT ILL HEALTH".

DECEMBER 1966

thur 1 BECK ARRIVES BACK IN LONDON.

fri 2 **UNION BALLROOM** BALDWIN-WALLACE COLLEGE, BEREA, OH, US. PLUS THE CHOIR. *4-PIECE YARDBIRDS PLAY A FEW NON-TOUR DATES.*

sat 3

sun 4 **SPRINGBROOK GARDENS TEEN CENTER** LIMA, OH, US. PLUS THE BREAKOUTS.

mon 5 **US RELEASE** 'SHAPES IN MY MIND' 45 BY KEITH RELF. *FOUR-MAN YARDBIRDS ARRIVE BACK IN LONDON.*

tue 6

wed 7

thu 8

fri 9

sat 10 **STUDENT UNION** UNIVERSITY OF BRISTOL, BRISTOL, ENGLAND. "GOING-DOWN DANCE". *UNOFFICIALLY AS 4-PIECE BAND STILL.*

sun 11

mon 12 BAND MEETING IN LONDON EARLY THIS WEEK TO INFORM BECK OFFICIALLY THAT HE IS NO LONGER A YARDBIRD.

tue 13 **UNIVERSITY OF ABERYSTWYTH** ABERYSTWYTH, CERE, WALES. *OFFICIALLY AS 4-PIECE BAND HEREAFTER.*

wed 14

thu 15 **CITY HALL** (KINGSTON UPON) HULL, ENGLAND. *VENUE POSSIBLY CHANGED TO THE CITY'S BEVERLEY ROAD BATHS.*

fri 16

sat 17

sun 18

mon 19

tue 20

wed 21

thu 22 **OLYMPIC STUDIOS** LONDON, RECORDING UNFINISHED TRACKS 'YOU STOLE MY LOVE', 'LSD'. PRODUCER: PAUL SAMWELL-SMITH.

fri 23

sat 24

sun 25 **US TOUR** STARTS WITH TRAVEL DAY FOR 4-PIECE YARDBIRDS.

mon 26 **WAR MEMORIAL AUDITORIUM** ROCHESTER, NY, US. PLUS ? & THE MYSTERIANS, ETC. "DICK CLARK'S CHRISTMAS TOUR".

tue 27 **FIFTH DIMENSION CLUB** ANN ARBOR, MI, US. PLUS RICHARD & THE YOUNG LIONS, (POSSIBLY) DECEMBER'S CHILDREN.

wed 28 **YOUTH BUILDING** EXPOSITION GARDENS, PEORIA, IL, US. PLUS THE FURNITURE, THE COACHMEN. *RELF SUFFERING LARYNGITIS ALREADY.*

thu 29 **KINGSTON MEMORIAL CENTRE** KINGSTON, ON, CANADA. "HOLIDAY TEEN DANCE". *YARDBIRDS NO-SHOW, ADVERSE WEATHER.*

fri 30 **UNKNOWN VENUE** UPSTATE NEW YORK, US, CANCELLED.

sat 31 **UNKNOWN VENUE**

JANUARY 1967

sun 1 **CAMBRIA COUNTY WAR MEMORIAL ARENA** JOHNSTOWN, PA, US. PLUS ? & THE MYSTERIANS, SYNDICATE OF SOUND, ETC.

mon 2 **LONG ISLAND ARENA** COMMACK, NY, US. PLUS ? & THE MYSTERIANS, SYNDICATE OF SOUND, ETC.

tue 3 WHILE IN NEW YORK CITY THIS WEEK FOR PRESS DUTIES SOME HASTILY-ARRANGED POST-TOUR DATES ARE ARRANGED.

wed 4

thu 5

fri 6

sat 7 **COMMODORE BALLROOM** LOWELL, MA, US. PLUS THE SHERWOODS.

sun 8

mon 9 **TRAVEL DAY** BACK TO LONDON.

tue 10 DURING THIS WEEK MANAGER SIMON NAPIER-BELL TRANSFERS HIS CONTRACT TO PETER GRANT, AND RECORDING TO MICKEY MOST.

wed 11

thu 12

fri 13

sat 14

sun 15 TRAVEL TO SINGAPORE FOR START OF AUSTRALASIA/FAR EAST TOUR. PETER GRANT NOW ATTENDING TO MANAGEMENT DUTIES.

mon 16

tue 17 **NATIONAL THEATRE** SINGAPORE (CITY), SINGAPORE. PLUS THE WALKER BROTHERS & THE QUOTATIONS, THE QUESTS.

wed 18

thu 19 **TRAVEL** TO AUSTRALIA.

fri 20

sat 21 **SYDNEY STADIUM** SYDNEY, AUSTRALIA. OZ DATES PLUS ROY ORBISON & WEBS, WALKER BROTHERS & QUOTATIONS, JOHNNY YOUNG.

sun 22

mon 23 **SYDNEY STADIUM** SYDNEY, NSW, AUSTRALIA.

tue 24

wed 25 **CENTENNIAL HALL** ADELAIDE, SOUTH AUS, AUSTRALIA.

thu 26 **FESTIVAL HALL** MELBOURNE, VICTORIA, AUSTRALIA.

fri 27 **FESTIVAL HALL** MELBOURNE, VICTORIA, AUSTRALIA. **UK RELEASE** *OVER UNDER SIDEWAYS DOWN EP.*

sat 28 **FESTIVAL HALL** BRISBANE, QUEENSLAND, AUSTRALIA.

sun 29 **TRAVEL** TO NEW ZEALAND.

mon 30 **THEATRE ROYAL** CHRISTCHURCH, NEW ZEALAND. NZ DATES ORBISON AND WALKERS, PLUS LEE GRANT, SANDY EDMONDS ETC.

tue 31 **TOWN HALL** WELLINGTON, NEW ZEALAND.

FEBRUARY 1967

wed 1 **FOUNDER'S THEATRE** HAMILTON, NEW ZEALAND. *AUSTRALASIA/ FAR EAST TOUR CONTINUES + ROY ORBISON, WALKER BROS, ETC.*

thu 2 **TOWN HALL** AUCKLAND, NEW ZEALAND.

fri 3 **TOUR** ENDS. FURTHER DATES IN HONG KONG, JAPAN AND POSSIBLY PHILLIPINES SCRAPPED. RELF, DREJA RETURN DIRECTLY TO LONDON; McCARTY BACK VIA NEW YORK CITY. PAGE GOES VIA

sat 4 BOMBAY, INDIA, TO TAKE SITAR LESSONS WITH RAVI SHANKAR.

sun 5

mon 6

tue 7

wed 8

thu 9

fri 10

sat 11 **LA LOCOMOTIVE** PARIS, FRANCE. **LE TUBE** AULNAY-SOUS-BOIS, PARIS, FRANCE.

sun 12

mon 13

tue 14

wed 15 **DE LANE LEA STUDIOS** LONDON. THIS WEEK OR NEXT, PROBABLE RECORDING OF SINGLE 'LITTLE GAMES'/'PUZZLES', WHICH IS FINISHED/DELIVERED MAR 6th.

thu 16

fri 17

sat 18 **CIVIC HALL** BARNSLEY, SOUTH YORKS, ENGLAND. *FIRST BRITISH DATE FOLLOWING OVERSEAS TOUR.*

sun 19

mon 20 **US RELEASE** *BLOWUP, THE ORIGINAL SOUNDTRACK LP.*

tue 21

wed 22

thu 23 **LOCARNO BALLROOM** COVENTRY, WEST MIDLANDS, ENGLAND.

fri 24 **SOPHIA GARDENS** CARDIFF, WALES.

sat 25 **LEAS CLIFF HALL** FOLKESTONE, KENT, ENGLAND. PLUS THE MIXED FEELINGS.

sun 26

mon 27 **LOCARNO BALLROOM** GLASGOW, SCOTLAND. PLUS DAVE BERRY & THE CRUISERS, STUDIO 6, CHRIS McCLURE SECTION, ETC.

tue 28

DE LANE LEA STUDIOS LONDON. MADE SOMETIME BETWEEN FEB AND APR IS A VIRTUALLY SOLO RECORDING BY PAGE OF 'WHITE SUMMER' WHICH AT FIRST IS REFERRED TO ON THE TAPE BOX AS 'ARABIC NUMBER'.

MARCH 1967

wed 1

thu 2 **UNKNOWN VENUE** IRELAND.

fri 3 **UNKNOWN VENUE** IRELAND.

sat 4 **UNKNOWN VENUE** IRELAND.

sun 5 SCHEDULED START OF RECORDING LP, LIKELY DELAYED; POSSIBLY FINISH 'LITTLE GAMES' / 'PUZZLES' 45 WHICH IS DELIVERED TO EMI TODAY.

mon 6

tue 7

wed 8 **TV STUDIO** PARIS, FRANCE, TAPING FOR *TETE EN BOIS*. CANCELLED, AS WERE FOLLOWING DATES, DUE TO LACK OF ADVANCE PAYMENT.

thu 9 **RADIO CAROLINE CLUB** PARIS, FRANCE. *CANCELLED*.

fri 10 **UNKNOWN VENUE** FRANCE. *CANCELLED*.

sat 11 **UNKNOWN VENUE** FRANCE. *CANCELLED*.

sun 12 **UNKNOWN VENUE** FRANCE. *CANCELLED*.

mon 13

tue 14

wed 15 **STADTHALLE** OFFENBACH, GERMANY. PERFORMING 5 SONGS INC 'OVER UNDER...', 'SHAPES...', 'HAPPENINGS...' FOR *BEAT BEAT BEAT*.

thu 16

fri 17

sat 18 **LONDON** PHOTO-SESSION FOR 'LITTLE GAMES' ADS.

sun 19

mon 20

tue 21

wed 22

thu 23

fri 24

sat 25

sun 26

mon 27 **DE LANE LEA STUDIOS** LONDON. (AROUND THIS TIME) LIKELY INITIAL "DAY" OF LP SESSIONS, LOOSELY DESCRIBED AS ABOUT 3

tue 28 DAYS BUT LIKELY SPREAD OVER MAR TO MAY. (SEE ALSO APR 23rd-25th & MAY 1st.)

wed 29

thu 30

fri 31

APRIL 1967

sat 1

sun 2 **UNKNOWN VENUE** ROTTERDAM ,BELGIUM. *CANCELLED*.

mon 3 **UNKNOWN VENUE** ROTTERDAM ,BELGIUM. *CANCELLED*; ALSO TOMORROW, 4th, SAME VENUE. **US RELEASE** 'LITTLE GAMES' 45.

tue 4 **BBC RADIO** LONDON, ENGLAND. TAPING 4 SONGS INC 'LITTLE GAMES', 'OVER UNDER...' FOR *SATURDAY CLUB* B/CAST APRIL 15th.

wed 5 **UNKNOWN VENUE** ABILDSø, OSLO, NORWAY. *DATE UNCONFIRMED*.

thu 6 **UNKNOWN VENUE** NORWAY.

fri 7 **RADIOHUSET** STOCKHOLM, SWEDEN. PERFORMING 8 SONGS INC 'LITTLE GAMES', 'OVER UNDER...', 'SHAPES...' FOR SWEDISH RADIO.

sat 8 **UNKNOWN VENUE** SWEDEN.

sun 9 **UNKNOWN VENUE** SWEDEN.

mon 10 **UNKNOWN VENUE** SWEDEN.

tue 11 **UNKNOWN VENUE** SWEDEN.

wed 12 **UNKNOWN VENUE** SWEDEN.

thu 13 **BOOM CLUB** AARHUS, DENMARK.

fri 14 **TEATERSALEN** FREDERIKSHAVN, DENMARK. **VERSTERHAVSHALLEN** RINGKøBING, DENMARK.

sat 15 **HOLTEHALLEN** HOLTE, DENMARK. **NøRREGÅRDESKOLEN** BRøNDBY, DENMARK. **BALLERUPHALLEN** BALLERUP, DENMARK.

sun 16 **REVENTLOWPARKEN** LOLLAND, DENMARK.

mon 17 **US RELEASE** *GREATEST HITS* LP. AFTER TOUR, BAND TRAVEL BACK TO LONDON TODAY.

tue 18

wed 19

thu 20

fri 21 **UK RELEASE** 'LITTLE GAMES' 45.

sat 22

sun 23 **DE LANE LEA STUDIOS** LONDON. LIKELY TIMING OF SECOND "DAY" OF LP SESSIONS. TRACKS RECORDED BY NOW INCLUDE 'NO

mon 24 EXCESS BAGGAGE', 'SMILE ON ME', 'DRINKING MUDDY WATER', 'DE LANE LEA LEE', 'STEALING STEALING', 'I REMEMBER THE NIGHT'.

tue 25 PREVIOUS "DAY" OF RECORDING LIKELY IN MAR (AND SEE ALSO MAY 1st).

wed 26

thu 27

fri 28

sat 29

sun 30 **MUGUET DE CHAVILLE FESTIVAL** PARIS, FRANCE. **TV STUDIO** PARIS, PERFORMING 4 SONGS ON *GRAND SPECTACLE DE JEUNES*.

MAY 1967

mon 1 **DE LANE LEA STUDIOS** LONDON. FINAL RECORDING NEW LP INC 'GLIMPSES', 'ONLY THE BLACK ROSE', 'SOLDIER BOY', 'NEVER MIND'.

tue 2

wed 3

thu 4

fri 5

sat 6 **ROYAL AGRICULTURAL COLLEGE** CHIPPENHAM, ENGLAND. "RAG RAVE/CHARITY APPEAL" PLUS CREAM, THE MINDBENDERS.

sun 7

mon 8 AN ANNOUNCED APPEARANCE BY THE YARDBIRDS IN CANNES, FRANCE FOR A SCREENING OF *BLOW-UP* MOVIE NEVER HAPPENS.

tue 9

wed 10 **UK RELEASE** *BLOW-UP, THE ORIGINAL SOUNDTRACK* LP.

thu 11

fri 12

sat 13

sun 14 **UNKNOWN VENUE** STRATFORD, LONDON, ENGLAND.

mon 15

tue 16

wed 17

thu 18 **UNKNOWN VENUE** VERSAILLES, FRANCE.

fri 19 **L'HERMITAGE** ELIZABETHVILLE, PARIS, FRANCE.

sat 20 **HEC BUSINESS SCHOOL** JOUY, FRANCE. "END OF YEAR PARTY". PLUS JOE DASSIN, JIMMY JAMES, JEAN-LUC PONTY, DEXTER GORDON.

sun 21

mon 22 **BBC RADIO** LONDON, ENGLAND. TAPING 'LITTLE GAMES', 'OVER UNDER...', 'ROCK ME' FOR *MONDAY MONDAY* B/CAST MAY 29th.

tue 23 **CORN EXCHANGE** BRISTOL, ENGLAND.

wed 24

thu 25

fri 26 **TILES** LONDON, ENGLAND.

sat 27 **SUPREME BALLROOM** RAMSGATE, KENT, ENGLAND. "ALL NIGHT RAVE".

sun 28

mon 29 **CITY FOOTBALL CLUB STADIUM** CAMBRIDGE, ENGLAND.

tue 30

wed 31

JUNE 1967

thur 1 **UNIVERSITY OF KENT** CANTERBURY, KENT, ENGLAND.

fri 2

sat 3

sun 4

mon 5

tue 6 **WINTER GARDENS** MALVERN WELLS, WORCS, ENGLAND.

wed 7

thu 8 **ASSEMBLY HALL** WORTHING, WEST SUSSEX, ENGLAND.

fri 9 **DREAMLAND BALLROOM** MARGATE, KENT, ENGLAND.

sat 10 **TOWN HALL** TORQUAY, TORBAY, ENGLAND. PLUS THE RIGHT ATTITUDE.

sun 11

mon 12

tue 13 **COLUMBIA STUDIOS** NEW YORK, NY, US. *SESSION MUSICIANS RECORD BACKING TRACK FOR 'HA HA SAID THE CLOWN' (SEE 19th).*

wed 14

thu 15

fri 16 **STUDENT UNION** UNIVERSITY OF EAST ANGLIA, NORWICH, NORFOLK, ENGLAND.

sat 17 **RAVEN CLUB** RAF WADDINGTON, LINCS, ENGLAND. PLUS PAUL & BARRY RYAN.

sun 18 **SAVILLE THEATRE** LONDON, ENGLAND. "CHARITY POP CONCERT" PLUS MANFRED MANN, THE NEW VAUDEVILLE BAND, THE SETTLERS.

mon 19 **EMI (ABBEY ROAD) STUDIOS** LONDON. *RELF DUBS VOCALS ON TO 'HA HA SAID THE CLOWN' BACKING TRACK (SEE 13th).*

tue 20

wed 21

thu 22

fri 23

sat 24 **TWENTY CLUB** MOUSCRON, BELGIUM. PLUS CAT STEVENS. *UNION DISPUTE LEADS TO YARDBIRDS' NON-APPEARANCE.*

sun 25 **UNKNOWN VENUE** FRANCE.

mon 26

tue 27

wed 28

thu 29

fri 30 **MUSIC HALL** SHREWSBURY, SHROPS, ENGLAND. PLUS THE KARAKTERS, THE ASTRONAUTS.

JULY 1967

sat 1

sun 2

mon 3

tue 4

wed 5 BAND SCHEDULED TO START TRAVEL TO NORTH AMERICA FOR TOUR, DELAYED AT LAST MINUTE.

thu 6

fri 7 **UNKNOWN VENUE** CANADA. *CANCELLED.*

sat 8 **UNKNOWN VENUE** MONTREAL, PQ, CANADA. *CANCELLED.*

sun 9 **UNKNOWN VENUE** OTTAWA, ON, CANADA. *CANCELLED.*

mon 10 **TEENSVILLE** THIENSVILLE, WI, US. *CANCELLED.*

tue 11 **THE NEW PLACE** ALGONQUIN, IL, US. *CANCELLED.*

wed 12 **CRIMSON COUGAR** AURORA, IL, US. *CANCELLED.*

thu 13

fri 14 BAND MAKE RESCHEDULED JOURNEY TO NORTH AMERICA FOR THE YARDBIRDS' 6th TOUR THERE.

sat 15 **THE BIG MOOSE SHOWCASE** LORAIN, OH, US.

sun 16

mon 17 **US RELEASE** 'HA HA SAID THE CLOWN' 45.

tue 18

wed 19 **CITY AUDITORIUM** COLORADO SPRINGS, CO, US.

thu 20 **LAKESIDE AMUSEMENT PARK** DENVER, CO, US.

fri 21 **RACING GRANDSTAND** SONOMA COUNTY FAIRGROUNDS, SANTA ROSA, CA, US. PLUS SIR DOUGLAS QUINTET, ETC.

sat 22 **CIVIC AUDITORIUM** SANTA MONICA, CA, US. PLUS STRAWBERRY ALARM CLOCK, CAPTAIN BEEFHEART, MOBY GRAPE, ETC.

sun 23

mon 24 **US RELEASE** *LITTLE GAMES* LP.

tue 25 **FILLMORE AUDITORIUM** SAN FRANCISCO, CA, US. PLUS JAMES COTTON BLUES BAND, RICHIE HAVENS.

wed 26 **FILLMORE AUDITORIUM** SAN FRANCISCO, CA, US. PLUS JAMES COTTON BLUES BAND, RICHIE HAVENS.

thu 27 **FILLMORE AUDITORIUM** SAN FRANCISCO, CA, US. PLUS JAMES COTTON BLUES BAND, RICHIE HAVENS.

fri 28 **GOVERNOR'S HALL** SACRAMENTO, CA, US. PLUS THE NEW BREED, PARRISH HALL BLUES BAND. *SHOW DELAYED BY BOMB SCARE.*

sat 29 **SAN RAMON HIGH SCHOOL** DANVILLE, CA, US. PLUS SIR DOUGLAS QUINTET, LOADING ZONE, BLUE LIGHT DISTRICT.

sun 30 **EAGLES AUDITORIUM** SEATTLE, WA, US. PLUS MAGIC FEARN.

mon 31 **KERRISDALE ARENA** VANCOUVER, BC, CANADA. PM CONCERT PLUS TOM NORTHCOTT ETC; EVE DANCE PLUS MAGIC FEARN ETC.

AUGUST 1967

tue 1

wed 2 **PROCHE'S POPULAR BALLROOM** ELLSWORTH, WI, US. PLUS THE BEDLAM FOUR. *LIKELY DATE AS 6th AMERICAN TOUR CONTINUES.*

thu 3 **NEW SOUND DANCE CLUB** YMCA, RACINE, WI, US.

fri 4 EXACT DATES AND VENUES UNCONFIRMED BUT LIKELY SUBURBAN CLUB APPEARANCES IN GREATER CHICAGO OVER THIS WEEKEND.

sat 5

sun 6

mon 7

tue 8

wed 9 **LAKE TIPPECANOE GARDENS** LEESBURG, IN, US. PLUS THE TRACES OF TIME.

thu 10

fri 11 **CANOBIE LAKE PARK BALLROOM** SALEM, NH, US.

sat 12 **MOUNTAIN PARK BALLROOM** HOLYOKE, MA, US.

sun 13

mon 14

tue 15 **LAKEVIEW CLUB/BALLROOM** LAKEVIEW AMUSEMENT PARK, MENDON, MA, US. "MIXER-HOP".

wed 16 **HUNT ARMORY** PITTSBURGH, PA, US. ONE NIGHT OF THE 6-DAY '67 TEEN FAIR'; OTHER NIGHTS FEATURED SPENCER DAVIS GROUP, ETC.

thu 17

fri 18 **UNKNOWN VENUE** FL, US. *REPORTED BUT UNCONFIRMED.*

sat 19 **UNKNOWN VENUE** FL, US. *REPORTED BUT UNCONFIRMED.*

sun 20 **UNKNOWN VENUE** FL, US. *REPORTED BUT UNCONFIRMED.*

mon 21

tue 22

wed 23

thu 24 **SURF CLUB** NANTASKET BEACH, HULL, MA, US.

fri 25 **VILLAGE THEATER** NEW YORK, NY, US. PLUS THE YOUNGBLOODS, JAKE HOLMES.

sat 26 **HIDDEN VALLEY** HUNTSVILLE, ON, CANADA. *BAND ARRIVE VERY LATE, AROUND 11pm.*

sun 27 **ROCKY POINT AMUSEMENT PARK** WARWICK NECK, RI, US. *6th NORTH AMERICAN TOUR ENDS.*

mon 28 PRESS DUTIES AT EPIC RECORDS OFFICES IN NEW YORK CITY.

tue 29 LIKELY TRAVEL DAY TO LONDON / END OF 6th US TOUR.

wed 30

thu 31

SEPTEMBER 1967

fri	1	A JAPANESE TOUR WAS ORIGINALLY SLATED SOME TIME THIS MONTH, FOLLOWING US TOUR, BUT THE PLAN WAS ABANDONED.
sat	2	
sun	3	
mon	4	
tue	5	
wed	6	
thu	7	
fri	8	
sat	9	
sun	10	
mon	11	
tue	12	
wed	13	
thu	14	
fri	15	
sat	16	

sun	17	
mon	18	
tue	19	
wed	20	
thu	21	
fri	22	
sat	23	
sun	24	
mon	25	**OLYMPIC STUDIOS** LONDON, RECORDING 'TEN LITTLE INDIANS' WITH RELF AND PAGE PLUS SESSION MUSICIANS.
tue	26	
wed	27	
thu	28	
fri	29	
sat	30	

OCTOBER 1967

RELF+PAGE+DREJA+McCARTY

sun	1	
mon	2	
tue	3	
wed	4	
thu	5	BAND MINUS McCARTY TRAVELS TODAY TO START 7th NORTH AMERICAN TOUR; McCARTY MISSES PLANE AND FIRST TWO DATES.
fri	6	**MEEHAN AUDITORIUM** BROWN UNIVERSITY, PROVIDENCE, RI, US. *YARDBIRDS CANCEL THEIR APPEARANCE, LACKING A DRUMMER.*
sat	7	**MOUNTAIN PARK BALLROOM** HOLYOKE, MA, US. PLUS THE RAMRODS. *YARDBIRDS PLAY WITH SUBSTITUTE DRUMMER.*
sun	8	**UNKNOWN VENUE** NORTH-EAST US. *YARDBIRDS PLAY WITH SUBSTITUTE DRUMMER.*
mon	9	THE BAND ARE BASED IN NEW YORK CITY DURING THE WEEK AND AWAIT THE ARRIVAL OF McCARTY.
tue	10	
wed	11	
thu	12	
fri	13	**FALK THEATER** UNIVERSITY OF TAMPA, TAMPA, FL, US. PLUS THE RAVENS, ETC. *McCARTY NOW BACK ON THE DRUM STOOL.*
sat	14	**UNKNOWN VENUE** COCOA BEACH, FL, US. **UNKNOWN VENUE** MELBOURNE, FL, US.
sun	15	**UNKNOWN VENUE** FL, US.
mon	16	**US RELEASE** 'TEN LITTLE INDIANS' 45.

tue	17	
wed	18	
thu	19	
fri	20	**PUSI-KAT CLUB** SAN ANTONIO, TX, US.
sat	21	**STUDIO CLUB** DALLAS, TX, US.
sun	22	**COTILLION BALLROOM** WICHITA, KS, US. *McCARTY PASSES OUT, TAKEN TO HOSPITAL; DRUMMER FROM AUDIENCE COMPLETES SET.*
mon	23	
tue	24	
wed	25	
thu	26	
fri	27	
sat	28	**FRANCIS FIELD HOUSE** WASHINGTON UNIVERSITY, ST LOUIS, MO, US. SUPPORTING RAMSEY LEWIS. *McCARTY BACK ON DRUMS.*
sun	29	**THE CHEETAH** CHICAGO, IL, US. PLUS LITTLE BOY BLUES; THE RUSH HOUR. *(VENUE ALSO KNOWN AS ARAGON BALLROOM.)*
mon	30	
tue	31	

NOVEMBER 1967

wed	1	
thu	2	
fri	3	**VILLAGE THEATER** NEW YORK, NY, US. PLUS VANILLA FUDGE, KINGDOM COME, TINY TIM. *7th US TOUR CONTINUES.*
sat	4	**SYRIA MOSQUE** PITTSBURGH, PA, US. PITTSBURGH UNIVERSITY "HOMECOMING WEEKEND" CONCERT, PLUS MITCH RYDER.
sun	5	
mon	6	
tue	7	
wed	8	
thu	9	
fri	10	**UNKNOWN VENUE** VANCOUVER, BC, CANADA. *UNCONFIRMED DATE.*
sat	11	**UNKNOWN VENUE** CALGARY, AB, CANADA.
sun	12	
mon	13	TOUR ENDS AND BAND FLY BACK TO LONDON.
tue	14	
wed	15	**PSYCHEDELIC SUPERMARKET** BOSTON, MA, US. *CANCELLED; SCHEDULED DATE NEVER FINALISED.*
thu	16	**PSYCHEDELIC SUPERMARKET** BOSTON, MA, US. *CANCELLED; SCHEDULED DATE NEVER FINALISED.*
fri	17	
sat	18	
sun	19	
mon	20	
tue	21	
wed	22	
thu	23	
fri	24	
sat	25	
sun	26	
mon	27	**UNKNOWN STUDIO** LONDON. REPORTED RECORDING "NEW SINGLE" SOME TIME THIS WEEK; APPARENTLY UNUSED.
tue	28	
wed	29	
thu	30	

DECEMBER 1967

fri	1	
sat	2	
sun	3	
mon	4	
tue	5	
wed	6	
thu	7	
fri	8	
sat	9	**TOWN HALL** EAST RETFORD, NOTTS, ENGLAND. *CANCELLED, BINGO THIS NIGHT INSTEAD.*
sun	10	
mon	11	PRESS RELEASE ANNOUNCES YET MORE TOUR DATES – IN SCANDINAVIA, HOLLAND AND AUSTRALIA – THAT FAIL TO HAPPEN.
tue	12	
wed	13	**OLYMPIA THEATRE** PARIS, FRANCE. PLUS DANTALIONS CHARIOT, PAN'S PEOPLE. *CANCELLED.*
thu	14	**OLYMPIA THEATRE** PARIS, FRANCE. PLUS DANTALIONS CHARIOT, PAN'S PEOPLE. *PLANNED SECOND NIGHT CANCELLED.*
fri	15	
sat	16	
sun	17	
mon	18	
tue	19	
wed	20	
thu	21	
fri	22	
sat	23	**MADISON SQUARE GARDEN** NEW YORK, NY, US. PLUS THE RASCALS, ROYAL GUARDSMEN, ETC. *CANCELLED.*
sun	24	
mon	25	REPORTED THEFT OF £3,000-WORTH OF GEAR FROM BAND VAN: PAGE'S ELECTRIC EQUIPMENT, 5 AMPS, PA, & McCARTY'S DRUMS.
tue	26	
wed	27	
thu	28	
fri	29	
sat	30	
sun	31	

JANUARY 1968

mon	1		
tue	2		
wed	3		
thu	4		
fri	5		
sat	6		
sun	7		
mon	8		
tue	9		
wed	10		
thu	11		
fri	12		
sat	13	**SATURDAY SCENE** CORN EXCHANGE, CHELMSFORD, ESSEX.
sun	14		
mon	15	PRESS RELEASE ANNOUNCES YARDBIRDS SCHEDULED TO RECORD A NEW SINGLE AND ALBUM SOON.
tue	16		

wed	17	
thu	18	
fri	19	**MIDDLE EARTH** LONDON, ENGLAND. PLUS RAINBOW REFLECTION, GOLD, DJ JEFF DEXTER.
sat	20	
sun	21	
mon	22	
tue	23	**UNKNOWN VENUE** POLAND. *CANCELLED.*
wed	24	**UNKNOWN VENUE** EUROPE. *CANCELLED.*
thu	25	
fri	26	**BINGLEY HALL** BIRMINGHAM, ENGLAND. "ALL-NIGHT RAVE".
sat	27	
sun	28	
mon	29	
tue	30	
wed	31	

DE LANE LEA STUDIOS LONDON, ENGLAND. LATE THIS MONTH, RECORDING 'GOODNIGHT SWEET JOSEPHINE', 'THINK ABOUT IT'.

FEBRUARY 1968

thu	1	
fri	2	
sat	3	
sun	4	
mon	5	PRESS RELEASE ANNOUNCES 'GOODNIGHT SWEET JOSEPHINE' AS UK SINGLE FOR MAR 1st.
tue	6	**DE LANE LEA STUDIOS** LONDON, ENGLAND (AROUND THIS TIME) POSSIBLE FURTHER WORK ON NEW SINGLE.
wed	7	
thu	8	
fri	9	**TOP RANK BALLROOM** CARDIFF, WALES.
sat	10	**BARLONG HALL** DAGENHAM, ESSEX, ENGLAND.
sun	11	
mon	12	PRESS RELEASE ANNOUNCES US TOUR APRIL AND AUSTRALIAN DATES AFTER; US GIGS MUCH REARRANGED; OZ DATES DROPPED.
tue	13	
wed	14	EMI RECORD COMPANY LOGS IN TAPES OF 'GOODNIGHT SWEET JOSEPHINE' (VERSION 1) AND 'THINK ABOUT IT'.
thu	15	
fri	16	**GOLDSMITH COLLEGE** UNIVERSITY OF LONDON, NEW CROSS, LONDON, ENGLAND. PLUS JIMMY JAMES, JETHRO TULL, CLOUDS.

sat	17	
sun	18	
mon	19	
tue	20	
wed	21	
thu	22	
fri	23	
sat	24	
sun	25	
mon	26	
tue	27	
wed	28	
thu	29	

MARCH 1968

fri 1 SCHEDULED RELEASE DATE OF 'GOODNIGHT SWEET JOSEPHINE' SINGLE IN UK DELAYED TO MAR 15th.

sat 2 **UNIVERSITY OF SOUTHAMPTON** SOUTHAMPTON, ENGLAND.

sun 3

mon 4

tue 5 **BBC RADIO** LONDON, ENGLAND, TAPING 3 SONGS INCLUDING 'GOODNIGHT SWEET JOSEPHINE' FOR *SATURDAY CLUB* b/c MAR 16th.

wed 6 **BBC RADIO** LONDON, TAPING 'GOODNIGHT...', 'THINK ABOUT IT', 'DAZED & CONFUSED', 'WHITE SUMMER' FOR *TOP GEAR* b/c MAR 10th.

thu 7

fri 8 **UNIVERSITY OF ASTON** BIRMINGHAM, ENGLAND. "PYJAMA HOP AT ASTON" PLUS SIMON DUPREE, ETC.

sat 9 **MAISON RADIO** PARIS, FRANCE, 4 SONGS LIVE TV FOR *BOUTON ROUGE*. **FACULTÉ DU DROIT** PARIS, PLUS BRIAN AUGER/JULIE DRISCOLL.

sun 10 **L'OMNIBUS** COLOMBES. ALSO, *PRIVATE PARTY AT MANSION IN PARIS SUBURBS FOR BARCLAY RECORDS HEAD, + JULIE DRISCOLL ETC.*

mon 11 PRESS RELEASE SAYS NEW 45 'GOODNIGHT SWEET JOSEPHINE' CANCELLED AS BAND "VERY DISAPPOINTED" AND WILL RE-RECORD IT.

tue 12

wed 13 **PYE STUDIOS** LONDON, ON OR ABOUT THIS DAY, 'JOSEPHINE' RE-RECORDED WITH SESSIONMEN-PLUS-PAGE ON BACKING TRACK.

thu 14

fri 15

sat 16 **LE TERMINUS** CORBEIL, PARIS, FRANCE **STUDENT UNION** LUTON COLLEGE TECHNOLOGY, BEDS, ENGLAND. POSTPONED TO JUL 7th.

sun 17

mon 18 EPIC RECORD COMPANY LOGS IN TAPES OF RE-RECORDED 'JOSEPHINE' SINGLE; SET FOR APR 1st RELEASE.

tue 19

wed 20

thu 21

fri 22

sat 23 **RETFORD COLLEGE** RETFORD, NOTTS, ENGLAND.

sun 24

mon 25

tue 26

wed 27 BAND TRAVEL TO US TO START YARDBIRDS' 8th NORTH AMERICAN TOUR, SUBJECT OF MANY REARRANGED AND RESCHEDULED DATES.

thu 28 **THE AERODROME** SCHENECTADY, NY, US.

fri 29 **CONARD HIGH SCHOOL** WEST HARTFORD, CT, US. "SENIOR CLASS CONCERT".

sat 30 **ANDERSON THEATER** NEW YORK, NY, US. *CONCERT OFFICIALLY RECORDED FOR PROPOSED LIVE ALBUM.*

sun 31

APRIL 1968

mon 1 **US RELEASE** 'GOODNIGHT SWEET JOSEPHINE' 45. *8th US TOUR CONTINUES; 2 DAYS OFF IN NYC LIKELY PREPARING FOR STUDIO.*

tue 2

wed 3 **COLUMBIA STUDIOS** NEW YORK, NY, RECORDING (3rd.) TAKING A HOLD OF ME'; (4th:) 'SPANISH BLOOD', 'KNOWING THAT I'M

thu 4 LOSING YOU'; (5th:) 'AVRON KNOWS', 'MY BABY', HEAR PRODUCER MANNY KELLEM'S MIXES OF LIVE ANDERSON THEATER TAPES.

fri 5 **GOLDEN CENTER** QUEEN'S COLLEGE OF NEW YORK, FLUSHING, NY, US. PLUS THE GOOD RATS.

sat 6 **CURRY HICKS CAGE** UNIVERSITY OF MASSACHUSETTS, AMHERST, MA, US. SUPPORTING THE ASSOCIATION.

sun 7

mon 8 **THEE IMAGE** MIAMI BEACH, FL, US. PLUS THE BLUES IMAGE, THE KOLLEKTION, THE BANGLES.

tue 9 **THEE IMAGE** MIAMI BEACH, FL, US. PLUS THE BLUES IMAGE, THE KOLLEKTION, THE BANGLES.

wed 10 **THEE IMAGE** MIAMI BEACH, FL, US. PLUS THE BLUES IMAGE, THE KOLLEKTION, THE BANGLES.

thu 11 **BOSTON TEA PARTY** MAGNA BUILDING, BOSTON, MA, US. "THURSDAY DANCE-NIGHT CONCERTS", PLUS STEVE MILLER BAND.

fri 12 **ACTION HOUSE** ISLAND PARK, NY, US. PLUS THE MUSIC BACHS.

sat 13 **ACTION HOUSE** ISLAND PARK, NY, US. PLUS THE MUSIC BACHS.

sun 14 **ACTION HOUSE** ISLAND PARK, NY, US. PLUS THE MUSIC BACHS.

mon 15 LIKELY TRAVEL DAY TO CHICAGO. *REPORTEDLY RELF & McCARTY THIS WEEK FORMALISE PLANS TO LEAVE THE BAND AT CLOSE OF TOUR.*

tue 16

wed 17

thu 18

fri 19 **BLUE VILLAGE** WESTMONT, IL, US. *EYEWITNESS REPORTS SUGGEST MEMBERS OF BAND VISIBLY DRUNK THIS NIGHT.*

sat 20 **THE CELLAR** ARLINGTON HEIGHTS, IL, US. PLUS FOUR DAYS & A KNIGHT. *PAGE HAS TROUBLE WITH HIS VOX AMPS THROUGHOUT.*

sun 21 **LE SCENE** INDIANAPOLIS, IN, US.

mon 22

tue 23

wed 24

thu 25 **PALACE THEATER** CLEVELAND, OH, US. **WUAB-TV STUDIOS** CLEVELAND, TAPING 'HEART FULL...' FOR *UPBEAT* B/CAST MAY 4th.

fri 26 **CONVENTION CENTER** CINCINATTI, OH, US. "ST XAVIER HIGH SCHOOL JUNIOR-SENIOR PROM".

sat 27 **WRISTON QUADRANGLE** BROWN UNIVERSITY, PROVIDENCE, RI, US. **CLARKSON COLLEGE** POTSDAM, NY, US.

sun 28 **UNKNOWN VENUE** UPSTATE NY UNIVERSITY, US. PLUS LINDA RONSTADT & THE STONE PONYS. *DATE UNCONFIRMED.*

mon 29

tue 30

MAY 1968

wed	1	
thu	2	
fri	3	**GRANDE BALLROOM** DEARBORN, MI, US. PLUS MC5, FROST, STUART AVERY ASSEMBLAGE, ETC. *LONG 8th AMERICAN TOUR CONTINUES.*
sat	4	**GRANDE BALLROOM** DEARBORN, MI, US. *SAME ACTS AS YESTERDAY.*
sun	5	**HULLABALOO SCENE** MENTOR, OH, US. PLUS JEAN PAUL JONES & THE AMERICAN NAVY.
mon	6	
tue	7	
wed	8	**HAL BABY'S** AURORA, CO, US. *DATE UNCONFIRMED.*
thu	9	
fri	10	**EARL WARREN SHOWGROUNDS** SANTA BARBARA, CA, US. PLUS DAVE DEE DOZY BEAKY MICK & TICH, TURQUOISE.
sat	11	
sun	12	**MELODYLAND THEATER** ANAHEIM, CA, US. PLUS THE TROGGS.
mon	13	LIKELY TIME OF TOUR BREAK IN LOS ANGELES.
tue	14	
wed	15	
thu	16	
fri	17	**FIELD HOUSE** UNIVERSITY OF PUGET SOUND, TACOMA, WA, US. PLUS THE CITY ZU.
sat	18	**CASEY'S** LEWISTON, ID, US. PLUS EASY CHAIR.
sun	19	**UNKNOWN OUTDOOR VENUE** CENTRALIA/CHEHALIS, WA, US. **FRANCISCO TORRES** UNIVERSITY OF CA, SANTA BARBARA, CA, US.
mon	20	
tue	21	
wed	22	
thu	23	**FILLMORE AUDITORIUM** SAN FRANCISCO, CA, US. PLUS CECIL TAYLOR, IT'S A BEAUTIFUL DAY; LIGHTS BY HOLY SEE.
fri	24	**FILLMORE AUDITORIUM** SAN FRANCISCO, CA, US. PLUS CECIL TAYLOR, IT'S A BEAUTIFUL DAY; LIGHTS BY HOLY SEE.
sat	25	**FILLMORE AUDITORIUM** SAN FRANCISCO, CA, US. PLUS CECIL TAYLOR, IT'S A BEAUTIFUL DAY; LIGHTS BY HOLY SEE.
sun	26	
mon	27	
tue	28	
wed	29	**CONCORD COLISEUM** CONCORD, CA, US. PLUS THE FLAMIN' GROOVIES.
thu	30	**THE PURPLE HAZE** RIVERSIDE, CA, US.
fri	31	**SHRINE EXPOSITION HALL** LOS ANGELES, CA, US. PLUS BB KING, THE SONS OF CHAMPLIN.

JUNE 1968

sat	1	**SHRINE EXPOSITION HALL** LOS ANGELES, CA, US. PLUS BB KING, SONS OF CHAMPLIN. *FINAL US TOUR AT LAST WINDING DOWN.*
sun	2	
mon	3	
tue	4	**INTERNATIONAL SPEEDWAY FAIRGROUNDS** MONTGOMERY, AL, US. "BIG SPRING FAIR"/"WBAM ALL-STAR SPECTACULAR".
wed	5	**INTERNATIONAL SPEEDWAY FAIRGROUNDS** MONTGOMERY, AL, US. "BIG SPRING FAIR"/"WBAM ALL-STAR SPECTACULAR".
thu	6	THE END OF WHAT WOULD TURN OUT TO BE THE YARDBIRDS' FINAL NORTH AMERICAN TOUR. McCARTY AND RELF RETURN TO BRITAIN; PAGE REMAINS BEHIND TO MEET UP WITH PETER GRANT IN NEW YORK CITY.
fri	7	
sat	8	
sun	9	
mon	10	PRESS RELEASE THIS WEEK ANNOUNCES A 6-WEEK US TOUR SCHEDULED TO START ON SEP 14th. THIS NEVER HAPPENS.
tue	11	
wed	12	PRESS RELEASE "TWO YARDBIRDS FLY" AROUND NOW NOTES RELF & McCARTY'S DEPARTURE; PAGE & DREJA TO CARRY ON AS YARDBIRDS.
thu	13	REPORTED DEPARTURE DATE FOR PAGE BACK TO LONDON, THOUGH POSSIBLY DELAYED TO THE WEEKEND.
fri	14	ONE REPORT HAS PAGE AT THE FILLMORE EAST, NEW YORK CITY, TO SEE THE JEFF BECK GROUP.
sat	15	
sun	16	
mon	17	
tue	18	
wed	19	
thu	20	
fri	21	
sat	22	PAGE BACK IN THE UK VISITING BILL WYMAN AT OLYMPIC STUDIOS AND PLAYING HIM YARDBIRDS RECORDINGS FROM APR SESSIONS.
sun	23	
mon	24	
tue	25	
wed	26	
thu	27	
fri	28	
sat	29	
sun	30	

EMI (ABBEY ROAD) STUDIOS LONDON, ENGLAND (MID-JUNE). *RELF & McCARTY'S FIRST NON-YARDBIRDS RECORDING SESSION: 'SHINING WHERE THE SUN HAS BEEN' (INITIALLY UNISSUED).*

JULY 1968

mon	1	
tue	2	
wed	3	
thu	4	
fri	5	
sat	6	**EMI (ABBEY ROAD) STUDIOS** LONDON. RELF & McCARTY AS "TOGETHER" RECORD 'LOVE MUM AND DAD' AND OTHERS.
sun	7	**STUDENT UNION** LUTON COLLEGE OF TECHONLOGY, LUTON, BEDS, ENGLAND. *LAST GIG BY ORIGINAL 1960s YARDBIRDS.*
mon	8	PRESS RELEASE ANNOUNCES *YARDBIRDS BREAK IN TWO,* SAYS NEW BAND REFORMED "UNDER SAME NAME BY PAGE & DREJA WHO SEEK
tue	9	2 NEW MEMBERS ... CONTINUE TO RECORD FOR EMI ... 10-DAY SCANDINAVIAN TOUR FROM SEP 14th, AND TO THE US IN OCT."
wed	10	SOME TIME THIS WEEK, WITH THE BAND ABSOLUTELY ENDED, PAGE APPROACHES VOCALIST TERRY REID WHO DECLINES OFFER TO JOIN
thu	11	HIM, BUT RECOMMENDS ROBERT PLANT. PLANT IS CONTACTED AND PAGE ARRANGES TO SEE HIM PERFORM. DREJA PHONES DRUMMER
fri	12	PAUL FRANCIS, WHO IS ABOUT TO GO OUT OF TOWN AND SO CANNOT YET COMMIT TO THE NEW GROUP.
sat	13	
sun	14	
mon	15	
tue	16	
wed	17	
thu	18	
fri	19	SESSION BASSIST JOHN PAUL JONES TODAY OR 20th PHONES PAGE OFFERING HIS SERVICES AFTER READING OF YARDBIRDS SPLIT.
sat	20	**TEACHER TRAINING COLLEGE** BIRMINGHAM. PAGE, DREJA AND PETER GRANT SEE PLANT PERFORM WITH HIS BAND HOBBSTWEEDLE.
sun	21	
mon	22	
tue	23	PLANT TRAVELS TO LONDON SOME TIME THIS WEEK TO TALK MUSIC WITH PAGE. PLANT AGREES TO JOIN, AND ALSO SUGGESTS HIS
wed	24	FORMER DRUMMER JOHN BONHAM (CURRENTLY IN MAJORCA).
thu	25	
fri	26	
sat	27	
sun	28	TIM ROSE AND BAND, INC DRUMMER JOHN BONHAM, BACK IN LONDON AFTER MAJORCA DATES; PLANT TRIES TO CONTACT HIM.
mon	29	
tue	30	
wed	31	**COUNTRY CLUB** HAMPSTEAD, LONDON. PAGE, PLANT & DREJA AT TIM ROSE DATE TO SEE BONHAM; GIG OFFERED BUT HE'S UNSURE.

AUGUST 1968

thu	1	
fri	2	AT THE START OF THIS MONTH DREJA DECIDES TO DROP OUT OF THE REFORMED YARDBIRDS AND PURSUE PHOTOGRAPHY AS A
sat	3	CAREER. JOHN PAUL JONES IS INVITED TO JOIN AND ACCEPTS ON THE SPOT. A CONCERTED EFFORT BEGINS TO PERSUADE BONHAM
sun	4	TO JOIN PAGE, PLANT AND JONES.
mon	5	PETER GRANT IN NEW YORK ISSUES PRESS RELEASE NOTING THAT JONES & PLANT ASKED BY PAGE "TO JOIN HIS NEW YARDBIRDS".
tue	6	
wed	7	
thu	8	
fri	9	
sat	10	
sun	11	
mon	12	AROUND THIS TIME BONHAM AGREES TO GIVE IT A TRY AFTER TELEGRAMS BOMBARD HIS LOCAL PUB FOR A FEW WEEKS.
tue	13	
wed	14	
thu	15	
fri	16	
sat	17	
sun	18	
mon	19	**REHEARSAL STUDIO** GERRARD ST, LONDON, AROUND THIS TIME, FIRST REHEARSAL OF YARDBIRDS: PAGE, PLANT, JONES, BONHAM.
tue	20	
wed	21	
thu	22	
fri	23	
sat	24	
sun	25	
mon	26	
tue	27	
wed	28	
thu	29	REHEARSALS IN LONDON AROUND THIS TIME FOR UPCOMING TOUR.
fri	30	
sat	31	

LANSDOWNE STUDIOS LONDON [MID-LATE AUG] "NEW" YARDBIRDS MEMBERS PLAY P J PROBY SESSION; 3 SONGS ISSUED.

SEPTEMBER 1968

sun 1

mon 2 REHEARSALS IN LONDON CONTINUE AROUND THIS TIME FOR UPCOMING TOUR.

tue 3

wed 4

thu 5

fri 6

sat 7 **GLADSAXE TEEN CLUB** GLADSAXE, DENMARK. **BRØNDBY POP-CLUB** BRøNDBY, DENMARK. *1ST GIGS FOR NEW LINE-UP.*

sun 8 **REVENTLOWPARKEN** LOLLAND, DENMARK. **FJORDVILLA** ROSKILDE, DENMARK. PLUS THE LADYBIRDS.

mon 9

tue 10

wed 11

thu 12 **STORA SCENEN** GRONA LUND, STOCKHOLM, SWEDEN.

fri 13 **INSIDE** STOCKHOLM, SWEDEN.

sat 14 **ÄNGBY PARK** KNIVSTA, SWEDEN. PLUS UNDECAYED JAZZ BLUES BAND, ATLANTIC OCEAN.

sun 15 **STJÄRNSCENEN** LISEBERG, GOTHENBURG, SWEDEN. *FURTHER SCANDINAVIAN DATES AFTER THIS ARE UNCONFIRMED & UNLIKELY.*

mon 16

tue 17

wed 18 AT JIMMY PAGE'S HOME IN PANGBOURNE, BERKSHIRE, AROUND THIS TIME MATERIAL FOR NEW LP IS REHEARSED, INC 'CHEST FEVER'.

thu 19

fri 20

sat 21

sun 22

mon 23

tue 24

wed 25

thu 26

fri 27 **OLYMPIC STUDIOS** BARNES, LONDON. LIKELY START DATE FOR NEW LINE-UP RECORDING, INC 'BABE I'M GONNA LEAVE YOU', 'YOU SHOOK ME'. TAPES INITIALLY HOUSED WITH EMI. SESSION

sat 28 SHEET LISTS ARTIST AS "YARDBIRDS", CLIENT AS "RAK/SUPER-HYPE". PRODUCERS: GLYN JOHNS/ JIMMY PAGE.

sun 29

mon 30

OCTOBER 1968

tue 1

wed 2 **OLYMPIC STUDIOS** BARNES, LONDON. EARLY THIS MONTH, SESSION FOR NEW LINE-UP'S 1st LP. REPORTEDLY, WHOLE ALBUM IS

thu 3 RECORDED IN 9 DAYS, USING A TOTAL OF JUST 30 STUDIO HOURS.

fri 4

sat 5

sun 6

mon 7

tue 8

wed 9

thu 10 **OLYMPIC STUDIOS** BARNES, LONDON. RECORDING 'TRIBUTE TO BERN BERNS' AKA 'BABY COME ON HOME'. LIKELY THE LAST DATE

fri 11 OF ALBUM SESSIONS, WITH POSSIBLE MIXING IN DAYS FOLLOWING.

sat 12

sun 13

mon 14 LIKELY NOW, DECISION MADE TO DROP YARDBIRDS NAME, AT LEAST IN PART PROMPTED BY LEGAL REQUEST FROM DREJA. LP TAPES NOW

tue 15 TO BE SHOPPED AROUND OUTSIDE EMI. PRESS RELEASE ANNOUNCES CHANGE OF NAME TO LED ZEPPELIN. DEBUT LP COMPLETED.

wed 16

thu 17

fri 18 **MARQUEE** LONDON, ENGLAND. *NEW BAND STILL BILLED AS THE YARDBIRDS.*

sat 19 **UNIVERSITY OF LIVERPOOL** LIVERPOOL, ENGLAND. *NEW BAND STILL BILLED AS THE YARDBIRDS.*

sun 20 NAME-CHANGE TO LED ZEPPELIN NOW EFFECTIVE.

mon 21

tue 22 REGISTRATION OF SUPERHYPE MUSIC INC, THE COMPANY FORMED BY PAGE AND GRANT, IS OFFICIAL THIS DAY.

wed 23

thu 24

fri 25 **SURREY UNIVERSITY** BATTERSEA, LONDON. PLUS THE GASS. *OFFICIAL FIRST LED ZEPPELIN DATE [THO' POSTERS STILL BILL "NEW YARDBIRDS"].*

sat 26 **BRISTOL BOXING CLUB** BRISTOL, ENGLAND. *NEW BAND BILLED AS LED ZEPPELIN.*

sun 27

mon 28 PETER GRANT IN NEW YORK CITY NEGOTIATING WITH ATLANTIC RECORDS; DEAL FOR LED ZEPPELIN COMPLETED OVER NEXT 2 WEEKS.

tue 29

wed 30

thu 31

These are the UK and US singles and LPs recorded during the original band's life, 1963 to 1968, plus significant recent reissues and compilations, all in chronological order of release date. (Many of the recordings have been released in various combinations in many other countries but are beyond the scope of this discography.)

The layout is intended to be simple, readable and informative. Record type (single, LP or CD) is followed by relevant title(s). Release date(s), record label(s) and catalogue number(s) are then given, and the composers are shown in brackets for each song. Information about the recording location, date and personnel is given where relevant. The listings are based on information from Greg Russo's *The Ultimate Rave-Up* (see our later Bibliography).

Single 'I Wish You Would'
(*Arnold*) / 'A Certain Girl' (*Neville*)
Recorded: Olympic, London, England, late March/early April 1964. Producer: Giorgio Gomelsky. Clapton line-up.
Released: **May 1st 1964** UK Columbia DB7823; August 17th 1964 US Epic 5-9709.

Single 'Good Morning Little Schoolgirl' (*Demarais*) / 'I Ain't Got You' (*Reed*)
Recorded: Olympic, London, England, August/September 1964. Producer: Giorgio Gomelsky. Clapton line-up.
Released: **October 30th 1964** UK Columbia DB 7391. No US issue.

LP *Five Live Yardbirds*
'Introduction' by Hamish Grimes
'Too Much Monkey Business' (*Berry*)
'Got Love If You Want It' (*Moore*)
'Smokestack lightning' (*Burnett*)
'Good Morning Little Schoolgirl'
  (*Demarais*)

'Respectable' (*O'K Isley/R. Isley/ R. Isley*)
'Five Long Years' (*Boyd*)
'Pretty Girl' (*McDaniel*)
'Louise' (*Hooker*)
'I'm A Man' (*McDaniel*)
'Here Tis' (*McDaniel*)
Recorded: live at the Marquee, London, England, probably March 20th 1964. Producer: Giorgio Gomelsky. Clapton line-up.
Released: **December 31st 1964** UK Columbia SX 1677 mono. No US issue.

Single 'For Your Love'
(*Gouldman*) / 'Got To Hurry' (*Gomelsky*)
Recorded: IBC, London, England, February 1st 1965 / Olympic, London, England, August or November 1964. Producer: Giorgio Gomelsky. Clapton line-up.
Released: **March 5th 1965** UK Columbia DB 7499; April 12th 1965 US Epic 5-9790.

Single 'Heart Full Of Soul'
(*Gouldman*) / 'Steeled Blues' (*Relf/Beck*)
Recorded: Advision, London, England, late April / March 15th 1965. Producer: Giorgio Gomelsky. Beck line-up.
Released: **June 4th 1965** UK Columbia DB 7594; July 19th 1965 US Epic 5-9823.

LP *For Your Love*
'For Your Love' (*Gouldman*)
'I'm Not Talking' (*Allison*)
'Putty (In Your Hands)'
  (*Rogers/Patton*)
'I Ain't Got You' (*Reed*)
'Got To Hurry' (*Gomelsky*)
'I Ain't Done Wrong' (*Relf*)
'I Wish You Would' (*Arnold*)
'A Certain Girl' (*Neville*)
'Sweet Music' (*Lance/Cobb/Bowie*)
'Good Morning Little Schoolgirl'
  (*Demarais*)
'My Girl Sloopy' (*Russell/Farrell*)
Recorded: Olympic/IBC/Advision,

London, England, between early 1964 and April 1965. Producer: Giorgio Gomelsky. Clapton and Beck line-ups.
Released: **July 5th 1965** US Epic LN 24167 mono, BN 26167 stereo. No UK release.

EP *Five Yardbirds* 'My Girl Sloopy' (*Russell/Farrell*) / 'I'm Not Talking' (*Allison*) / 'I Ain't Done Wrong' (*Relf*)
Recorded: Advision, London, England, March/April 1965. Producer: Giorgio Gomelsky. Beck line-up.
Released: **August 6th 1965** UK Columbia SEG 8421. No US release.

Single 'Evil Hearted You'
(*Gouldman*) / 'Still I'm Sad' (*Samwell-Smith/McCarty*)
Recorded: Advision, London, England, August 23rd 1965 / Olympic, London, England, July 27th 1965 & Advision, London, England, mid August 1965. Producer: Giorgio Gomelsky. Beck line-up.
Released: **October 1st 1965** UK Columbia DB 7706. No US issue (but see following).

Single 'I'm A Man' (*McDaniel*) / 'Still I'm Sad' (*Samwell-Smith/McCarty*)
Recorded: Chess, Chicago, IL, US, September 19th 1965 & Columbia, New York, NY, US, September 21st 1965 / Olympic, London, England, July 27th 1965 & Advision, London, mid August 1965. Producer: Giorgio Gomelsky. Beck line-up.
Released: **October 11th 1965** US Epic 5-9857. No UK issue (but see previous).

LP *Having A Rave Up With The Yardbirds*
'You're A Better Man Than I'
  (*M.Hugg/B.Hugg*)
'Evil Hearted You' (*Gouldman*)
'I'm A Man' (*McDaniel*)
'Heart Full Of Soul' (*Gouldman*)

'Still I'm Sad' (*Samwell-Smith/
   McCarty*)
'The Train Kept A-Rollin'
   (*Bradshaw/Mann/Kay*)
'Smokestack Lightning' (*Burnett*)
'Respectable' (*O'K Isley/R. Isley/
   R. Isley*)
'I'm A Man' (*McDaniel*)
'Here Tis' (*McDaniel*)
Recorded: Sun, Memphis, TN,
US/Chess, Chicago, IL,
US/Advision, London,
England/Marquee, London,
England, between March 1964 and
September 1965. Producer: Giorgio
Gomelsky. Clapton & Beck line-ups.
Released: **November 20th 1965** US
Epic LN 24177 mono, BN 26177
stereo. No UK release.

LP *Sonny Boy Williamson And The Yardbirds*

'Bye Bye Bird' (*Williamson*)
'Pontiac Blues' (*Williamson*)
'Take It Easy Baby' (*Williamson*)
'I Don't Care No More' SBW solo
   (*Williamson*)
'Do The Weston' (*Williamson*)
'Mister Downchild' (*Williamson*)
'23 Hours Too Long' (*Williamson*)
'Out On The Water Coast'
   (*Williamson*)
'Baby Don't Worry' SBW solo
(*Williamson*)
Recorded: live Craw Daddy,
Richmond, London, England,
December 8th 1963. Clapton line-up.
Released: **January 7th 1966** UK
Fontana TL 5277 mono; February
7th 1966 US Mercury MG 21071
mono, SR 61071 stereo.

Single 'Questa Volta'

(*Satti/Dinamo/Mogol*) /
'Pafff…Bum' (*Reverberi/Bardotti/
Samwell-Smith*)
Recorded: Columbia, New York, NY,
US, January 17th 1966.
Producer: Giorgio Gomelsky.
Beck line-up.
Released: **February 1966** Italy
Ricordi SIR 20-010. No UK or
US issue.

Single 'Shapes Of Things'

(*Samwell-Smith/Relf/McCarty*) /
'You're A Better Man Than I'
(*M.Hugg/B.Hugg*)
Recorded: Chess, Chicago, IL, US,
December 21st/22nd 1965 &
Columbia, Los Angeles, CA, US
January 7th 1966 / Sun, Memphis,
TN, US, September 12th 1965 &
Columbia, New York, NY, US,
September 21st 1965. Producer:
Giorgio Gomelsky. Beck line-up.
Released: **February 25th 1966** UK
Columbia DB 7848. No US issue
(but see following).

Single 'Shapes Of Things'

(*Samwell-Smith/Relf/McCarty*) /
'New York City Blues' (*Relf/Dreja*)
Recorded: Chess, Chicago, IL, US,
December 21st/22nd 1965 &
Columbia, Los Angeles, CA, US
January 7th 1966 / Columbia, New
York, NY, US September 21st 1965.
Producer: Giorgio Gomelsky.
Beck line-up.
Released: **March 28th 1966** US Epic
5-10006 (also shortlived version
February 28th with 'I'm Not Talking'
b-side). No UK release (but see
previous).

Single by Keith Relf 'Mr Zero'

(*Lind*) / 'Knowing' (*Relf*)
Recorded: De Lane Lea, London,
England, mid April 1966.
Producer: Simon Napier-Bell.
Released: **May 13th 1966** UK
Columbia DB 7920; July 4th 1966
US Epic 5-10044.

Single 'Over Under Sideways Down'

(*Dreja/McCarty/Beck/
Relf/Samwell-Smith*) /
'Jeff's Boogie' (*Dreja/
McCarty/Beck/Relf/Samwell-Smith*)
Recorded: Advision, London,
England, April 19th-20th 1966.
Producer: Simon Napier-Bell/Paul
Samwell-Smith. Beck line-up.
Released: **May 27th 1966** UK
Columbia DB 7928; June 13th
1966 US Epic 5-10035.

LP *The Yardbirds (aka "Roger The Engineer")*

'Lost Woman' (*Dreja/McCarty
   Beck/Relf/Samwell-Smith*)
'Over Under Sideways Down'
   (*Dreja/McCarty/Beck/Relf/
Samwell-Smith*)
'The Nazz Are Blue' (*Dreja/McCarty/
   Beck/Relf/Samwell-Smith*)
'I Can't Make Your Way' (*Dreja/
   McCarty/Beck/Relf/Samwell-Smith*)
'Rack My Mind' (*Dreja/
   McCarty/Beck/Relf/Samwell-Smith*)
'Farewell' (*Dreja/McCarty/Beck/
   Relf/Samwell-Smith*)
'Hot House Of Omargararshid'
(*Dreja/McCarty/Beck/Relf/
   Samwell-Smith*)
'Jeff's Boogie' (*Dreja/McCarty/
   Beck/Relf/Samwell-Smith*)
'He's Always There' (*Dreja/
   McCarty/Beck/Relf/Samwell-Smith*)
'Turn Into Earth' (*Samwell-Smith/Simon*)
'What Do You Want' (*Dreja/
   McCarty/Beck/Relf/Samwell-Smith*)
'Ever Since The World Began' (*Dreja/
   McCarty/Beck/Relf/Samwell-Smith*)
Recorded: Advision, London,
England, April 19th/20th,
May 31st–June 4th, & mid-June
1966. Producer: Simon Napier-
Bell/Paul Samwell-Smith.
Beck line-up.
Released: **July 15th 1966** UK
Columbia SX 6063 mono, SCX
6063 stereo. No US release (but
following *Over Under…* is similar).

LP *Over Under Sideways Down*

'Lost Woman' (*Dreja/McCarty/
   Beck/Relf/Samwell-Smith*)
'Over Under Sideways Down' (*Dreja/
   McCarty/Beck/Relf/Samwell-Smith*)
'I Can't Make Your Way' (*Dreja/
   McCarty/Beck/Relf/Samwell-Smith*)
'Farewell' (*Dreja/McCarty/Beck/
   Relf/Samwell-Smith*)
'Hot House Of Omargararshid' (*Dreja/
McCarty/Beck/Relf/Samwell-Smith*)
'Jeff's Boogie' (*Dreja/McCarty/
   Beck/Relf/Samwell-Smith*)
'Turn Into Earth' (*Samwell-Smith/Simon*)

'He's Always There' (*Dreja/McCarty/ Beck/Relf/Samwell-Smith*)
'What Do You Want' (*Dreja/ McCarty/Beck/Relf/Samwell-Smith*)
'Ever Since The World Began' (*Dreja/ McCarty/Beck/Relf/Samwell-Smith*)
Recorded: Advision, London, April 19th/20th, May 31st-June 4th, mid-June 1966. Producer: Simon Napier-Bell/Paul Samwell-Smith. Beck line-up.
Released: **August 1st 1966** US Epic LN 24210 mono, BN 26210 stereo. No UK release (but previous *The Yardbirds* is similar).

Single 'Happenings Ten Years Time Ago' (*Yardbirds*) / 'Psycho Daisies' (*Dreja/McCarty/Beck/ Relf/Samwell-Smith*)
Recorded: De Lane Lea, London, England, September 20th & October 3rd 1966. Producer: Simon Napier-Bell. A-side Beck & Page line-up; B-side Beck/Page/McCarty only.
Released: **October 21st 1966** UK Columbia DB 8024. No US issue (but see following).

Single 'Happenings Ten Years Time Ago' (*Yardbirds*) / 'The Nazz Are Blue' (*Dreja/McCarty/ Beck/Relf/Samwell-Smith*)
Recorded: De Lane Lea, London, England, September 20th & October 3rd 1966 / Advision, London, England, May 31st–June 4th 1966. A-side Beck+Page line-up; B-side Beck line-up. Producer: Simon Napier-Bell.
Released: **October 31st 1966** US Epic 5-10094. No UK issue (but see previous).

Single by Keith Relf 'Shapes In My Mind' (*Napier-Bell*) / 'Blue Sands' by The Outsiders.
Recorded: Sunset Sound, Los Angeles, CA, US, late August 1966 & Columbia, New York, NY, US, September 8th 1966.
Producer: Simon Napier-Bell.
Released: **November 25th 1966** UK Columbia DB 8084; December 5th 1966 US Epic 5-10110.

EP *Over Under Sideways Down* 'Over Under Sideways Down' (*Dreja/McCarty/Beck/ Relf/Samwell-Smith*) / 'I Can't Make Your Way' (*Dreja/McCarty/Beck/ Relf/Samwell-Smith*) / 'He's Always There' (*Dreja/McCarty/Beck/Relf/ Samwell-Smith*) / 'What Do You Want' (*Dreja/McCarty/Beck/Relf/ Samwell-Smith*)
Recorded: Advision, London, England, April/June 1966. Producer: Simon Napier-Bell. Beck line-up.
Released: **January 27th 1967** UK Columbia SEG 8521. No US release.

LP *Blowup Original Soundtrack*
'Stroll On' (*Relf/Beck/Page/Dreja*) (Rest of album is incidental film music, including pieces by Herbie Hancock.)
Yardbirds track recorded: Sound Techniques, London, England, early October 1966. Producer: Simon Napier-Bell. Beck & Page two-guitar line-up.
Released: **February 20th 1967** US MGM E-4447 mono, SE-4447 stereo; May 10th 1967 UK MGM C 8039 mono, CS 8039 stereo.

Single 'Little Games' (*Wainman/Spiro*) / 'Puzzles' (*Relf/Page/McCarty/Dreja*)
Recorded: De Lane Lea, London, England, February/March 1967. Producer: Mickie Most. Page line-up.
Released: **April 3rd 1967** US Epic 5-10156; April 21st 1967 UK Columbia DB 8165.

LP *Greatest Hits*
'Shapes Of Things' (*Samwell-Smith/ Relf/McCarty*)
'Still I'm Sad' (*Samwell-Smith/ McCarty*)
'New York City Blues' (*Relf/Dreja*)
'For Your Love' (*Gouldman*)
'Over Under Sideways Down' (*Dreja/ McCarty/Beck/Relf/Samwell-Smith*)
'I'm A Man' (*McDaniel*)
'Heart Full Of Soul' (*Gouldman*)

'Happenings Ten Years Time Ago' (*Yardbirds*)
'Smokestack Lightning' (*Burnett*)
'I'm Not Talking' (*Allison*)
Various studios/producers/line-ups.
Released: **April 17th 1966** US Epic LN 24246 mono, BN 24246 stereo. No UK release.

Single 'Ha Ha Said The Clown' (*Hazzard*) / 'Tinker Tailor Soldier Sailor' (*Page/McCarty*)
Recorded: Columbia, New York, NY, US, June 13th 1967 & EMI Abbey Road, London, England, June 19th 1967 / De Lane Lea, London, England, March/April 1967.
Producer: Simon Napier-Bell. Page line-up.
Released: **July 17th 1967** US Epic 5-10204. No UK issue.

LP *Little Games*
'Little Games' (*Wainman/Spiro*)
'Smile On Me' (*Relf/Page/ McCarty/Dreja*)
'White Summer' (*trad arr Page*)
'Tinker Tailor Soldier Sailor' (*Page/McCarty*)
'Glimpses' (*Relf/Page/ McCarty/ Dreja*)
'Drinking Muddy Water' (*Relf/Page/ McCarty/Dreja*)
'No Excess Baggage' (*Atkins/D'Errico*)
'Stealing Stealing' (*trad arr Relf/ Page/McCarty/Dreja*)
'Only The Black Rose' (*Relf*)
'Little Soldier Boy' (*Relf/Page/ McCarty*)
Recorded: De Lane Lea, London, England, March to May 1967. Producer: Mickie Most. Page line-up.
Released: **July 24th 1966** US Epic LN 24313 mono, BN 26313 stereo. No UK issue.

Single 'Ten Little Indians' (*Nilsson*) / 'Drinking Muddy Water' (*Relf/Page/McCarty/Dreja*)
Recorded: Olympic, London, England, September 25th 1967 / De Lane Lea, London, March/April

1967. Producer: Mickie Most. Page line-up.
Released: **October 16th 1967** US Epic 5-10248. No UK issue.

Single 'Goodnight Sweet Josephine' (*Hazzard*) / 'Think About It' (*Relf/McCarty/Page*) Recorded: Pye, London, England, mid March 1968 / De Lane Lea, London, England, late January 1968. Producer: Mickie Most.
Released: **April 1st 1968** US Epic 5-10303.

LP *Live Yardbirds! Featuring Jimmy Page*
'The Train Kept A-Rollin' (*Bradshaw/Mann/Kay*)
'You're A Better Man Than I' (*M.Hugg/B.Hugg*)
'I'm Confused' [='Dazed And Confused'] (*Holmes arr Yardbirds*)
'My Baby' (*Shuman/Ragovoy*)
'Over Under Sideways Down' (*Dreja/ McCarty/Beck/Relf/Samwell-Smith*)
'Drinking Muddy Water' (*Relf/Page/McCarty/Dreja*)
'Shapes Of Things' (*Samwell-Smith/ Relf/McCarty*)
'White Summer' (*trad arr Page*)
'I'm A Man' (*McDaniel*)
Recorded: live at the Anderson Theater, New York, NY, US, March 30th 1968. Producer: Manny Kellem. Page line-up.
Released: **September 1971** US Epic E 30615 stereo.

CD box-set *Train Kept A-Rollin: Complete Giorgio Gomelsky Productions*
Live Craw Daddy, Richmond, London, England, December 8th 1963; Yardbirds: 'Smokestack Lightning' (*Burnett*); 'You Can't Judge A Book By Its Cover' (*Dixon*); 'Let It Rock' (*Berry*); 'I Wish You Would' (*Arnold*); 'Who Do You Love' (*McDaniel*); 'Honey In Your Hips' (*Relf*); **Sonny Boy Williamson & The Yardbirds:** 'Bye Bye Bird' (*Williamson*); 'Mister Downchild' (*Williamson*); 'The

River Rhine' (*Williamson*); '23 Hours Too Long' (*Williamson*); 'A Lost Care' (*Williamson*); 'Pontiac Blues' (*Williamson*); 'Take It Easy Baby' (*Williamson*); 'Out On The Water Coast' (*Williamson*); 'I Don't Care No More' (*Williamson*); 'Western Arizona' [='Do The Weston'] (*Williamson*); 'Take It Easy Baby' (*Williamson*).
Early studio recordings: 'Baby What's Wrong' (*Boyd*); 'Boom Boom' (*Hooker*); 'Honey In Your Hips' (*Relf*); 'Talkin Bout You' (*Berry*); 'I Wish You Would' (*Arnold*); 'A Certain Girl' (*Neville*).
Live Birmingham Town Hall, Birmingham, England, February 28th 1964; Sonny Boy Williamson & The Yardbirds: 'Slow Walk' (*Williamson*); 'Highway 69' (*Williamson*); 'My Little Cabin' (*Williamson*).
Live Marquee, London, England, around March 20th 1964: 'Too Much Monkey Business' (*Berry*); 'Got Love If You Want It' (*Moore*); 'Smokestack Lightning' (*Burnett*); 'Good Morning Little Schoolgirl' (*Demarais*); 'Respectable' (*O'K Isley/R. Isley/R. Isley*); 'Five Long Years' (*Boyd*); 'Pretty Girl' (*McDaniel*); 'Louise' (*Hooker*); 'I'm A Man' (*McDaniel*); 'Here Tis' (*McDaniel*).
More studio recordings: 'I Wish You Would' (*Arnold*); 'A Certain Girl' (*Neville*); 'Good Morning Little Schoolgirl' three takes (*Demarais*); 'I Ain't Got You' (*Reed*); 'For Your Love' (*Gouldman*); 'Got To Hurry' three takes (*Gomelsky*); 'Putty (In Your Hands)' (*Rogers/Patton*); 'Sweet Music' two takes (*Lance/Cobbs/ Bowie*); 'I'm Not Talking' (*Allison*); 'I Ain't Done Wrong' (*Relf*); 'My Girl Sloopy' (*Russell/Farrell*); 'Heart Full Of Soul' two takes, one with sitar (*Gouldman*); 'Steeled Blues' (*Relf/Beck*); 'Evil Hearted You' (*Gouldman*); 'Still I'm Sad' (*Samwell-Smith/McCarty*); 'Shapes Of Things' (*Samwell-Smith/Relf/McCarty*);

'You're A Better Man Than I' (*M.Hugg/B.Hugg*); 'I'm A Man' (*McDaniel*); 'New York City Blues' (*Relf/Dreja*); 'The Train Kept A-Rollin' (*Bradshaw/Mann/Kay*); 'Pafff...Bum' two takes (*Reverberi/Bardotti/ Samwell-Smith*); 'Questa Volta' (*Satti/Dinamo/Mogol*); 'Mr Zero' by Keith Relf (*Lind*); 'Knowing' by Keith Relf (*Relf*); 'Jeff's Blues' [='The Nazz Are Blue' instrumental] two takes (*Beck*); 'Someone To Love' four takes (*Beck/McCarty/Dreja/Relf/Samwell -Smith*); 'Like Jimmy Reed Again' (*Beck/McCarty/Dreja/Relf/Samwell -Smith*); 'Chris' Number' (*Beck/ McCarty/Dreja/Relf/Samwell-Smith*); 'Pounds And Stomps' [='He's Always There' instrumental] two takes (*Beck/ McCarty/Dreja/Relf/Samwell-Smith*); 'What Do You Want' four takes (*Beck/McCarty/Dreja/Relf/Samwell -Smith*); 'Here Tis' instrumental two takes (*McDaniel*); 'Crimson Curtain' (*Young*); 'Stroll On' [='Train Kept A-Rollin' rearranged for *Blowup*] (*Relf/Beck/Page/Dreja*).
Live, Germany 1967: 'I'm A Man' (*McDaniel*); 'Shapes Of Things' (*Samwell-Smith/Relf/McCarty*). Various studios/producers/line-ups.
Released: **May 1993** UK 4-CD box-set Charly LIKBOX3. *Really is virtually all the Gomelsky-era recordings.*

CD *Where The Action Is!*
Recordings made in radio studios for broadcast.
For the BBC, at various studios, England, recording dates as noted: 'I Ain't Got You' (*Reed*), 'For Your Love' (*Gouldman*), 'I'm Not Talking' (*Allison*) Mar 22nd 65; 'I Wish You Would' (*Arnold*) Jun 1st 65; 'Heart Full Of Soul' (*Gouldman*) Jun 1st or 9th 65; 'I Ain't Done Wrong' (*Relf*) Jun 9th 65; 'Too Much Monkey Business' (*Berry*), 'Love Me Like I Love You' (*Dreja/McCarty/Samwell-Smith/ Relf*), 'I'm A Man' (*McDaniel*) Aug 6th 65; 'Evil Hearted You' (*Gouldman*), 'Still I'm Sad' (*Samwell-Smith/McCarty*), 'My Girl Sloopy'

(Russell/Farrell) Sep 27th 65; 'Smokestack Lightning' *(Burnett)*, 'You're A Better Man Than I' *(M.Hugg/B.Hugg)*, 'The Train Kept A-Rollin' *(Bradshaw/Mann/Kay)* Nov 16th 65; 'Shapes Of Things' *(Samwell-Smith/Relf/McCarty)*, 'Dust My Broom' *(Johnson)* Feb 28th 66; 'Baby Scratch My Back' *(Dreja/McCarty/Beck/Relf/Samwell-Smith)*, 'Over Under Sideways Down' *(Dreja/McCarty/Beck/Relf/Samwell Smith)*; 'The Sun Is Shining' *(James)*, 'Shapes Of Things' *(Samwell-Smith/Relf/McCarty)* May 6th 66; 'Most Likely You'll Go Your Way' *(Dylan)*, 'Little Games' *(Wainman/Spiro)*, 'Drinking Muddy Water' *(Relf/Page/McCarty/Dreja)* Apr 4th 67; 'Think About It' *(Relf/McCarty/Page)*, 'Goodnight Sweet Josephine' *(Hazzard)*, 'My Baby' *(Shuman/Ragovoy)* Mar 5th 68.

For Swedish radio, at Radiohuset, Stockholm, Sweden, April 7th 1967: 'Shapes Of Things' *(Samwell-Smith/Relf/ McCarty)*; 'Heart Full Of Soul' *(Gouldman)*; 'You're A Better Man Than I' *(M.Hugg/B.Hugg)*; 'Most Likely You'll Go Your Way' *(Dylan)*; 'Over Under Sideways Down' *(Dreja/McCarty/Beck/Relf/Samwell-Smith)*; 'Little Games' *(Wainman/Spiro)*; 'My Baby' *(Shuman/Ragovoy)*; 'I'm A Man' *(McDaniel)*.
Released: **May 1997** UK 2-CD New Millennium Productions PILOT10. *The best showing of the BBC radio recordings, plus some Swedish airshots too.*

Audio/Video CD *Cumular Limit*
Live at Stadthalle, Offenbach, Germany for German TV, March 15th 1967: 'Shapes Of Things' *(Samwell-Smith/Relf/ McCarty)*; 'Happenings Ten Years Time Ago' *(Yardbirds)*; 'Over Under Sideways Down' *(Dreja/McCarty/ Beck/Relf/Samwell-Smith)*; 'I'm A Man' *(McDaniel)*.
Other studio recordings: 'Tinker Sailor Soldier Sailor' alternative *(Page/McCarty)*; 'White Summer' alternative *(trad arr Page)*; 'Ten Little Indians' take 1 *(Nilsson)*; 'Glimpses' alternative *(Relf/Page/McCarty/Dreja)*; 'You Stole My Love' take 5 *(Gouldman)*; 'De Lane Lea Lee' *(Relf/Dreja/McCarty)*.

Columbia Studios, New York, NY, US, April 1968: 'Avron Knows' *(Yardbirds)*; 'Spanish Blood' *(Yardbirds)*; 'My Baby' *(Shuman/Ragovoy)*; 'Taking A Hold On Me' *(Yardbirds)*.

Live at Maison Radio, Paris, France for French TV, March 9th 1968: 'Dazed And Confused' *(Holmes arr Yardbirds)*.
(Plus various video selections.)
Various studios/producers.
Released: **August 2000** UK 2-CD Burning Airlines PILOT24. *Adds an otherwise elusive Page-era session alongside some bonus live outings.*

CD *The Yardbirds' Ultimate!*
'Boom Boom' *(Hooker)*; 'Honey In Your Hips' *(Relf)*; 'A Certain Girl' *(Neville)*; 'I Wish You Would' *(Arnold)*; 'Too Much Monkey Business' *(Berry)*; 'Got Love If You Want It' *(Moore)*; 'Smokestack Lightning' *(Burnett)*; 'Here Tis' *(McDaniel)*; 'Good Morning Little Schoolgirl' *(Demarais)*; 'Got To Hurry' *(Gomelsky)*; 'I Ain't Got You' *(Reed)*; 'For Your Love' *(Gouldman)*; 'I'm Not Talking' *(Allison)*; 'Steeled Blues' *(Relf/Beck)*; 'Heart Full Of Soul' *(Gouldman)*; 'I Ain't Done Wrong' *(Relf)*; 'You're A Better Man Than I' *(M.Hugg/B.Hugg)*; 'Shapes Of Things' *(Samwell-Smith/Relf/ McCarty)*; 'The Train Kept A-Rollin' *(Bradshaw/Mann/Kay)*; 'New York City Blues' *(Relf/Dreja)*; 'Evil Hearted You' *(Gouldman)*; 'I'm A Man' *(McDaniel)*; 'Still I'm Sad' *(Samwell-Smith/McCarty)*; 'Questa Volta' *(Satti/Dinamo/Mogol)*; 'Pafff...Bum' *(Reverberi/Bardotti/Samwell-Smith)*; 'Lost Woman' *(Dreja/McCarty/Beck/Relf/Samwell-Smith)*; 'Over Under Sideways Down' *(Dreja/McCarty/Beck/Relf/Samwell-Smith)*; 'The Nazz Are Blue' *(Dreja/McCarty/Beck/Relf/Samwell-Smith)*; 'I Cant Make Your Way' *(Dreja/McCarty/Beck/Relf/Samwell-Smith)*; 'Rack My Mind' *(Dreja/McCarty/Beck/Relf/Samwell-Smith)*; 'Hot House Of Omagararshid' *(Dreja/McCarty/Beck/Relf/Samwell-Smith)*; 'Jeff's Boogie' *(Dreja/McCarty/Beck/Relf/Samwell-Smith)*; 'He's Always There' *(Dreja/McCarty/Beck/Relf/Samwell-Smith)*; 'Turn Into Earth' *(Samwell-Smith/Simon)*; 'What Do You Want' *(Dreja/McCarty/Beck/Relf/Samwell-Smith)*; 'Happenings Ten Years Time Ago' *(Yardbirds)*; 'Psycho Daisies' *(Dreja/McCarty/Beck/Relf/Samwell-Smith)*; 'Stroll On' *(Relf/Beck/Page/Dreja)*; 'Little Games' *(Wainman/Spiro)*; 'Puzzles' *(Relf/Page/McCarty/Dreja)*; 'White Summer' *(trad arr Page)*; 'Tinker Tailor Soldier Sailor' *(Page/McCarty)*; 'No Excess Baggage' *(Atkins/D'Errico)*; 'Drinking Muddy Water' *(Relf/Page/McCarty/Dreja)*; 'Only The Black Rose' *(Relf)*; 'Ten Little Indians' *(Nilsson)*; 'Ha Ha Said The Clown' *(Hazzard)*; 'Goodnight Sweet Josephine' *(Hazzard)*; 'Think About It' *(Relf/McCarty/Page)*; 'Knowing' *(Relf)*; 'Mr Zero' *(Lind)*; 'Shapes In My Mind' *(Napier-Bell)*.
Various studios/producers/line-ups.
Released: **July 2001** US 2-CD Rhino R2 79825; August 2001 UK 2-CD Rhino 8122 798252. *The first definitive compilation of the best of The Yardbirds, with material from all four line-ups: Clapton; Beck; Beck & Page; and Page.*

AUTHOR'S THANKS

More than certain other books of this nature written by me, I have gained the trust of my subjects. Indeed, I have a long and ongoing professional and personal association with Jim McCarty, mainstay of the present-day Yardbirds.

I have drawn too from past conversations with other of the *dramatis personnae* – notably Chris Dreja and Paul Samwell-Smith, as well as April Relf and Richard Mackay (editor of *Yardbirds World*) who both retold the ancient saga and turned up new and rediscovered insights and information.

Whether they were aware of providing assistance in varying degrees or not, let's have a round of applause too for Hans Alehag, Sue Allen, Ian 'Tich' Amey, Richard Barnes, Roger Barnes, Peter Barton, Jeff Beck, Dave Berry, Stuart Booth, Chris Britton, Carol Boyer, Bruce Brand, Chris Britton, Trevor Burton, Clem Cattini, Billy Childish, Pete Cox, Don Craine, Trevor 'Dozy' Davies, Denis D'Ell, Kevin Delaney, Rod Demick, Peter Doggett, Lonnie Donegan, Ray Dorset, Ian Drummond, Tim Fagan, Wayne Fontana, Pete Frame, Ann Freer, Steve Gibbons, Alan Glen, Gary Gold, 'Wreckless' Eric Goulden, Keith Grant, Brian Hinton, Detroit John Idan, Garry Jones, Chris 'Ace' Kefford, Graham Larkbey, Spencer Leigh, Jon Lewin, Brendan MacAlpine, Elisabeth McCrae, Tom McKee, Jacqui McShee, Steve Maggs, Phil May, Gypie Mayo, Colin Miles, Adrian Moulton, Les Payne, Dave Pegg, Mike Pender, Chris Phipps, Reg Presley, Alan Robinson, Mike Robinson, Twinkle Rogers, Jane Relf, Dave Sampson, Mike and Anja Stax (of *Ugly Things*), the late Lord David Sutch, Dick Taylor, Vic Thomas, John Tobler, John Townsend, Paul Tucker, Hilton Valentine, Clifford White, Robb Woodward (Shel Naylor), and Alan Zipper – plus a big 'hello' to Mike Ober.

To Harry, Jack and Inese, I owe my usual debts.

Finally, it may be obvious to the reader that I have received help from sources that prefer not to be mentioned. Nevertheless, I wish to express my appreciation for what they did.

DOUG HINMAN & JOE McMICHAEL, compilers of the
Diary section, would like to thank: Chris Hjort, Andy Neill (the Colindale man), Keith Badman & Bob Eliot (BBC & TV/radio), Greg E. Shaw, Stu Rosenberg, Jason Brabazon, Benoit Pascal & Christophe LePublic (the French connection), Steve Kolanjian (for access to the files), Dave Lewis (TBL), Bill Tikellis (Australia), Richard McKay (*Yardbirds World*), John Spencer, Peter Moody, Gary Peterson & Bill Inglot (Rhino Records), Greg Russo (with acknowledgement for info on the Cyrkle session coup and the 1968 legal matters), Neal Skok, Richard Groothuizen, Jerry Fuentes, Andrew Sandoval, Ed Halbrook, Clark Besch, Greg Shaw (Bomp), Barry Tucker, Tom Tourville, Russ Garrett, Gordon Linden, Lou Newman, Andy Mitchell, Gerry Clarke, Dennis Keller, Michael Stelke, Jon Paris, "cowboybeeps", Sam Rapollo, the late John Platt, the late & great Alan Betrock, Mike Carlton, Ron Starkle, Doug Calgaro, Jim Bonfanti, Richard Arfin, Marc Muller, Lee Burton, John Holcomb, Bob Gonzalez, Joey Barbosa, Don Cameron, Tom Sielck, Bob Blackburn, Steven Moore, Steve Ingless, Peter Stupar, Lawrie Read, Peter Robinson, Bobby Poe, Ed Martz, Tim Doherty, Chris Klein, Ronnie Warner, Kenny Collins, Bill Small, Craig Moore, Mike Ober, Piers Hemmingsen, Glen Anderson, Julian Bailey, Phil Cohen, Alec Palao, Mark Ritucci, Cheryl Jennings, Dick Wyzanski, David Terralavoro, Marianne Spellman, Mark Ranson, Pedro, not forgetting Paul Samwell-Smith, Giorgio Gomelsky and Simon Napier-Bell. Anyone we missed, please accept our apologies but please know that your assistance has been very much appreciated. Every gesture of help and support means the world to us. A special thanks to all the librarians and archivists around the world; far too many to mention in this small space, but you are our favourite people in the whole world. Personal thanks to our families, Pam & Maggie and Nancy, Ned & Amie. And let's not forget Jim McCarty, Chris Dreja and the early-21st-century-model Yardbirds, still rockin' and better than ever.

PHOTOGRAPHS reproduced in this book come from a number
of sources. Pictures, photographers and (where relevant) agencies and/or owners are identified in the following key, organised by page number and subject. 2/3: Gerry Clarke. 11: Beck line-up, Michael Ochs Archives/Redfern's. 17: main pic, Tony Gale/Pictorial Press; Lord Ted, Express Newspapers/Archive Photos/Hulton Archives. 18: red-Tele Eric, Rex Features; O'Neill & Clapton, Jacqueline Ryan. 19: harping Relf, Pace/Hulton Getty; record shop, Jeremy Fletcher/Redfern's. 20: main pic, Tony Gale/Pictorial Press. 21: TV studio (top), S&G/Redfern's; suits pose, Rex Features; TV studio (bottom), Dezo Hoffman/Rex Features. 22: TV studio, Pictorial Press; red background pose, Michael Ochs Archives/Redfern's. 22/23: American TV, Chuck Boyd/Redfern's. 23: blue sky pose, Rex Features. 24: McCarty sticks, Pictorial Press; TV studio (bottom), Pictorial Press. 25: TV studio (top), S&G/Redfern's; Beck, Rex Features. 26/27: All shots, Pictorial Press. 28: Page & Beck on-stage (top), Gordon Linden; Page & Les Paul, Chuck Boyd/Redfern's. 29: on the rocks, Chuck Boyd/Redfern's; cameras, Rex Features; pose, Michael Ochs Archives/Redfern's. 30: shirts, Rex Features. 31: early Zep, Graham Wiltshire/Redfern's; neckerchiefs (bottom), Ivan Keenan/Redfern's. 35: all shots, Judy Totton. 35: McCarty, Pictorial Press. 45: Samwell-Smith, Redfern's. 57: Relf, Pictorial Press. 65: Clapton line-up, Michael Ochs Archives/Redfern's. 73: Beck, Pictorial Press. 81: Dreja, Pictorial Press. 91: Samwell-Smith, Pictorial Press. 101: Page, Pictorial Press. 111: Relf, Rex Features. 161: Page, Pictorial Press.

MEMORABILIA illustrated in this book, including ads,
newspaper cuttings, posters, record sleeves, snaps and 8-track cartridges, came from the collections of Andy Babiuk, Tony Bacon, Alan Clayson, Doug Hinman, and the National Sound Archive (London).

THE PUBLISHERS would like to thank Andy Babiuk, Keith
Badman, Christopher Hjort, Mikael Jansson, Gordon Linden, Joe McMichael, Greg Prevost, and Paul Quinn. **Special thanks** to Douglas Hinman for detailing the Diary, and for help and guidance beyond the call of duty.

UPDATES? The publisher welcomes any new information for
future editions. Write to Yardbirds, Backbeat UK, 115J Cleveland Street, London W1T 6PU, England, or you can email us at yardbirds@backbeatuk.com.

THE YARDBIRDS

BIBLIOGRAPHY
If you want any more, you really ought to write it yourself. Otherwise, the author recommends the following four source books for further reading.

Richard McKay & Mike Ober *Yardbirds World* (Yardbirds World Publications, 1989) and **Richard McKay** *Over Under Sideways Down: Yardbirds World 2* (Yardbirds World Publications, 1992). Here you can digest much enjoyable food for thought in two carefully-wrought labours of love culled from back-issues of the *Yardbirds World* fanzine, from Mr Mackay's first-hand knowledge, and his meticulous trawls through vast hoard of archives. The two volumes also make the most of willing assistance from various past and present Yardbirds, participants in associated projects, and a supporting cast of fellow travellers reminiscing about matters that either could have emerged on the eve of publication or were pertinent up to 30 years before. Raw fact is balanced, however, by enthusiastic opinion that never takes a party-line at face value.

John Platt, Jim McCarty, Chris Dreja *The Yardbirds* (Sidgwick & Jackson, 1983). You don't have to be into The Yardbirds' music to be entertained by this insider's perspective on the group's prehistory and the sunshine and showers of its years of maximum impact. Written in a level-headed but humorously self-effacing style, it's sort of Gilbert-and-Sullivan to, say, the Wagner of either of the more recent autobiographies by each of the Kink brothers.

Greg Russo *Yardbirds: The Ultimate Rave-Up* third edition (Crossfire Publications, 2001; contact PO Box 20406, Floral Park, NY 11002). A rather dry commentary on The Yardbirds' career and beyond prefaces the most comprehensive consumer's guide to their official disc releases (including composer credits) and associated merchandise ever published, making for an eye-stretching cornucopia. Our own discography was based on the material in this book.

Also useful to the producers of this book were six further volumes.
Tony Bacon *London Live* (Balafon/Miller Freeman, 1999).
Annette Carson *Jeff Beck: Crazy Fingers* (Backbeat, 2001).
Christopher Hjort & Doug Hinman *Jeff's Book* (Rock'n'Roll Research Press, 2000; contact PO Box 4759, Rumford, RI 02916, US).
Giorgio Gomelsky & Phil Cohen *The Yardbirds: The Train Kept A-Rollin'* CD booklet (Charly Records, 1993).
Dave Lewis & Simon Pallett *Led Zeppelin: The Concert File* (Omnibus, 1997).
Mike Ober *Then Play On* (privately published, 1992).
Marc Roberty *Clapton: The Complete Chronicle* (Pyramid, 1991).
We also consulted: *Beat Instrumental; Making Music; Melody Maker; Rolling Stone;* and the CNN website.

"Recollected attractions blend into a simpler and denser unit of pleasure than ever really existed." *Samuel Johnson*